Lecture Notes in Computer Science   10608

Commenced Publication in 1973
Founding and Former Series Editors:
Gerhard Goos, Juris Hartmanis, and Jan van Leeuwen

More information about this series at http://www.springer.com/series/7407

Mohammad Reza Mousavi · Jiří Sgall (Eds.)

Topics in Theoretical Computer Science

Second IFIP WG 1.8 International Conference, TTCS 2017
Tehran, Iran, September 12–14, 2017
Proceedings

 Springer

Editors
Mohammad Reza Mousavi ⓘ
University of Leicester
Leicester
UK

Jiří Sgall
Charles University
Prague
Czech Republic

ISSN 0302-9743   ISSN 1611-3349 (electronic)
Lecture Notes in Computer Science
ISBN 978-3-319-68952-4   ISBN 978-3-319-68953-1 (eBook)
DOI 10.1007/978-3-319-68953-1

Library of Congress Control Number: 2017956068

LNCS Sublibrary: SL1 – Theoretical Computer Science and General Issues

Printed on acid-free paper

This Springer imprint is published by Springer Nature
The registered company is Springer International Publishing AG
The registered company address is: Gewerbestrasse 11, 6330 Cham, Switzerland

Preface

Welcome to the Second IFIP International Conference on Topics in Theoretical Computer Science (TTCS 2017), held during September 12–14, 2017, at the School of Computer Science, Institute for Research in Fundamental Sciences (IPM), Tehran, Iran.

This volume contains the papers accepted for presentation at TTCS 2017. For this edition of TTCS, we received 20 submissions from 10 different countries. An international Program Committee comprising 32 leading scientists from 13 countries reviewed the papers thoroughly providing on average four review reports for each paper. We accepted eight submissions, which translates into 40% of all submissions. This means that the process was selective and only high-quality papers were accepted. The program also includes four invited talks by the following world-renowned computer scientists:

- Mahdi Cheraghchi, Imperial College, UK
- Łukasz Jeż, University of Wrocław, Poland
- Jaco van de Pol, University of Twente, The Netherlands
- Peter Csaba Ölveczky, University of Oslo, Norway

Additionally, the program features two talks and one tutorial in the PhD Forum, which are not included in the proceedings.

We thank IPM, and in particular the Organizing Committee, for having provided various facilities and for their generous support. We are also grateful to our Program Committee for their professional and hard work in providing expert review reports and thorough discussions leading to a very interesting and strong program.

We also acknowledge the excellent facilities provided by the EasyChair system, which were crucial in managing the process of submission, selection, revision, and publication of the manuscripts included in these proceedings.

September 2017   Mohammad Reza Mousavi
                                                                              Jiří Sgall

The original version of this book was revised: The paper starting on p. 41 was moved from the topical section heading "Logic, Semantics, and Programming Theory" to "Algorithms and Complexity". The erratum to this book is available at https://doi.org/10.1007/978-3-319-68953-1_10

Organization

General Chair

Hamid Sarbazi-azad   IPM, Iran; Sharif University of Technology, Iran

Local Organization Chair

Hamid Reza Shahrabi   IPM, Iran

Publicity Chair

Mahmoud Shirazi   IPM, Iran

Program Committee

Farhad Arbab	CWI and Leiden University, The Netherlands
Amitabha Bagchi	Indian Institute of Technology, Delhi, India
Sam Buss	University of California, San Diego, USA
Jarek Byrka	University of Wroclaw, Poland
Ilaria Castellani	Inria Sophia Antipolis, France
Amir Daneshgar	Sharif University of Technology, Iran
Anna Gal	University of Texas at Austin, USA
Fatemeh Ghassemi	University of Tehran, Iran
Mohammad T. Hajiaghayi	University of Maryland, College Park, USA
Hossein Hojjat	Rochester Institute of Technology, Rochester, New York, USA
Mohammad Izadi	Sharif University of Technology, Iran
Sung-Shik T.Q. Jongmans	Open University of The Netherlands, Imperial College London, UK
Ramtin Khosravi	University of Tehran, Iran
Jan Kretinsky	Masaryk University, Czech Republic
Amit Kumar	IIT Delhi, India
Bas Luttik	Eindhoven University of Technology, The Netherlands
Mohammad Mahmoody	University of Virginia
Larry Moss	Indiana University, USA
Mohammad Reza Mousavi	University of Leicester, UK
Rolf Niedermeier	TU Berlin, Germany
Giuseppe Persiano	Università degli Studi di Salerno, Italy
Jörg-Rüdiger Sack	Carleton University, Canada
Mehrnoosh Sadrzadeh	Queen Mary University of London, UK
Rahul Santhanam	University of Edinburgh, UK
Gerardo Schneider	Chalmers, University of Gothenburg, Sweden

Jiří Sgall	Computer Science Institute of Charles University, Czech Republic
Subodh Sharma	Indian Institute of Technology Delhi, India
Mirco Tribastone	IMT Institute for Advanced Studies Lucca, Italy
Kazunori Ueda	Waseda University, Japan
Vijay Vazirani	Georgia Tech, USA
Gerhard Woeginger	RWTH Aachen, Germany
Hamid Zarrabi-Zadeh	Sharif University of Technology, Iran

Additional Reviewers

Abd Alrahman, Yehia
Bagga, Divyanshu
Baharifard, Fatemeh
Bentert, Matthias
Klinz, Bettina
Krämer, Julia
Maggi, Alessandro
Meggendorfer, Tobias

Mirjalali, Kian
Molter, Hendrik
Neruda, Roman
van der Woude, Jaap
van Oostrom, Vincent
Vegh, Laszlo
Łukaszewski, Andrzej

Abstracts of Invited Talks

The Coding Lens in Explicit Constructions

Mahdi Cheraghchi

Department of Computing, Imperial College London, UK
m.cheraghchi@imperial.ac.uk

Abstract. The theory of error-correcting codes, originally developed as a fundamental technique for a systematic study of communications systems, has served as a pivotal tool in major areas of mathematics, computer science and electrical engineering. Understanding problems through a "coding lens" has consistently led to breakthroughs in a wide spectrum of research areas, often seemingly foreign from coding theory, including discrete mathematics, geometry, cryptography, signal processing, algorithms and complexity, to name a few. This talk will focus on the role of coding theory in pseudorandomness, and particularly, explicit construction problems in sparse recovery and signal processing.

Online Packet Scheduling

Łukasz Jeż

Institute of Computer Science, University of Wrocław, Poland

Packet Scheduling, also known as *Buffer Management with Bounded Delay*, is a problem motivated by managing the buffer of a network switch or router (hence the latter name), but also an elementary example of a job scheduling problem: a job j has unit processing time ($p_j = 1$), arbitrary weight w_j, as well as arbitrary release time $r_j \in \mathbb{Z}$ and deadline $d_j \in \mathbb{Z}$ such that $r_j < d_j$. A given set of such jobs is to be scheduled on a single machine so as to maximize the total weight of jobs completed by their deadlines.

The *online* variant is of particular interest, given the motivation: Think of an algorithm that has to schedule jobs on the fly, at time slot t knowing only those (and their parameters) which were already released. From the algorithm's perspective, the computation proceeds in rounds, corresponding to time slots; in round t, the following happen: first, jobs with deadlines t expire (and are since ignored), then any set of new jobs with release time t may arrive, and finally the algorithm can choose one pending job; next, this job is completed, yielding reward equal to its weight, and the computation proceeds to the next round.

Though an online algorithm knows nothing of the future jobs arrivals, we require worst-case performance guarantees on the complete instance when it ends. Specifically, we say an algorithm is *R-competitive* if on *every* instance I its gain is at least a $1/R$ fraction of the optimum gain on I.

It is easy to give bounds on the competitive ratio: an upper bound of 2 is attained by a simple greedy algorithm that chooses the heaviest pending job in each slot; for a lower bound, it suffices to consider an instance merely two slots long. These can of course be improved: a careful analysis of a natural generalization of the lower bound instance yields a lower bound of $\varphi \approx 1.618$, which is the best known. Better algorithms, with rather involved analyses, are also known: the best, dating back to 2007, is 1.828-competitive.

These bounds do not match, despite simple problem statement and significant effort since the early 2000s. One consequence is a number of restricted classes of instances that were considered. I will survey known results, on both deterministic and randomized algorithms, presenting some of them in more detail.

We will start by noting that packet scheduling is a special case of maximum-weight matching problem, where the jobs and the time slots form the two partitions, and each job j is connected by an edge of weight w_j to each of the time slots in $[r_j, d_j) \cap \mathbb{Z}$. This has twofold implications: Firstly, online algorithms designed for the matching problem apply, one of them (randomized) in fact the best known even for our special case. Secondly, optimal offline algorithms, though not our primary interest, grant structural insight into optimal schedules, helping in the online setting too.

Parallel Algorithms for Model Checking

Jaco van de Pol

University of Twente, Formal Methods and Tools, Enschede, The Netherlands
J.C.vandePol@utwente.nl

Model checking [1, 5] is an automated verification procedure, which checks that a model of a system satisfies certain properties. These properties are typically expressed in some temporal logic, like LTL and CTL. Algorithms for LTL model checking (linear time logic) are based on automata theory and graph algorithms, while algorithms for CTL (computation tree logic) are based on fixed-point computations and set operations.

The basic model checking procedures examine the state space of a system exhaustively, which grows exponentially in the number of variables or parallel components. Scalability of model checking is achieved by clever abstractions (for instance counter-example guided abstraction refinement), clever algorithms (for instance partial-order reduction), clever data-structures (for instance binary decision diagrams) and, finally, clever use of hardware resources, for instance algorithms for distributed and multi-core computers.

This invited lecture will provide a number of highlights of our research in the last decade on high-performance model checking, as it is implemented in the open source LTSmin tool set[1] [10], focusing on the algorithms and datastructures in its multi-core tools.

A lock-free, scalable hash-table maintains a globally shared set of already visited state vectors. Using this, parallel workers can semi-independently explore different parts of the state space, still ensuring that every state will be explored exactly once. Our implementation proved to scale linearly on tens of processors [12].

Parallel algorithms for NDFS. Nested Depth-First Search [6] is a linear-time algorithm to detect accepting cycles in Büchi automata. LTL model checking can be reduced to the emptiness problem of Büchi automata, i.e. the absence of accepting cycles. We introduced a parallel version of this algorithm [9], despite the fact that Depth-First Search is hard to parallelize. Our multi-core implementation is compatible with important state space reduction techniques, in particular state compression and partial-order reduction [11, 15] and generalizes to timed automata [13].

A multi-core library for Decision Diagrams, called Sylvan [7]. Binary Decision Diagrams (BDD) have been introduced as concise representations of sets of Boolean vectors. The CTL model checking operations can be expressed directly on the BDD representation [4]. Sylvan provides a parallel implementation of BDD operations for shared-memory, multi-core processors. We also provided successful experiments on

---

[1] http://ltsmin.utwente.nl, https://github.com/utwente-fmt/ltsmin.

distributed BDDs over a cluster of multi-core computer servers [14]. Besides BDDs, Sylvan also supports Multi-way and Multi-terminal Decision Diagrams.

Multi-core algorithms to detect Strongly Connected Components. An alternative model-checking algorithm is based on the decomposition and analysis of Strongly Connected Components (SCCs). We have implemented a parallel version of Dijkstra's SCC algorithm [2, 8]. It forms the basis of model checking LTL using generalized Büchi and Rabin automata [3]. SCCs are also useful for model checking with fairness, probabilistic model checking, and implementing partial-order reduction.

References

1. Baier, C., Katoen, J.P.: Principles of Model Checking. The MIT Press (2008)
2. Bloemen, V., Laarman, A., van de Pol, J.: Multi-core on-the-fly SCC decomposition. In: PPoPP'16, pp. 8:1–8:12. ACM (2016)
3. Bloemen, V., Duret-Lutz, A., van de Pol, J.: Explicit state model checking with generalized Büchi and Rabin automata. In: SPIN'17: Model Checking of Software. ACM SIGSOFT (2017)
4. Burch, J.R., Clarke, E.M., McMillan, K.L., Dill, D.L., Hwang, L.J.: Symbolic model checking: 10^20 states and beyond. Inf. Comput. **98**(2), 142–170 (1992)
5. Clarke, E.M., Grumberg, O., Peled, D.: Model Checking. The MIT Press (1999)
6. Courcoubetis, C., Vardi, M.Y., Wolper, P., Yannakakis, M.: Memory-efficient algorithm for the verification of temporal properties. Formal Methods Syst. Des. **1**, 275–288 (1992)
7. van Dijk, T., van de Pol, J.: Sylvan: multi-core framework for decision diagrams. Int. J. Softw. Tools Technol. Transfer (2016)
8. Dijkstra, E.W.: A Discipline of Programming. Prentice-Hall (1976)
9. Evangelista, S., Laarman, A., Petrucci, L., van de Pol, J.: Chakraborty, S., Mukund, M. (eds.) ATVA 2012. LNCS, vol. 7561, pp. 269–283. Springer, Heidelberg (2012)
10. Kant, G., Laarman, A., Meijer, J., van de Pol, J., Blom, S., van Dijk, T.: LTSmin: high-performance language-independent model checking. In: Baier, C., Tinelli, C. (eds.) TACAS 2015. LNCS, vol. 9035, pp. 692–707. Springer, Heidelberg (2015)
11. Laarman, A., Pater, E., van de Pol, J., Hansen, H.: Guard-based partial-order reduction. STTT **18**(4), 427–448 (2016)
12. Laarman, A., van de Pol, J., Weber, M.: Boosting multi-core reachability performance with shared hash tables. In: FMCAD 2010, pp. 247–255 (2010)
13. Laarman, A.W., Olesen, M.C., Dalsgaard, A.E., Larsen, K.G., van de Pol, J.C.: Multi-core emptiness checking of timed Büchi automata using inclusion abstraction. In: Sharygina, N., Veith, H. (eds.) CAV 2013. LNCS, vol. 8044, pp. 968–983. Springer, Heidelberg (2013)
14. Oortwijn, W., van Dijk, T., van de Pol, J.: Distributed binary decision diagrams for symbolic reachability. In: SPIN'17: Model Checking of Software. ACM SIGSOFT (2017)
15. Valmari, A.: A stubborn attack on state explosion. Formal Methods Syst. Des. **1**(4), 297–322 (1992)

Design and Validation of Cloud Storage Systems Using Formal Methods

Peter Csaba Ölveczky

University of Oslo, Oslo, Norway
peterol@ifi.uio.no

Abstract. To deal with large amounts of data while offering high availability and throughput and low latency, cloud computing systems rely on distributed, partitioned, and replicated data stores. Such cloud storage systems are complex software artifacts that are very hard to design and analyze. Formal specification and model checking should therefore be beneficial during their design and validation. In particular, I propose rewriting logic and its accompanying Maude tools as a suitable framework for formally specifying and analyzing both the correctness and the performance of cloud storage systems. This abstract of an invited talk gives a short overview of the use of rewriting logic at the University of Illinois' Assured Cloud Computing center on industrial data stores such as Google's Megastore and Facebook/Apache's Cassandra. I also briefly summarize the experiences of the use of a different formal method for similar purposes by engineers at Amazon Web Services.

Contents

Invited Talk

Design and Validation of Cloud Storage Systems Using Formal Methods

Peter Csaba Ölveczky$^{(\boxtimes)}$

University of Oslo, Oslo, Norway
`peterol@ifi.uio.no`

Abstract. To deal with large amounts of data while offering high availability and throughput and low latency, cloud computing systems rely on distributed, partitioned, and replicated data stores. Such cloud storage systems are complex software artifacts that are very hard to design and analyze. Formal specification and model checking should therefore be beneficial during their design and validation. In particular, I propose rewriting logic and its accompanying Maude tools as a suitable framework for formally specifying and analyzing both the correctness and the performance of cloud storage systems. This abstract of an invited talk gives a short overview of the use of rewriting logic at the University of Illinois Assured Cloud Computing center on industrial data stores such as Google's Megastore and Facebook/Apache's Cassandra. I also briefly summarize the experiences of the use of a different formal method for similar purposes by engineers at Amazon Web Services.

1 Introduction

Cloud computing relies on dealing with large amounts of data safely and efficiently. To ensure that data are always available—even when parts of the network are down—data should be *replicated* across widely distributed data centers. Data may also have to be *partitioned* to obtain the elasticity expected from cloud computing. However, given the cost of the communication needed to coordinate the different replicas in a replicated and possibly partitioned distributed data store, there is a trade-off between efficiency on the one hand, and maintaining consistency across the different replicas and the transactional guarantees provided on the other hand. Many data stores therefore provide weaker forms of consistency and weaker transactional guarantees than the traditional ACID guarantees.

Designing cloud data stores that satisfy certain performance and correctness requirements is a highly nontrivial task, and so is the validation that the design actually meets its requirements. In addition, although cloud storage systems are not traditionally considered to be "safety-critical" systems, as more and more applications migrate to the cloud, it becomes increasingly crucial that storage systems do not lose potentially critical user data. However, as argued in, e.g., [4,15], standard system development and validation techniques are not

Published by Springer International Publishing AG 2017. All Rights Reserved
M.R. Mousavi and J. Sgall (Eds.): TTCS 2017, LNCS 10608, pp. 3–8, 2017.
DOI: 10.1007/978-3-319-68953-1_1

well suited for designing data stores with high assurance that they satisfy their correctness and quality-of-service requirements: Executing and simulating new designs may require understanding and modifying large code bases; furthermore, although system executions and simulations can give an idea of the performance of a design, they cannot give any (quantified) assurance about the system performance, and they cannot be used to verify correctness properties.

In [4], colleagues at the University of Illinois at Urbana-Champaign (UIUC) and I argue for the use of executable formal methods during the design of cloud storage system, and to provide high levels of assurance that the designs satisfy desired correctness and performance requirements. The key thing is that an executable formal model can be directly simulated; it can be also be subjected to various model checking analyses that automatically explore all possible system behaviors from a given initial system configuration. From a system developer's perspective, such model checking can be seen as a powerful debugging and testing method that automatically executes a comprehensive "test suite" for complex fault-tolerant systems. Having an abstract executable formal system model also allow us to quickly and easily explore many design options and to validate designs as early as possible.

However, finding an executable formal method that can handle large and complex distributed systems and that supports reasoning about both the system's *correctness* and its *performance* is not an easy task. *Rewriting logic* [14] and its associated Maude tool [5] and their extensions should be a promising candidate. Rewriting logic is a simple, intuitive, and expressive executable specification formalism for distributed systems. In rewriting logic, data types are defined using algebraic equational specifications and the dynamic behavior of a system is defined by conditional rewrite rules $t \longrightarrow u$ **if** *cond*, where the terms t and u denote state fragments. Such a rewriting logic specification can be directly simulated, from a given initial system state, in Maude. However, such a simulation only covers one possible system behavior. Reachability analysis and LTL model checking can then be used to analyze all possible behaviors from a given initial system state to check, respectively, whether a certain state pattern is reachable from the initial state and whether all possible behaviors from the initial state satisfy a linear temporal logic (LTL) property.

Cloud storage systems are often real-time systems; in particular, to analyze their performance we need timed models. The specification and analysis of real-time systems in rewriting logic are supported by the Real-Time Maude tool [17,19]. In particular, randomized Real-Time Maude simulations have been shown to predict system performance as well as domain-specific simulation tools [18]. Nevertheless, such ad hoc randomized simulations cannot give a quantified measure of confidence in the accuracy of the performance estimations. To achieve such guarantees about the performance of a design, we can specify our design as a *probabilistic rewrite theory* and subject it to *statistical model checking* using the PVeStA tool [1]. Such statistical model checking performs randomized simulations to estimate the expected average value of a given expression, until the desired level of statistical confidence in the outcome has been reached.

In this way we can obtain statistical guarantees about the expected performance of a design.

2   Applications

This section gives a brief overview of how Jon Grov, myself, and colleagues at the Assured Cloud Computing center at the UIUC have applied rewriting logic and its associated tools to model and analyze cloud storage systems. A more extensive overview of parts of this research can be found in the report [4].

Google's Megastore. Megastore [3] is a key component in Google's celebrated cloud infrastructure and is used for Gmail, Google+, Android Market, and Google AppEngine. Megastore is a fault-tolerant replicated data store where the data are divided into different *entity groups* (for example, "Peter's emails" could be one such entity group). Megastore's trade-off between consistency and performance is to provide consistency only for transactions accessing a single entity group. Jon Grov and I had some ideas on how to extend Megastore to also provide consistency for transactions accessing multiple entity groups, without sacrificing performance.

Before experimenting with extensions of Megastore, we needed to understand the Megastore design in significant detail. This was a challenging task, since Megastore is a complex system whose only publicly available description was the short overview paper [3]. We used Maude simulation and model checking extensively throughout the development of a Maude model (with 56 rewrite rules) of the Megastore design [6]. In particular, model checking from selected initial states could be seen as our "test suite" that explored all possible behaviors from those states. Our model also provided the first detailed publicly available description of the Megastore design.

We could then experiment with our design ideas for extending Megastore, until we arrived at a design with 72 rewrite rules, called Megastore-CGC, that also provided consistency for certain sets of transactions that access multiple entity groups [7]. To analyze our conjecture that the extension should have a performance similar to that of Megastore, we ran randomized Real-Time Maude simulations on both models.

An important point is that even *if* we would have had access to Megastore's code base, understanding and extending it would have been much more time-consuming than developing our own models/executable prototypes.

Apache Cassandra. Apache Cassandra [8] is an open-source key-value data store originally developed at Facebook that is currently used by, e.g., Amadeus, Apple, IBM, Netflix, Facebook/Instagram, GitHub, and Twitter. Colleagues at UIUC wanted to experiment with whether some alternative design choices would lead to better performance. In contrast to our Megastore efforts, the problem in this case was that to understand and experiment with different design choices would require understanding and modifying Cassandra's 345,000 lines of code. After studying this code base, Si Liu and others developed a 1,000-line Maude model that captured all the main design choices of Cassandra [13]. The authors used their models and Maude model checking to analyze under what circumstances Cassandra provides stronger consistency properties than "eventual consistency."

They then transformed their models into fully probabilistic rewrite theories and used statistical model checking with PVESTA to evaluate the performance of the original Cassandra design and their alternative design (where the main performance measure is how often strong consistency is satisfied in practice) [12]. To investigate whether the performance estimates thus obtained are realistic, in [12] the authors compare their model-based performance estimates with the performance obtained by actually executing the Cassandra code itself.

RAMP. RAMP [2] is a partitioned data store, developed by Peter Bailis and others at UC Berkeley, that provide efficient multi-partition transactions with a weak transactional guarantee: read atomicity (either all or none of a transaction's updates are visible to other transactions). The RAMP developers describe three main RAMP algorithms in [2]; they also sketch a number of other design alternatives without providing details or proofs about their properties. In [11], colleagues at UIUC and I develop Maude models of RAMP and its sketched designs, and use Maude model checking to verify that also the sketched designs satisfy the properties conjectured by Bailis et al.

But how efficient are the alternative designs? Bailis *et al.* only provide simulation results for their main designs, probably because of the effort required to develop simulation models of a design. Having higher-level smaller formal models allowed us to explore the design state of RAMP quite extensively. In particular, in [10] we used statistical model checking to evaluate the performance along a number of parameters, with many different distributions of transactions. In this way, we could evaluate the performance of a number RAMP designs not explored by Bailis et al., and for many more parameters and workloads than evaluated by the RAMP developers. This allow us to discover the most suitable version of RAMP for different kinds of applications with different kinds of expected workloads. We also experimented with some design ideas of our own, and discovered that one design, RAMP-Faster, has many attractive performance properties, and that, while not guaranteeing read atomicity, provides read atomicity for more than 99% of the transactions for certain workloads.

P-Store. In [16] I analyzed the partially replicated transactional data store P-Store [20] that provides some fault tolerance, serializability of transactions, and limited use of atomic multicast. Although this protocol supposedly was verified by its developers, Maude reachability analysis found a nontrivial bug in the P-Store algorithm that was confirmed by one of the P-Store developers.

3   Formal Methods at Amazon

Amazon Web Services (AWS) is the world's largest provider of cloud computing services. Key components of its cloud computing infrastructure include the DynamoDB replicated database and the Simple Storage System (S3).

In their excellent paper "How Amazon Web Services Uses Formal Methods" [15], engineers at AWS explain how they used the formal specification language TLA+ [9] and its associated model checker TLC during the development of S3, DynamoDB, and other components. Their experiences of using formal methods in an industrial setting can be briefly summarized as follows:

– Model checking finds subtle "corner case" bugs that are not found by the standard validation techniques used in industry.
– A formal specification is a valuable short, precise, and testable description of an algorithm.
– Formal methods are surprisingly feasible for mainstream software development and give good returns on investment.
– Executable formal specifications makes it quick and easy to experiment with different design choices.

The paper [15] concludes that "formal methods are a big success at AWS" and that management actively encourages engineers to use formal methods during the development of new features and design changes.

The weakness reported by the AWS engineers was that while TLA+ was effective at finding bugs, it was not (or could not be) used to analyze performance. It seems that TLC does not support well the analysis of real-time system, and neither does TLA+ come with a probabilistic or statistical model checker. This seems to be one major difference between the formal methods used at AWS and the Maude-based formal method that we propose: we have showed that the Maude tools are useful for analyzing both the correctness and the expected performance of the design.

Acknowledgments. I am grateful to Jon Grov, José Meseguer, Indranil Gupta, Si Liu, Muntasir Rahman, and Jatin Ganhotra for the collaboration on the work summarized in this abstract. I would also like to thank the organizers of TTCS 2017 for giving me the opportunity to present these results as a keynote speaker.

References

1. AlTurki, M., Meseguer, J.: PVeStA: a parallel statistical model checking and quantitative analysis tool. In: Corradini, A., Klin, B., Cîrstea, C. (eds.) CALCO 2011. LNCS, vol. 6859, pp. 386–392. Springer, Heidelberg (2011). doi:10.1007/978-3-642-22944-2_28
2. Bailis, P., Fekete, A., Hellerstein, J.M., Ghodsi, A., Stoica, I.: Scalable atomic visibility with RAMP transactions. In: Proceedings SIGMOD 2014. ACM (2014)
3. Baker, J., et al.: Megastore: Providing scalable, highly available storage for interactive services. In: CIDR 2011 (2011). www.cidrdb.org

4. Bobba, R., Grov, J., Gupta, I., Liu, S., Meseguer, J., Ölveczky, P.C., Skeirik, S.: Design, formal modeling, and validation of cloud storage systems using Maude. Technical report, Department of Computer Science, University of Illinois at Urbana-Champaign (2017). http://hdl.handle.net/2142/96274

5. Clavel, M., Durán, F., Eker, S., Lincoln, P., Martí-Oliet, N., Meseguer, J., Talcott, C.: All About Maude - A High-Performance Logical Framework: How to Specify, Program and Verify Systems in Rewriting Logic. LNCS, vol. 4350. Springer, Heidelberg (2007)

6. Grov, J., Ölveczky, P.C.: Formal modeling and analysis of Google's Megastore in Real-Time Maude. In: Iida, S., Meseguer, J., Ogata, K. (eds.) Specification, Algebra, and Software. LNCS, vol. 8373, pp. 494–519. Springer, Heidelberg (2014). doi:10.1007/978-3-642-54624-2_25

7. Grov, J., Ölveczky, P.C.: Increasing consistency in multi-site data stores: Megastore-CGC and its formal analysis. In: Giannakopoulou, D., Salaün, G. (eds.) SEFM 2014. LNCS, vol. 8702, pp. 159–174. Springer, Cham (2014). doi:10.1007/978-3-319-10431-7_12

8. Hewitt, E.: Cassandra: The Definitive Guide. O'Reilly Media, Sebastopol (2010)

9. Lamport, L.: Specifying Systems: The TLA+ Language and Tools for Hardware and Software Engineers. Addison-Wesley, Boston (2002)

10. Liu, S., Ölveczky, P.C., Ganhotra, J., Gupta, I., Meseguer, J.: Exploring design alternatives for RAMP transactions through statistical model checking. In: Proceedings of ICFEM 2017. LNCS, vol. 10610. Springer (2017, to appear)

11. Liu, S., Ölveczky, P.C., Rahman, M.R., Ganhotra, J., Gupta, I., Meseguer, J.: Formal modeling and analysis of RAMP transaction systems. In: Proceedings of SAC 2016. ACM (2016)

12. Liu, S., Ganhotra, J., Rahman, M., Nguyen, S., Gupta, I., Meseguer, J.: Quantitative analysis of consistency in NoSQL key-value stores. Leibniz Trans. Embed. Syst. 4(1), 03:1–03:26 (2017)

13. Liu, S., Rahman, M.R., Skeirik, S., Gupta, I., Meseguer, J.: Formal modeling and analysis of Cassandra in Maude. In: Merz, S., Pang, J. (eds.) ICFEM 2014. LNCS, vol. 8829, pp. 332–347. Springer, Cham (2014). doi:10.1007/978-3-319-11737-9_22

14. Meseguer, J.: Conditional rewriting logic as a unified model of concurrency. Theoret. Comput. Sci. 96, 73–155 (1992)

15. Newcombe, C., Rath, T., Zhang, F., Munteanu, B., Brooker, M., Deardeuff, M.: How Amazon Web Services uses formal methods. Commun. ACM 58(4), 66–73 (2015)

16. Ölveczky, P.C.: Formalizing and validating the P-Store replicated data store in Maude. In: Proceedings of WADT 2016. LNCS. Springer (2017, to appear)

17. Ölveczky, P.C., Meseguer, J.: Semantics and pragmatics of Real-Time Maude. Higher-Order Symbolic Comput. 20(1–2), 161–196 (2007)

18. Ölveczky, P.C., Thorvaldsen, S.: Formal modeling, performance estimation, and model checking of wireless sensor network algorithms in Real-Time Maude. Theoret. Comput. Sci. 410(2–3), 254–280 (2009)

19. Ölveczky, P.C.: Real-Time Maude and its applications. In: Escobar, S. (ed.) WRLA 2014. LNCS, vol. 8663, pp. 42–79. Springer, Cham (2014). doi:10.1007/978-3-319-12904-4_3

20. Schiper, N., Sutra, P., Pedone, F.: P-Store: genuine partial replication in wide area networks. In: Proceedings of SRDS 2010. IEEE Computer Society (2010)

Algorithms and Complexity

A Characterization of Horoidal Digraphs

Ardeshir Dolati[(✉)]

Department of Computer Science, Shahed University,
PoBox 18151-159, Tehran, Iran
dolati@shahed.ac.ir

Abstract. In this paper we investigate the upward embedding problem on the horizontal torus. The digraphs that admit upward embedding on this surface are called *horoidal digraphs*. We shall characterize the horoidal digraphs, combinatorially. Then, we construct a new digraph from an arbitrary digraph in such a way that the new digraph has an upward embedding on sphere if and only if it is horoidal. By using these constructed digraphs, we show that the decision problem whether a digraph has an upward embedding on the horizontal torus is NP-Complete.

Keywords: Upward embedding · Sphericity testing · Horizontal torus · Computational complexity · Horoidal st-graphs

1 Introduction

We call a digraph *horoidal* if it has an upward drawing with no edge crossing on the *horizontal torus*; an embedding of its underlying graph so that all directed edges are monotonic and point to the direction of z-axis. Throughout this paper, by surfaces we mean two-dimensional compact orientable surfaces such as sphere, torus and connected sum of tori with a fixed embedding in three-dimensional space $\mathbb{R}^3$. In this paper we deal with upward drawing with no edge crossing (hereafter it will be referred as *upward embedding*) on a special embedding of the ring torus in $\mathbb{R}^3$ which we call the horizontal torus. This surface is denoted by $\mathbf{T_h}$.

There are major differences between graph embedding and upward embedding of digraphs. Despite the fact that the vertical torus and the horizontal torus are two special embeddings of the ring torus in three-dimensional space $\mathbb{R}^3$, and are topologically equivalent, Dolati, Hashemi and Khosravani [11] have shown that a digraph with the underlying graph with genus one, may have an upward embedding on the vertical torus, and may fail to have an upward embedding on the horizontal torus. In addition, while Filotti, Miller and Reif [12] have shown that the question whether an undirected graph has an embedding on a fixed surface has polynomial time algorithm, the decision problem of upward embedding testing is NP-complete, even on sphere and plane. In the following we review the results on upward embedding from the characterization and computational complexity point of view.

© IFIP International Federation for Information Processing 2017
Published by Springer International Publishing AG 2017. All Rights Reserved
M.R. Mousavi and J. Sgall (Eds.): TTCS 2017, LNCS 10608, pp. 11–25, 2017.
DOI: 10.1007/978-3-319-68953-1_2

1.1 Plane

A digraph is called *upward planar* if it has an upward embedding on the plane.

Characterization. An st-digraph is a single source and single sink digraph in which there is an arc from the source to the sink. Di Battista and Tamassia [7] and Kelly [19], independently, characterized the upward planarity of digraphs.

Theorem 1.1 *(Di Battista and Tamassia [7], Kelly [19]). A digraph is upward planar if and only if it is a spanning subgraph of an st-digraph with planar underlying graph.*

Testing. The decision problem associated with plane is stated as follows.

Problem 1 *Upward embedding testing on plane (Upward planarity testing)*
INSTANCE: *Given a digraph D.*
QUESTION: *Does D have an upward embedding on plane?*

This decision problem has polynomial time algorithms for some special cases; Bertolazzi, Di Battista, Liotta, and Mannino [5] have given a polynomial-time algorithm for testing the upward planarity of three connected digraphs. Thomassen [21] has characterized upward planarity of the single source digraphs in terms of forbidden circuits. By combining Thomassen's characterization with a decomposition scheme Hutton and Lubiw [18] have given a polynomial-time algorithm to test if a single source digraph with n vertices is upward planar in $O(n^2)$. Bertolazzi, Di Battista, Mannino, and Tamassia [6] have presented an optimal algorithm to test whether a single source digraph is upward planar in the linear time. Papakostas [20] has given a polynomial-time algorithm for upward planarity testing of outerplanar digraphs.

The results for the general case is stated in the following theorem.

Theorem 1.2 *(Garg, Tamassia [13,14], Hashemi, Rival, Kisielewicz [17]) Upward planarity testing is NP-Complete.*

1.2 Round Sphere

A digraph is called *spherical* if it has an upward embedding on the sphere.

Characterization. The following theorem characterizes the sphericity of digraphs.

Theorem 1.3 *(Hashemi, Rival, Kisielewicz [15,17]). A digraph is spherical if and only if it is a spanning subgraph of a single source and single sink digraph with planar underlying graph.*

Testing. The decision problem associated with this surface is as follows.

Problem 2 *Upward embedding testing on sphere (Upward sphericity testing)*
INSTANCE: *Given a digraph D.*
QUESTION: *Does D have an upward embedding on the round sphere?*

Dolati and Hashemi [10] have presented a polynomial-time algorithm for upward sphericity testing of the embedded single source digraphs. Recently, Dolati [9] has presented an optimal linear algorithm for upward sphericity testing of this class of digraphs.

The results of the general case is stated in the following theorem.

Theorem 1.4 *(Hashemi, Rival, Kisielewicz [17]) Upward sphericity testing is NP-Complete.*

1.3   Horizontal Torus

Another surface to be mentioned is horizontal torus. Here we recall its definition. The surface obtained by the revolving of the curve $c : (y-2)^2 + (z-1)^2 = 1$ round the line $L : y = 0$ as its axis of the revolution in the yz-plane. In this case the part of $\mathbf{T_h}$ resulting from the revolving of that part of c in which $y \leq 2$ is called *inner layer*. The other part of $\mathbf{T_h}$ resulting from the revolving of that part of c in which $y \geq 2$ is called *outer layer*. The curves generating from revolving points $(0, 2, 0)$ and $(0, 2, 2)$ round the axis of revolution are minimum and maximum of the torus and are denoted by c_{min} and c_{max}, respectively. According to our definition, it is clearly seen that c_{min} and c_{max} are common between the inner layer and the outer layer. Our main results bear characterization of the digraphs that have upward embedding on the horizontal torus; we call them the horoidal digraphs. Note that, this characterization can not be applied for vertical torus. Because the set of all digraphs that admit upward embedding on horizontal torus is a proper subset of the set of all digraphs that have upward embedding on vertical torus.

Characterization. In the next section we will characterize the horoidal digraphs. Let D be a horoidal digraph that is not spherical. As we will show, in the new characterization, a proper partition of the arcs into two parts will be presented. This partition must be constructed in such a way that the induced subdigraph on each part is spherical. Moreover, the common sources and the common sinks of the two induced subdigraphs must be able to be properly identified. Note that, the arcs set of one of these parts can be considered as $\emptyset$. Therefore, the set of spherical digraphs is a proper subset of the set of horoidal digraphs.

Testing. It has been shown that the following corresponding decision problem is not easy [8]. We will investigate its complexity in details in the next sections.

Problem 3 *Upward embedding testing on* $\mathbf{T_h}$
INSTANCE: *Given a digraph D.*
QUESTION: *Does D have an upward embedding on the horizontal torus* $\mathbf{T_h}$ *?*

Dolati, Hashemi, and Khosravani [11] have presented a polynomial-time algorithm to decide whether a single source and single sink digraph has an upward embedding on $\mathbf{T_h}$. In this paper, by using a reduction from the sphericity testing decision problem, we show that this decision problem is NP-Complete.

Recently, Auer et al. in [1–4] consider the problem by using the fundamental polygon of the surfaces. They use a vector field for defining the direction of the arcs. By their definition, acyclicity condition is not a necessary condition for a digraph to have upward embedding.

The rest of this paper is organized as follows. After some preliminaries in Sect. 2 we present a characterization of a digraph to have an upward embedding on $\mathbf{T_h}$ in Sect. 3. Then we show that the decision problem to decide whether a digraph has an upward embedding on the horizontal torus belongs to NP. In Sect. 4 we shall present a polynomial reduction from the sphericity decision problem to the upward embedding testing on $\mathbf{T_h}$. In Sect. 5 we present conclusions and some related open problems.

2   Preliminaries

Here, we introduce some definitions and notations which we use throughout the paper. By a digraph D we mean a pair $D = (V, A)$ of vertices V, and arcs A. In this paper all digraphs are finite and simple (without loops and multiple edges). A necessary condition for a digraph to have an upward embedding on a surface is that it has no directed cycle, i.e. it is acyclic. For any two vertices u and v of a digraph D, the symbol (u, v) denotes an arc in D that originates from u and terminates at v. A *source* of D is a vertex with no incoming arcs. A *sink* of D is a vertex with no outgoing arcs. An *internal* vertex of D has both incoming and outgoing arcs. Let x be a vertex of D, by $od(x)$ we mean the number of the outgoing arcs of x and by $id(x)$ we mean the number of the incoming arcs to x. A *directed path* of a digraph D is a list $v_0, a_1, v_1, \ldots, a_k, v_k$ of vertices and arcs such that, for $1 \leq i \leq k$; $a_i = (v_{i-1}, v_i)$. An *undirected path* of a digraph D is a list $v_0, a_1, v_1, \ldots, a_k, v_k$ of vertices and arcs such that, for $1 \leq i \leq k$; $a_i = (v_{i-1}, v_i)$ or $a_i = (v_i, v_{i-1})$. If D is a digraph, then its *underlying graph* is the graph obtained by replacing each arc of D by an (undirected) edge joining the same pair of vertices. A digraph D is *weakly connected* or simply *connected* if, for each pair of vertices u and v, there is a undirected path in D between u and v. We use of the following equivalence relation $\mathbf{R}$ on the arcs of a digraph, introduced by Dolati et al. in [11].

Definition 2.5 *Given a digraph* $D = (V, A)$. *We say two arcs* $a, a' \in A(D)$ *are in relation* $\mathbf{R}$ *if they belong to a directed path or there is a sequence* $P_1, P_2, \ldots, P_k$, *for some* $k \geq 2$, *of directed paths with the following properties:*

(i) $a \in P_1$ and $a' \in P_k$.
(ii) Every $P_i, i = 1, \ldots, k - 1$, has at least one common vertex with P_{i+1} which is an internal vertex.

This partition is used directly in the following theorem.

Theorem 2.6 *(Dolati, Hashemi, Khosravani* [11]*). Given a digraph D. In every upward embedding of D on* $\mathbf{T_h}$*, all arcs that belong to the same class* $\mathbf{R}$ *must be drawn on the same layer.*

3   Characterization

In this section we present a characterization of a digraph that has an upward embedding on the horizontal torus. Then, by using the characterization we show that the decision problem to decide whether a digraph has an upward embedding on the horizontal torus belongs to NP. Here, for the sake of the simplicity, by $D = (V, A, S, T)$ we mean a digraph D with vertex set V, arc set A, source set S, and sink set T. For each $A_1 \subseteq A$, by $D(A_1)$ we mean the induced subdigraph on A_1. A bipartition A_1 and A_2 of A is called an *ST-bipartition* and denoted by $[A_1, A_2]$ if the source set and sink set of both $D(A_1)$ and $D(A_2)$ are S and T, respectively. Such a bipartition is called a *stable ST-bipartition* if all arcs of each equivalence class of $\mathbf{R}$ belong to exactly one part. If $[A_1, A_2]$ is a stable ST-bipartition for which $D(A_1)$ and $D(A_2)$ are spherical then we call it a *consistent stable ST-bipartition*. See Fig. 1. As we will prove, a necessary condition for a digraph $D = (V, A, S, T)$ to be horoidal is that D is a spanning subdigraph of a digraph $D' = (V, A', S', T')$ with a consistent stable $S'T'$-bipartition.

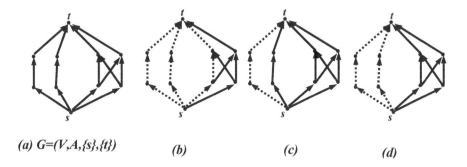

(a) $G=(V,A,\{s\},\{t\})$ **(b)**   **(c)**   **(d)**

Fig. 1. (a) A horoidal digraph $G = (V, A, \{s\}, \{t\})$, (b) A non-stable $\{s\}\{t\}$-bipartition of G, (c) An inconsistent stable $\{s\}\{t\}$-bipartition of G, (d) A consistent stable $\{s\}\{t\}$-bipartition of G

We need to introduce two more notions. For the sphere $S = \{(x, y, z) : x^2 + y^2 + z^2 = 1\}$ by the c-circle we mean one obtained from the intersection of

S with the plane $z = c$. For a finite set S, by a *permutation* π_S of S we mean a linear ordering of S.

Let $D = (V, A, S, T)$ be a spherical digraph and π_S and σ_T be two permutations for S and T, respectively. The digraph D is called *ordered spherical* with respect to π_S and σ_T if it has an upward embedding in which the vertices in S and T lie on c_1-circle and c_2-circle for some $-1 < c_1 < c_2 < 1$, and are ordered (cyclically) by π_S and σ_T, respectively. A digraph $D = (V, A, S, T)$ is called *bispherical* if there is a consistent stable ST-bipartition $[A_1, A_2]$ of A.

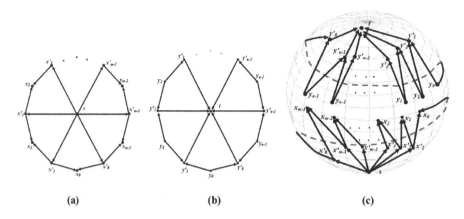

(a)   (b)   (c)

Fig. 2. (a) A super source of type m. (b) A super sink of type n. (c) An upward embedding of this super source (super sink) on sphere whose sinks (sources) lie on a c_1-circle (c_2-circle) for some $-1 < c_1 < c_2 < 1$.

Let π_S and σ_T be two permutations for S and T, respectively. A digraph $D = (V, A, S, T)$ is called *ordered bispherical* with respect to π_S and σ_T, if there is a consistent stable ST-bipartition $[A_1, A_2]$ of A such that $D(A_1)$ and $D(A_2)$ are ordered spherical with respect to π_S and σ_T. A *super source* of type m is denoted by S_m and is a single source digraph of order $2m+1$ whose vertex set is $V(S_m) = \{s, x_0, x_1, \ldots, x_{m-1}, x'_0 x'_1, \ldots, x'_{m-1}\}$ and its arc set is $A(S_m) = \{(s, x'_i) : i = 0, 1, \ldots, m - 1\} \cup \{(x'_i, x_i), (x'_i, x_{i-1}) : i = 0, 1, \ldots, m - 1\}$; here the indices are considered modulo m, see Fig. 2. The vertices $\{x_0, x_1, \ldots, x_{m-1}\}$ are the sinks of S_m. A *super sink* of type n is denoted by T_n and is a single sink digraph of order $2n + 1$ whose vertex set is $V(T_n) = \{t, y_0, y_1, \ldots, y_{n-1}, y'_0, y'_1, \ldots, y'_{n-1}\}$ and its arc set is $A(T_n) = \{(y'_i, t) : i = 0, 1, \ldots, n - 1\} \cup \{(y_i, y'_i), (y_i, y'_{i-1}) : i = 0, 1, \ldots, n-1\}$; here the indices are considered modulo n. See Fig. 2. The vertices $\{y_0, y_1, \ldots, y_{n-1}\}$ are the sources of T_n. Let D and H be two digraphs such that $V(D) \cap V(H) = \emptyset$. Also suppose that $\{u_1, \ldots, u_m\} \subseteq V(D)$ and $\{v_1, \ldots, v_m\} \subseteq V(H)$, by $D \ltimes \{(u_1 = v_1) \ldots (u_m = v_m)\} \rtimes H$ we mean the digraph obtained from D and H by identifying the vertices u_i and v_i, for $i = 1, \ldots, m$. Suppose that $D = (V, A, S, T)$ is a digraph whose source set is $S = \{s_1, s_2, \ldots, s_m\}$ and its sink set is $T = \{t_1, t_2, \ldots, t_n\}$. Assume that π_S and σ_T are permutations for S and T, respectively. Suppose that S_m is a super source whose sink set is $\{x_0, x_1, \ldots, x_{m-1}\}$ and T_n is a super sink whose source set is $\{y_0, y_1, \ldots, y_{n-1}\}$. Let us denote the single source and single sink digraph obtained as

$$(S_m \ltimes \{(x_0 = s_{\pi(0)}) \ldots (x_{m-1} = s_{\pi(m-1)})\} \ltimes D) \ltimes \{(t_{\sigma(0)} = y_0) \ldots (t_{\sigma(n-1)} = y_{n-1})\} \ltimes T_n$$

by $\pi_S D \sigma_T$.

Lemma 3.7 *Let $D = (V, A, S, T)$ be a digraph and π_S and σ_T be permutations for S and T, respectively. The digraph is ordered spherical with respect to the permutations π_S and σ_T if and only if $\pi_S D \sigma_T$ is spherical.*

Proof. If $\pi_S D \sigma_T$ is spherical, then it is not hard to observe that, we can redraw the graph, if necessary, to obtain an upward embedding of $\pi_S D \sigma_T$ in which the vertices of S lie on a c_1-circle and also the vertices of T lie on a c_2-circle preserving their permutations. The proof of the other side of the lemma is obvious. ∎

Consider the round sphere $\mathbf{S} = \{(x, y, z) | x^2 + y^2 + z^2 = 1\}$, by $\mathbf{S}_z^\epsilon$ we mean the portion of the sphere between the two level curves obtained by cutting the sphere with parallel planes $Z = z$ and $Z = z + \epsilon$, for all $-1 < z < 1$ and all $0 < \epsilon < 1 - z$. Note that, every upward embedding of a digraph D on sphere $\mathbf{S}$ can be redrawn to be an upward embedding on $\mathbf{S}_z^\epsilon$, for all $-1 < z < 1$ and all $0 < \epsilon < 1 - z$. According to this observation, we can show that for upward embedding of digraphs, each layer of $\mathbf{T_h}$ is equivalent to the round sphere. It is summarized in the following proposition.

Proposition 3.8 *The digraph D has an upward embedding on a layer of $\mathbf{T_h}$ if and only if it has an upward embedding on the round sphere $\mathbf{S} = \{(x, y, z) | x^2 + y^2 + z^2 = 1\}$.*

By the following theorem we characterize the horoidal digraphs. We assume w.l.o.g. that the digraphs have no isolated vertex.

Theorem 3.9 *The digraph $D = (V, A, S, T)$ has an upward embedding on the horizontal torus if and only if there are subsets $S' \subseteq S$ and $T' \subseteq T$ and there are permutations $\pi_{S'}$ and $\sigma_{T'}$ such that by adding new arcs, if necessary, the digraph can be extended to a digraph $D' = (V, A', S', T')$ which is ordered spherical or ordered bispherical with respect to $\pi_{S'}$ and $\sigma_{T'}$.*

Proof Suppose that $D = (V, A, S, T)$ has an upward embedding on T_h. There are two cases that can be happen for D.

Case 1. D has an upward embedding on a layer of T_h. In this case, according to Proposition 3.8 it has an upward embedding on sphere. By Theorem 1.3 we conclude that D is a spanning subdigraph of a single source and single sink digraph $D' = (V, A', S', T')$. That means the assertion for this case follows. Because D' is an ordered spherical with respect to the unique permutation of S' and T'.

Case 2. D has no upward embedding on a layer of T_h. In this case we consider an upward embedding of D on T_h. Suppose that, the subset of sources (sinks) that must be placed on $c_{min}(c_{max})$ is denoted by $S'(T')$. Now, we add a set of new arcs F to this embedding in such way that all of them point up, they do not generate crossing and for each source node in $S \setminus S'$ (sink node in $T \setminus T'$) there will be an arc in F incoming to (emanating from) it. By adding this set of arcs we have an upward embedding of a superdigraph $D' = (V, A', S', T')$ of $D = (V, A, S, T)$ in which $A' = A \cup F$. Suppose that we denote by π'_S and σ'_T the permutations of S' and T' according to their order of their placement on c_{min} and c_{max}, respectively. Let A_{in} and A_{out} be the set of arcs drawn on the inner layer and outer layer of T_h, respectively. The digraphs $D'(A_{in})$ and $D'(A_{out})$ are order spherical with respect to π'_S and σ'_T. In other words, $D' = (V, A', S', T')$ is a superdigraph of $D = (V, A, S, T)$ and is ordered bispherical with respect to π'_S and σ'_T.

Conversely, suppose that, there is a superdigraph $D' = (V, A', S', T')$ of D that is an ordered spherical with respect to some permutations of S' and T', for some $S' \subset S$ and $T' \subset T$. In this case, D' is a horoidal digraph and therefore its subdigraph D is also horoidal.

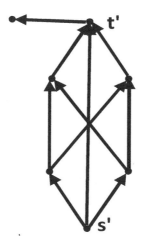

Fig. 3. A digraph $D = (V, A, \{s'\}, \{t'\})$ that is not horoidal

Now, suppose that there are some subsets $S' \subset S$ and $T' \subset T$ and some permutations π'_S and σ'_T for them such that a superdigraph $D' = (V, A', S', T')$ of D is ordered bispherical with respect to π'_S and σ'_T. Let $[A_1, A_2]$ be its corresponding consistent stable $S'T'$-bipartition. In this case, the digraphs $D'(A_1)$ and $D'(A_2)$ are ordered spherical with respect to π'_S and σ'_T. Therefore, the digraph $D'(A_1)$ and $D'(A_2)$ can be embedded upwardly on inner layer and outer layer of T_h, respectively such that these upward embeddings imposes an upward embedding for D' on T_h. In other words, D' and therefore D has an upward embedding on the horizontal torus.   ∎

We characterize the horoidal digraphs by the above theorem. Note that, one can not apply it for characterization the digraphs that admit upward embedding on vertical torus. As an example, all arcs in A in every stable $\{s'\}\{t'\}$-bipartition of every super graph $D' = (V, A', \{s'\}, \{t'\})$ of digraph $D = (V, A, \{s'\}, \{t'\})$ depicted in Fig. 3 belong to one part. That means it is inconsistent. Because $k_{3,3}$ is a subgraph of the underlying graph of indeced subdigraph on the aforementioned part. Therefore, this digraph is not horoidal. However, one of its upward embeddings on vertical torus is depicted in [11].

Now, by using the characterization stated in Theorem 3.9 we show that Problem 3 belongs to NP. It is summarized in the following theorem.

Theorem 3.10 *The upward embedding testing on T_h belongs to NP.*

Proof The candidate solution consists of a superdigraph $D' = (V, A', S', T')$ of the instance D whose sources and sinks are subsets of the sources and sinks of D, two cyclic permutations π'_S and σ'_T for S' and T' and a consistent stable $S'T'$-bipartition $[A_1, A_2]$, if necessary. For checking the correctness of this solution in polynomial time, one can check the conditions of Theorem 3.9. To this end, the Step 1 of the following two steps can be considered and if it is not sufficient (i.e., if the answer of Step 1 is not true) then another step must be considered, too.

Step 1. Check if the digraph D' is an ordered spherical with respect to π'_S and σ'_T.

Step 2. Check if the digraphs $D'(A_1)$ and $D'(A_2)$ are ordered spherical with respect to π'_S and σ'_T.

For checking Step 1, it suffices to check if the single source and single sink digraph $\pi'_S D' \sigma'_T$ is spherical. According to Theorem 1.3 it can be done by checking if its underlying graph is planar. Therefore this checking step can be done in polynomial time. If it is revealed that its underlying graph is not planar then by using $[A_1, A_2]$ we have to consider Step 2. For checking Step 2 it is sufficient to check if the single source and single sink digraphs $D'(A_1)$ and $D'(A_2)$ are ordered spherical with respect to π'_S and σ'_T. Similarly, this step can be checked in polynomial time. Therefore the candidate solution can be checked in polynomial time. That means the assertion follows.   ∎

4   Source-In-Sink-Out Graph of Adigraph

In this section we want to show that the upward embedding testing problem on $\mathbf{T_h}$ is an NP-hard problem. We do this by a polynomial time reduction from the upward sphericity testing decision problem. Let x and y be two vertices of a digraph D. By $y \prec x$ we mean the vertex x is *reachable* from the vertex y. That means there is a directed path from y to x in D, especially y is reachable from itself by the trivial path. By $N^+(y)$ we mean all the reachable vertices from y and by $N^-(y)$ we mean all the vertices for which y is a reachable vertex. A subgraph $D_x^O = (V(D_x^O), A(D_x^O))$ is an *out-subgraph* rooted at vertex x if $V(D_x^O) = N^+(x)$ and $A(D_x^O)$ consists of all the arcs of all the directed paths in D from x to every other vertex in $V(D_x^O)$. A subgraph $D_x^I = (V(D_x^I), A(D_x^I))$ is an *in-subgraph* rooted at vertex x if $V(D) = N^-(x)$ and $A(D_x^I)$ consists of all the arcs of all the directed paths in D from every other vertex in $V(D_x^O)$ to x. In Fig. 4 an out-subgraph rooted at a source vertex is depicted. Now, we are ready to introduce some useful properties of these defined subgraphs.

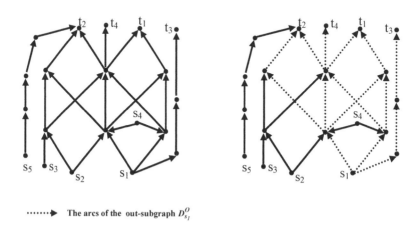

........▶ **The arcs of the out-subgraph** $D_{s_1}^O$

Fig. 4. A digraph D and the arcs of $D_{s_1}^O$.

Lemma 4.11 *Let x be an internal vertex of a digraph D, then all the arcs in $A(D_x^O) \cup A(D_x^I)$ belong to the same equivalence class with respect to the relation* **R**.

Proof The internal vertex x has both incoming and outgoing arcs. Let a and a' be an incoming arc of x and an outgoing arc of x, respectively. For each arc in $A(D_x^O)$ there is a directed path containing that arc and a, therefore they belong to the same equivalence class. Similarly, for each arc in $A(D_x^I)$ there is a directed path containing that arc and a', therefore they belong to the same equivalence class. On the other hand, there is a directed path containing a and a', that means they belong to the same equivalence class too. According to the transitive property of **R** the proof is completed.   ■

The relation between the arcs of the out-subgraph rooted at a source vertex and the relation between the arcs of the in-subgraph rooted at a sink vertex are shown in the following lemma.

Lemma 4.12 *Let s and t be a source vertex and a sink vertex of a digraph D, respectively.*

(i) *If $od(s) = 1$ then all the arcs of D_s^O belong to the same equivalence class with respect to the relation* **R**.

(ii) *If $id(t) = 1$ then all the arcs of D_t^I belong to the same equivalence class with respect to the relation* **R**.

Proof Suppose that $od(s) = 1$ and let a be the outgoing arc of s. Obviously, for each arc of D_s^O there is a directed path containing that arc and a, therefore they belong to the same equivalence class. That means all the arcs of D_s^O belong to the same equivalence class with respect to the relation **R**. Similarly, the second part of the lemma can be proved. ∎

Now, we define the *source-in-sink-out graph* of a digraph $D = (V, A)$ that is denoted by $SISO(D)$. Suppose that $D = (V, A)$ is a digraph with the set of source vertices S and the set of sink vertices T. Let $\mathcal{S} = \{s \in S \mid od(s) > 1\}$ and let $\mathcal{T} = \{t \in T \mid id(t) > 1\}$. In other words, $\mathcal{S}$ is the set of sources for which the number of their outgoing arcs is more than one and $\mathcal{T}$ is the set of sinks for which the number of their incoming arcs is more than one. Construction of the digraph $SISO(D)$ from the digraph D is done as follows. For each source vertex $s \in \mathcal{S}$, we add a new vertex s' and a new arc from the new vertex s' to the vertex s. Also, for each sink vertex $t \in \mathcal{T}$, we add a new vertex t' and a new arc from the vertex t to the new vertex t' (see Fig. 5). Obviously, s' is a source vertex, t' is a sink vertex, and s and t are two internal vertices of $SISO(D)$. With respect to the construction of $SISO(D)$, we can immediately conclude the following lemma.

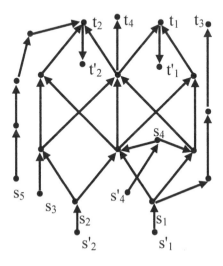

Fig. 5. The source-in-sink-out graph of the depicted graph in Fig. 4

Lemma 4.13 *Let D be a digraph.*

(i) If s is a source vertex of $SISO(D)$ then $od(s) = 1$.
(ii) If t is a sink vertex of $SISO(D)$ then $id(t) = 1$.

By Definition 2.5 two arcs of a digraph belong to the same equivalence class if they belong to a directed path. In the following lemma we show that two arcs of a source-in-sink-out graph belong to the same class if they belong to the same undirected path (not necessarily directed).

Lemma 4.14 *Suppose that D is a digraph. If P is an undirected path in $SISO(D)$, then all the arcs of P belong to the same equivalence class with respect to the relation $\mathbf{R}$.*

Proof It is sufficient to show that each pair of consecutive arcs in P belong to the same equivalence class. To this end let a and a' be an arbitrary pair of consecutive arcs of P, and let v be their common vertex. Since the number of the arcs incident with v is at least two, by Lemma 4.13, the vertex v is neither a source vertex of $SISO(D)$ nor a sink vertex of $SISO(D)$. That means v is an internal vertex of $SISO(D)$. Therefore by Lemma 4.11, the arcs a and a' belong to the same equivalence class.   ∎

The following theorem states a key property of the source-in-sink-out graph of a digraph.

Proposition 4.15 *Let D be a connected digraph, all the arcs of $SISO(D)$ belong to the same equivalence class with respect to $\mathbf{R}$.*

Proof Let $a = (x, y)$ and $a' = (x', y')$ be an arbitrary pair of arcs of D. Because of the connectivity of D, there is an undirected path P' between x to y'. If P' does not contain a, we add it to P'. In this case the starting point of the obtained undirected path is the vertex y. Similarly, we can add the arc a' to the undirected path, if it does not contain this arc. In other words, there is an undirected path P in D that contains a and a'. Thus, by Lemma 4.14, a and a' belong to the same equivalence class.   ∎

In the following theorem we observe that either both digraphs D and $SISO(D)$ or none of them have upward embeddings on sphere.

Proposition 4.16 *The digraph D has an upward embedding on sphere if and only if $SISO(D)$ has an upward embedding on sphere.*

Proof Suppose that we have an upward embedding of D on the round sphere $\mathbf{S} = \{(x, y, z) | x^2 + y^2 + z^2 = 1\}$. Let $\mathcal{S}$ be the set of sources for which the number of their outgoing arcs is more than one and let $\mathcal{T}$ be the set of sinks of D for which the number of their incoming arcs is more than one. Without loss of generality, we can assume that none of the sources (sinks) of $\mathcal{S}$ ($\mathcal{T}$) is located at south (north) pole. Otherwise, we may modify the upward embedding to provide an upward embedding on the sphere with this property. Let $s \in \mathcal{S}$ be an arbitrary source in S with z its height (its z-coordinate) and consider $\mathbf{S}^{\epsilon}_{z-\epsilon}$, where ϵ is small enough so that this portion contains no vertices of D in its interior. This portion may be partitioned into connected regions bounded by the monotonic curves corresponding to the arcs of D. We consider a point s' as an arbitrary point on the circle obtained by cutting the sphere with plane $Z = z - \epsilon$ so that the point s and s' are on the boundary of a region. Now, we draw the arc (s', s) in the mentioned region by a monotonic curve. Similarly, if we draw an arc (t, t') for each sink $t \in \mathcal{T}$ by a monotonic curve without any crossing with other arcs. Then we have an upward embedding for $SISO(D)$ on the round sphere. Conversely, if we have an upward embedding of $SISO(D)$ on the round sphere. By deleting all added arcs (s', s) and (t, t') in construction of $SISO(D)$ from D, we have an upward embedding of D on sphere. ∎

Proposition 4.17 *Let D be a digraph, $SISO(D)$ has an upward embedding on sphere if and only if it has an upward embedding on $\mathbf{T_h}$.*

Proof Suppose that $SISO(D)$ has an upward embedding on sphere. Since, for upward embedding, sphere and each layer of $\mathbf{T_h}$ are equivalent we can conclude that $SISO(D)$ has an upward embedding on a layer of $\mathbf{T_h}$ and therefore on $\mathbf{T_h}$. Conversely, suppose that $SISO(D)$ has an upward embedding on $\mathbf{T_h}$. By Proposition 4.15, all the arcs of each connected component of $SISO(D)$ belong to the same equivalence class with respect to relation $\mathbf{R}$. Therefore, by Theorem 2.6 in any upward embedding of $SISO(D)$ on $\mathbf{T_h}$ all the arcs of each connected component of $SISO(D)$ must be drawn on a layer of $\mathbf{T_h}$. Suppose that $SISO(D)$ has k connected components and let $H_1, H_2, \ldots, H_k$ be its connected components. Assume that $-1 < z < 1$ is a real number. We set $\epsilon = \frac{1-z}{k+1}$, and embed the component H_j on the portion $\mathbf{S}^{\epsilon}_{z+(j-1)\epsilon}$ upwardly, for $j = 1, \ldots, k$. In other words, we can have an upward embedding of $SISO(D)$ on the round sphere. ∎

Now, by Propositions 4.16 and 4.17 we have the following theorem:

Proposition 4.18 *The digraph D has an upward embedding on sphere if and only if $SISO(D)$ has an upward embedding on $\mathbf{T_h}$.*

Obviously, the construction of $SISO(D)$ from D can be done in $O(n)$ time, where n is the number of vertices of D. By this fact and Proposition 4.18 the NP-hardness of upward embedding testing on $\mathbf{T_h}$ is proved, this is summarized in the following theorem.

Theorem 4.19 *The upward embedding testing on $\mathbf{T_h}$ is an NP-hard problem.*

By Theorems 3.10 and 4.19 we have one of the main results of the paper as follows.

Theorem 4.20 *The upward embedding testing on $\mathbf{T_h}$ is an NP-Complete problem.*

5   Conclusion and Some Open Problems

In this paper, we have presented a characterization for a digraph to have an upward embedding on $\mathbf{T_h}$. By that characterization we have shown that the decision problem to decide whether a digraph has an upward embedding on the horizontal torus belongs NP. We have constructed a digraph from a given digraph in such a way that it is horoidal if and only if it is spherical. Finally, we have presented a polynomial time reduction from the sphericity testing decision problem to the upward embedding testing on $\mathbf{T_h}$. That means we have shown that the upward embedding testing decision problem on $\mathbf{T_h}$ is NP-Complete.

The following are some open problems:
Dolati et al. in [11] presented a polynomial time algorithm to decide whether a single source and single sink digraph has an upward embedding on $\mathbf{T_h}$.

Problem 1: Is it possible to find polynomial time algorithms for upward embedding testing of some other classes of digraphs on $\mathbf{T_h}$?
Problem 2: Characterize those digraphs which they are spherical if and only if they are horoidal.

Acknowledgements. I am very thankful to Dr. Masoud Khosravani for his helpful discussions. I am also very grateful to anonymous referees for their useful suggestions and comments.

References

1. Auer, C., Bachmaier, C., Brandenburg, F.J., Gleißner, A.: Classification of planar upward embedding. In: van Kreveld, M., Speckmann, B. (eds.) GD 2011. LNCS, vol. 7034, pp. 415–426. Springer, Heidelberg (2012). doi:10.1007/978-3-642-25878-7_39

2. Auer, C., Bachmaier, C., Brandenburg, F.J., Gleißner, A., Hanauer, K.: The duals of upward planar graphs on cylinders. In: Golumbic, M.C., Stern, M., Levy, A., Morgenstern, G. (eds.) WG 2012. LNCS, vol. 7551, pp. 103–113. Springer, Heidelberg (2012). doi:10.1007/978-3-642-34611-8_13

3. Auer, C., Bachmaier, C., Brandenburg, F.J., Hanauer, K.: Rolling upward planarity testing of strongly connected graphs. In: Brandstädt, A., Jansen, K., Reischuk, R. (eds.) WG 2013. LNCS, vol. 8165, pp. 38–49. Springer, Heidelberg (2013). doi:10.1007/978-3-642-45043-3_5

4. Auer, C., Bachmaier, C., Brandenburg, F.J., Gleiner, A., Hanauer, K.: Upward planar graphs and their duals. Theor. Comput. Sci. **571**, 36–49 (2015)

5. Bertolazzi, P., Di Battista, G., Liotta, G., Mannino, C.: Upward drawing of triconnected digraphs. Algorithmica **12**(6), 476–497 (1994)

6. Bertolazzi, P., Di Battista, G., Mannino, C., Tamassia, R.: Optimal upward planarity testing of single source digraphs. SIAM J. Comput. **27**(1), 132–169 (1998)

7. Di Battista, G., Tamassia, R.: Algorithms for plane representations of acyclic digraphs. Theoret. Comput. Sci. **61**, 175–198 (1988)

8. Dolati, A.: Digraph embedding on T_h. In: Proceeding of Seventh Cologne Twente Workshop on Graphs and Combinatorial Optimization, CTW 2008, University of Milan, pp. 11–14 (2008)

9. Dolati, A.: Linear sphericity testing of 3-connected single source digraphs. Bull. Iran. Math. Soc. **37**(3), 291–304 (2011)
10. Dolati, A., Hashemi, S.M.: On the sphericity testing of single source digraphs. Discrete Math. **308**(11), 2175–2181 (2008)
11. Dolati, A., Hashemi, S.M., Khosravani, M.: On the upward embedding on the torus. Rocky Mt. J. Math. **38**(1), 107–121 (2008)
12. Filotti, I.S., Miller, G.L., Reif, J.: On determining the genus of a graph in $O(v^{O(g)})$ steps. In: Proceeding of the 11th Annual Symposium on Theory of Computing, pp. 27–37. ACM, New York (1979)
13. Garg, A., Tamassia, R.: On the computational complexity of upward and rectilinear planarity testing. In: Tamassia, R., Tollis, I.G. (eds.) GD 1994. LNCS, vol. 894, pp. 286–297. Springer, Heidelberg (1995). doi:10.1007/3-540-58950-3_384
14. Garg, A., Tamassia, R.: Upward planarity testing. Order **12**(2), 109–133 (1995)
15. Hashemi, S.M.: Digraph embedding. Discrete Math. **233**, 321–328 (2001)
16. Hashemi, S.M., Rival, I.: Upward drawings to fit surfaces. In: Bouchitté, V., Morvan, M. (eds.) ORDAL 1994. LNCS, vol. 831, pp. 53–58. Springer, Heidelberg (1994). doi:10.1007/BFb0019426
17. Hashemi, S.M., Rival, I., Kisielewicz, A.: The complexity of upward drawings on spheres. Order **14**, 327–363 (1998)
18. Hutton, M., Lubiw, A.: Upward planar drawing of single-source acyclic digraph. SIAM J. Comput. **25**(2), 291–311 (1996)
19. Kelly, D.: Fudemental of planar ordered sets. Discrete Math. **63**, 197–216 (1987)
20. Papakostas, A.: Upward planarity testing of outerplanar dags (extended abstract). In: Tamassia, R., Tollis, I.G. (eds.) GD 1994. LNCS, vol. 894, pp. 298–306. Springer, Heidelberg (1995). doi:10.1007/3-540-58950-3_385
21. Thomassen, C.: Planar acyclic oriented graphs. Order **5**, 349–361 (1989)

Gomory Hu Tree and Pendant Pairs
of a Symmetric Submodular System

Saeid Hanifehnezhad and Ardeshir Dolati[✉]

Department of Mathematics, Shahed University, Tehran, Iran
{s.hanifehnezhad,dolati}@shahed.ac.ir

Abstract. Let $\mathcal{S} = (V, f)$, be a symmetric submodular system. For two distinct elements s and l of V, let $\Gamma(s,l)$ denote the set of all subsets of V which separate s from l. By using every Gomory Hu tree of $\mathcal{S}$ we can obtain an element of $\Gamma(s,l)$ which has minimum value among all the elements of $\Gamma(s,l)$. This tree can be constructed iteratively by solving $|V| - 1$ minimum sl-separator problem. An ordered pair (s,l) is called a pendant pair of $\mathcal{S}$ if $\{l\}$ is a minimum sl-separator. Pendant pairs of a symmetric submodular system play a key role in finding a minimizer of this system. In this paper, we obtain a Gomory Hu tree of a contraction of $\mathcal{S}$ with respect to some subsets of V only by using contraction in Gomory Hu tree of $\mathcal{S}$. Furthermore, we obtain some pendant pairs of $\mathcal{S}$ and its contractions by using a Gomory Hu tree of $\mathcal{S}$.

Keywords: Symmetric submodular system · Contraction of a system · Pendant pair · Maximum adjacency ordering · Gomory-Hu tree

1 Introduction

Let V be a finite set. A set function $f : 2^V \mapsto \mathbb{R}$ is called a submodular function if and only if for all $X, Y \in 2^V$, we have

$$f(X) + f(Y) \geq f(X \cup Y) + f(X \cap Y). \tag{1}$$

Submodular functions play a key role in combinatorial optimization, see [3] for further discussion. Rank functions of matroids, cut capacity functions and entropy functions are some well known examples of submodular functions. For a given system $\mathcal{S} = (V, f)$, let $f : 2^V \mapsto \mathbb{R}$ be a submodular function. The problem in which we want to find a subset $X \subseteq V$, for which $f(X) \leq f(Y)$ for all $Y \subseteq V$ is called submodular system minimization problem. Minimizing a submodular system is one of the most important problems in combinatorial optimization. Many problems in combinatorial optimization, such as finding minimum cut and minimum st-cut in graphs, or finding the largest common independent set in two matroids can be modeled as a submodular function minimization. Image segmentation [1,8,9], speech analysis [11,12], wireless and power networks [20] are

© IFIP International Federation for Information Processing 2017
Published by Springer International Publishing AG 2017. All Rights Reserved
M.R. Mousavi and J. Sgall (Eds.): TTCS 2017, LNCS 10608, pp. 26–33, 2017.
DOI: 10.1007/978-3-319-68953-1_3

only a small part of applications of minimizing submodular functions. Grotchel, Lovasz and Scherijver have developed the first weakly and strongly polynomial time algorithm for minimizing submodular systems in [6] and [13], respectively. Each of them is designed based on the ellipsoid method. Then, nearly simultaneously Scherijver [18] and Iwata, Fleischer, and Fujishige [7] gave a combinatorial strongly polynomial time algorithms for this problem. Later, a faster algorithm for minimizing submodular system was proposed by Orlin [16]. To the best of our knowledge, the fastest algorithm to find a minimizer of a submodular system $\mathcal{S} = (V, f)$ is due to Lee et al. [10]. Their algorithm runs in $O(|V|^3 log^2 |V|\tau + |V|^4 log^{O(1)} |V|)$ time, where τ is the time taken to evaluate the function.

Stoer and Wagner [19] and Frank [2] independently have presented an algorithm that finds a minimum cut of a graph $G = (V, E)$ in $O(|E||V| + |V|^2 \log |V|)$ time. Their algorithms are based on Nagamochi and Ibaraki's algorithm [15] which finds a minimum cut of an undirected graph. Queyranne [17] developed a faster algorithm to find a minimizer in a special case of a submodular system. This algorithm was proposed to find a minimizer of a symmetric submodular system $\mathcal{S} = (V, f)$. It is a generalization of Stoer and Wagner's algorithm [19] and runs in $O(|V|^3)$ time. This algorithm, similar to Stoer and Wagner's algorithm uses pendant pairs to obtain a minimizer of a symmetric submodular system.

For a given weighted undirected graph $G = (V, E)$, Gomory and Hu constructed a weighted tree, named as Gomory Hu tree [5]. By using a Gomory Hu tree of the graph G, one can solve the all pairs minimum st-cut problem with $|V| - 1$ calls to the maximum flow subroutine instead of the $\binom{|V|}{2}$ calls. Goemans and Ramakrishnan [4] illustrated that for every symmetric submodular system, there exists a Gomory-Hu tree. It is worth to mention that, there is neither an algorithm to construct a Gomory Hu tree of a symmetric submodular system by using pendant pairs nor any method to obtain pendant pairs of a symmetric submodular system by using a Gomory Hu tree of it.

In this paper, we obtain a Gomory Hu tree of a contraction of a symmetric submodular system $\mathcal{S} = (V, f)$, under some subsets of V only by using a Gomory Hu tree of $\mathcal{S}$. In other words, without solving any minimum st-separator problem of the contracted system, we obtain a Gomory Hu tree of it only by contracting the Gomory Hu tree of the original system. Furthermore, we obtain some pendant pairs of a symmetric submodular system $\mathcal{S}$ and its contractions by using a Gomory Hu tree of $\mathcal{S}$.

The outline of this paper is as follows. Section 2 provides preliminaries and basic definitions. In Sect. 3, we obtain some pendant pairs of a symmetric submodular system by using a Gomory Hu tree of the system. In Sect. 4, we construct a Gomory Hu tree of a contracted system by using a Gomory Hu tree of the original system.

2   Preliminaries

Let V be a finite nonempty set. A function $f : 2^V \mapsto \mathbb{R}$ is called a set function on V. For every $X \subseteq V, x \in X$ and $y \in V \backslash X$, we use $X + y$ and $X - x$ instead of $X \cup \{y\}$ and $X \backslash \{x\}$, respectively. Also, for $x \in V$ we use $f(x)$ instead of $f(\{x\})$.

A pair $\mathcal{S} = (V, f)$, is called a system if f is a set function on V. A system $\mathcal{S} = (V, f)$ is called a submodular system if for all $X, Y \subseteq V$, we have

$$f(X) + f(Y) \geq f(X \cup Y) + f(X \cap Y). \tag{2}$$

Furthermore, it is called a symmetric system if for every $X \subseteq V$, we have

$$f(X) = f(V \backslash X). \tag{3}$$

Consider a symmetric submodular system $\mathcal{S} = (V, f)$. Suppose that A and B are two disjoint subsets of V. A subset $X \subseteq V$ is called an AB-separator in $\mathcal{S}$, if $X \cap (A \cup B) = A$ or $X \cap (A \cup B) = B$. Let $\Gamma(A, B)$ denote the set of all AB-separators in $\mathcal{S}$. A subset $X \in \Gamma(A, B)$ is called a minimum AB-separator in $\mathcal{S}$ if $f(X) = min_{Y \in \Gamma(A,B)} f(Y)$. If A and B are singletones $\{a\}$ and $\{b\}$, then we use ab-separator and $\Gamma(a, b)$ instead of $\{a\}\{b\}$-separator and $\Gamma(\{a\}, \{b\})$, respectively.

Let $G = (V, E)$ be a weighted undirected graph with the weight function $w : E \mapsto \mathbb{R}^+ \cup \{0\}$. Suppose that X is a nonempty proper subset of V. The set of all edges connecting X to $V \backslash X$, is called the cut associated with X and is denoted by $\delta(X)$. The capacity of $\delta(X)$ is denoted by $C(X)$ and defined by

$$C(X) = \sum_{e \in \delta(X)} w(e). \tag{4}$$

By setting $C(\emptyset) = C(V) = 0$, (V, C) is a symmetric submodular system [14]. For two distinct vertices u and v of G, every minimum uv-separator of (V, C) is a minimum uv-cut of G.

Let $T = (V, F)$ be a tree and uv be an arbitrary edge of it. By $T - uv$, we mean the forest obtained from T by removing uv. The set of vertices of two components of $T - uv$ which respectively contain u and v, is denoted by $V_u(T - uv)$ and $V_v(T - uv)$. Also, for $uv \in F$, define $\mathcal{F}_u(T - uv) = \{X | u \in X \subseteq V_u(T - uv)\}$, $\mathcal{F}_v(T - uv) = \{X | v \in X \subseteq V_v(T - uv)\}$.

Suppose that X is a nonempty subset of vertices of a given graph $G = (V, E)$. We denote by $G_{>X<}$ the graph obtained from G by contracting all the vertices in X into a single vertex.

Let $\mathcal{S} = (V, f)$ be a symmetric submodular system. Suppose that $T = (V, F)$ is a weighted tree with the weight function $w : E \mapsto \mathbb{R}^+$. If for all $u, v \in V$, the minimum weight of the edges on the path between u and v in T is equal to minimum uv-separator in $\mathcal{S}$, then T is called a flow equivalent tree of $\mathcal{S}$. Also, we say that T has the cut property with respect to $\mathcal{S}$ if $w(e) = f(V_u(T - uv)) = f(V_v(T - uv))$ for every $e = uv \in F$. A flow equivalent tree of $\mathcal{S}$ is called a Gomory Hu tree of $\mathcal{S}$ if it has cut property with respect to $\mathcal{S}$.

Consider a system $\mathcal{S} = (V, f)$. A pair of elements (x, y) of V is called a pendant pair for $\mathcal{S}$, if $\{y\}$ is a minimum xy-separator in $\mathcal{S}$.

Let $\mathcal{S} = (V, f)$ be a symmetric submodular system. Suppose that $\rho = (v_1, v_2, \cdots, v_{|V|})$ is an ordering of the elements of V, where v_1 can be chosen arbitrarily. If for all $2 \leq i \leq j \leq |V|$, we have

$$f(V_{i-1} + v_i) - f(v_i) \leq f(V_{i-1} + v_j) - f(v_j), \tag{5}$$

where $V_i = \{v_1, v_2, \cdots, v_i\}$, then ρ is called a maximum adjacency ordering (MA-ordering) of $\mathcal{S}$.

For a symmetric submodular system $\mathcal{S} = (V, f)$, Queyranne [17] showed that the last two elements $(v_{|V|-1}, v_{|V|})$ of an MA-ordering of $\mathcal{S}$, is a pendant pair of this system.

Let $\mathcal{S} = (V, f)$ be a system and X be an arbitrary subset of V. By $\varphi(X)$, we mean a single element obtained by unifying all elements of X. The contraction of $\mathcal{S}$ with respect to a subset $A \subseteq V$ is denoted by $\mathcal{S}_A = (V_A, f_A)$ and defined by $V_A = (V \setminus A) + \varphi(A)$ and

$$f_A(X) = \begin{cases} f(X) & if \ \varphi(A) \notin X \\ f((X - \varphi(A)) \cup A) & if \ \varphi(A) \in X. \end{cases} \tag{6}$$

Suppose that A and B are two nonempty disjoint subsets of V. We denote by $(\mathcal{S}_A)_B$, the contraction of $\mathcal{S}_A$ with respect to B.

3   Obtaining Pendant Pairs from a Gomory Hu Tree

Stoer and Wagner [19] obtained a pendant pair of a weighted undirected graph $G = (V, E)$ by using MA-ordering in $O(|E| + |V| \log |V|)$ time. By generalizing their algorithm to a symmetric submodular system $\mathcal{S} = (V, f)$, Queyranne [17] obtained a pendant pair of this system in $O(|V|^2)$ time.

In this section, by using the fact that there exists a Gomory Hu tree for a symmetric submodular system $\mathcal{S} = (V, f)$, we obtain some pendant pairs of it from a Gomory Hu tree of this system. Also, we show that a Gomory Hu tree of a symmetric submodular system can be constructed by pendant pairs. Firstly, we prove the following lemma.

Lemma 1. *Let $T = (V, F)$ be a flow equivalent tree of a symmetric submodular system $\mathcal{S} = (V, f)$ with the weight function $w : E \mapsto \mathbb{R}^+$. If $e = uv$ is an arbitrary edge of T, then for every $A \in \mathcal{F}_u(T - uv)$ and $B \in \mathcal{F}_v(T - uv)$, we have $w(e) \leq min\{f(X)|X \in \Gamma(A, B)\}$.*

Proof. Since T is a flow equivalent tree of $\mathcal{S}$, then the value of a minimum uv-separator in $\mathcal{S}$ is equal to $w(e)$. In other words $w(e) = min\{f(X)|X \in \Gamma(u, v)\}$. Since $\mathcal{F}_u(T - uv)$ and $\mathcal{F}_v(T - uv)$ are two subsets of $\Gamma(u, v)$, then $w(e) \leq min\{f(X)|X \in \Gamma(A, B)\}$.

Theorem 1. *Let $T = (V, F)$ be a Gomory Hu tree of a symmetric submodular system $\mathcal{S} = (V, f)$ with the weight function $w : E \mapsto \mathbb{R}^+$. If $e = uv$ is an arbitrary edge of T, then for every $A \in \mathcal{F}_u(T - uv)$ and $B \in \mathcal{F}_v(T - uv)$, $V_v(T - uv)$ is a minimum AB-separator in $\mathcal{S}$.*

Proof. Since T has the cut property, then $w(e) = f(V_v(T - uv))$. Now, according to Lemma 1 we have $f(V_v(T - uv)) \leq min\{f(X)|X \in \Gamma(A, B)\}$. On the other hand, $V_v(T - uv)$ is one of the elements of $\Gamma(A, B)$ then $f(V_v(T - uv)) = min\{f(X)|X \in \Gamma(A, B)\}$, and the proof is completed.

The following theorem is immediate from Theorem 1.

Theorem 2. *Let $T = (V, F)$ be a Gomory Hu tree of a symmetric submodular system $\mathcal{S} = (V, f)$. If $e = uv$ is an arbitrary edge of T, then $(\varphi(A), \varphi(V_v(T - uv))$ for every $A \in \mathcal{F}_u(T - uv)$ is a pendant pair of $(\mathcal{S}_A)_{V_v(T - uv)}$.*

Theorem 2 shows that every Gomory Hu tree of a symmetric submodular system can be obtained by using pendant pairs. We know that every Gomory Hu tree of a symmetric submodular system $\mathcal{S}$ is a flow equivalent tree having the cut property. We show by an example that Theorem 2 is not necessarily true for every flow equivalent tree of $\mathcal{S}$. Let $V = \{1, 2, 3, 4\}$. Consider the symmetric submodular system $\mathcal{S} = (V, f)$ presented in Table 1.

Table 1. A symmetric submodular system $\mathcal{S} = (V, f)$.

A	$\{1\}$	$\{2\}$	$\{3\}$	$\{4\}$	$\{1, 2\}$	$\{1, 3\}$	$\{1, 4\}$	V
$f(A) = f(V \backslash A)$	4	6	3	5	4	5	9	0

It can be shown that the tree $T = (V, f)$ depicted in Fig. 1 is a flow equivalent tree of $\mathcal{S}$. Suppose that $w : E \mapsto \mathbb{R}^+$ is the weight function of T. By considering the edge $e = 24$ of T, we have $V_4(T - 24) = \{4\}$. Now, choose the element $\{2\}$ from $\mathcal{F}_2(T - 24)$. According to Fig. 1, $\{4\}$ is a minimum 24-cut and $w(24) = 4$. Since T is a flow equivalent tree of $\mathcal{S}$, then the value of minimum 24-separator in $\mathcal{S}$ is equal to 4. However, in the given system we have $f(\{4\}) = 5$. Therefore, $(2, 4)$ cannot be a pendant pair of $\mathcal{S}$.

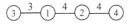

Fig. 1. Flow equivalent tree of $\mathcal{S}$.

Theorem 3. *Let $T = (V, F)$ be a flow equivalent tree of a symmetric submodular system $\mathcal{S} = (V, f)$ with the weight function $w : F \mapsto \mathbb{R}^+$. If for every edge $e = uv$ of T, there exists a set $A \in \mathcal{F}_u(T - uv)$ such that $(\varphi(A), \varphi(V_v(T - uv))$ is a pendant pair of $(\mathcal{S}_A)_{V_v(T - uv)}$, then T is a Gomory Hu tree.*

Proof. Since for every $e = uv$ of T, there exists a subset A in $\mathcal{F}_u(T - uv)$, that $(\varphi(A), \varphi(V_v(T - uv))$ is a pendant pair of $(\mathcal{S}_A)_{V_v(T-uv)}$ then $w(e) = f(V_v(T - uv))$. Thus, T has the cut property. Therefore, T is a Gomory Hu tree of $\mathcal{S}$.

In the rest of this section, we will prove some properties of pendant pairs of a system.

Theorem 4. *Let (s,l) be a pendant pair of a system $\mathcal{S} = (V, f)$. For every $A \subseteq V \backslash \{s,l\}$, (s,l) is a pendant pair of $\mathcal{S}_A$.*

Proof. Since (s,l) is a pendant pair of $\mathcal{S}$, then $f(l) = min\{f(X)|X \in \Gamma(s,l)\}$. From (6) we have $f(l) = f_A(l) = min\{f_A(X)|X \in \Gamma(s,l)\}$.
   Thus, (s,l) is a pendant pair of $\mathcal{S}_A$. The proof is completed.

Note that, the converse of Theorem 4 is not generally true. Consider the given system in Table 1. Table 2 contains MA-orderings of $\mathcal{S}$ and $\mathcal{S}_{\{1,3\}}$ and also pendant pairs, obtained from these MA-orderings.

Table 2. MA-orderings of $\mathcal{S}$ and $\mathcal{S}_{\{1,3\}}$.

System	MA-ordering	Pendant pair
$\mathcal{S}$	$4, 2, 1, 3$	$(1, 3)$
$\mathcal{S}_{\{1,3\}}$	$13, 2, 4$	$(2, 4)$

It can be observed that $(2,4)$ is a pendant pair of $\mathcal{S}_{\{1,3\}}$; however, it is not a pendant pair of $\mathcal{S}$.

Proposition 1. *If (s,l) is a pendant pair of a system $\mathcal{S} = (V, f)$, then (l, s) is a pendant pair of $\mathcal{S}$ iff $f(l) = f(s)$.*

Proof. Let (l, s) be a pendant pair of $\mathcal{S}$. Thus, $f(l) = min\{f(X)|X \in \Gamma(s,l)\}$. Since (s,l) is also a pendant pair of $\mathcal{S}$, then $f(s) = f(l)$. Now, suppose that $f(s) = f(l)$. Since (s,l) is a pendant pair of $\mathcal{S}$, then (l, s) is also a pendant pair of $\mathcal{S}$.

4   Gomoru Hu Tree of the Contraction of a System

Let $T = (V, F)$ be a tree. A subset $X \subseteq V$ is called a *T-connected* subset of V, if the graph induced by X in T is a subtree. The following theorem shows that by having a flow equivalent tree T of a symmetric submodular system $\mathcal{S} = (V, f)$, we can easily obtain a flow equivalent tree of $\mathcal{S}_X$ for every T-connected subset of V.

Theorem 5. *Let $T = (V, F)$ be a flow equivalent tree of a symmetric submodular system $\mathcal{S} = (V, f)$. If X is a T-connected subset of V, then $T_{>X<}$ is a flow equivalent tree of $\mathcal{S}_X = (V_X, f_X)$.*

Proof. Let u and v be two distinct elements of V_X. Consider the path P_{uv} connecting u and v in T. Suppose that $T' = (V', F')$ is the induced subtree by X in T. Let E' be the set of edges in P_{uv} with the minimum weight. If $E' \not\subseteq F'$, then there is nothing to prove. Now, suppose that E' is a subset of F'. Assume that $m_1 = min\{f_X(A)|A \in \Gamma(u, \varphi(X))\}$, $m_2 = min\{f_X(A)|A \in \Gamma(\varphi(X), v)\}$ and $m^* = min\{f_X(A)|A \in \Gamma(u, v)\}$. Obviously, the values of the minimum $u\varphi(X)$-cut, the minimum $\varphi(X)v$-cut and the minimum uv-cut in tree $T_{>X<}$ are equal to m_1, m_2 and $min\{m_1, m_2\}$, respectively. Thus, to show that $T_{>X<}$ is a flow equivalent tree of $\mathcal{S}_X$ it suffices to prove that $m^* = min\{m_1, m_2\}$. Let T' be a flow equivalent tree of $\mathcal{S}_X$ and P'_{uv} be a path connecting u and v in T'. Now, we have two cases: case (i), $\varphi(X)$ is appeared in P'_{uv}. Therefore, the value of uv-separator in $\mathcal{S}_X$ is equal to $min\{m_1, m_2\}$ which is equal to the value of minimum uv-cut in $T_{>X<}$. Case (ii), if $\varphi(X)$ is not appeared in P'_{uv}, then we can easily conclude that the value of minimum uv-cut in T' and $T_{>X<}$ are equal. The proof is completed.

Theorem 6. *Let $T = (V, F)$ be a Gomory Hu tree of a symmetric submodular system $\mathcal{S} = (V, f)$. If X is a T-connected subset of V, then $T_{>X<}$ is a Gomory Hu tree of $\mathcal{S}_X = (V_X, f_X)$.*

Proof. According to Theorem 5, $T_{>X<}$ is a flow equivalent of $\mathcal{S}_X$. Furthermore, from (6), $T_{>X<}$ has the cut property. Then, $T_{>X<}$ is a Gomory Hu tree of $\mathcal{S}_X$.

Then, by having a Gomory Hu tree of a symmetric submodular system $\mathcal{S} = (V, f)$, we can find a Gomory Hu tree of the contracted system, with respect to a connected set X, without finding any minimum st-separators in $\mathcal{S}_X$. Also, we can deduce that $T_{>V_v(T-uv)<}$ is a Gomory Hu tree of $\mathcal{S}_{V_v(T-uv)}$.

Corollary 1. *Let $T = (V, f)$ be a Gomory Hu tree of a symmetric submodular system $\mathcal{S} = (V, f)$ and uv be an arbitrary edge of T. For every $A \in \mathcal{F}_u(T - uv)$, for which A is a connecting set in T, the tree $T_{>A\cup V_v(T-uv)<}$ is a Gomory Hu tree of $(\mathcal{S}_A)_{V_v(T-uv)}$.*

5   Conclusion

In this paper, we obtained some pendant pairs of a symmetric submodular system by using its Gomory Hu tree. Furthermore, for a contraction of $\mathcal{S}$ with respect to a connected set, we constructed a Gomory Hu tree only by contracting the connected set in Gomory Hu tree of $\mathcal{S}$.

Acknowledgements. The authors would like to thank the anonymous referees for their helpful suggestions and comments to improve the paper.

References

1. Boykov, Y., Veksler, O., Zabih, R.: Fast approximate energy minimization via graph cuts. IEEE Trans. Pattern Anal. Mach. Intell. **23**(11), 1222–1239 (2001)
2. Frank, A.: On the edge-connectivity algorithm of Nagamochi and Ibaraki. Laboratoire Artemis, IMAG, Universit J. Fourier, Grenoble (1994)
3. Fujishige, S.: Submodular Functions and Optimization. Elsevier (2005)
4. Goemans, M.X., Ramakrishnan, V.S.: Minimizing submodular functions over families of sets. Combinatorica **15**(4), 499–513 (1995)
5. Gomory, R.E., Hu, T.C.: Multi-terminal network flows. J. Soc. Ind. Appl. Math. **9**(4), 551–570 (1961)
6. Grötschel, M., Lovász, L., Schrijver, A.: The ellipsoid method and its consequences in combinatorial optimization. Combinatorica **1**(2), 169–197 (1981)
7. Iwata, S., Fleischer, L., Fujishige, S.: A combinatorial strongly polynomial algorithm for minimizing submodular functions. J. ACM (JACM) **48**(4), 761–777 (2001)
8. Kohli, P., Kumar, M.P., Torr, P.H.: P3 & Beyond: move making algorithms for solving higher order functions. IEEE Trans. Pattern Anal. Mach. Intell. **31**(9), 1645–1656 (2009)
9. Kohli, P., Torr, P.H.S.: Dynamic graph cuts and their applications in computer vision. In: Cipolla, R., Battiato, S., Farinella, G.M. (eds.) Computer Vision. Studies in Computational Intelligence, vol. 285, pp. 51–108. Springer, Heidelberg (2010). doi:10.1007/978-3-642-12848-6_3
10. Lee, Y.T., Sidford, A., Wong, S.C.: A faster cutting plane method and its implications for combinatorial and convex optimization. In: IEEE 56th Annual Symposium on Foundations of Computer Science (FOCS), pp. 1049–1065. IEEE, October 2015
11. Lin, H., Bilmes, J.: An application of the submodular principal partition to training data subset selection. In: NIPS Workshop on Discrete Optimization in Machine Learning, December 2010
12. Lin, H., Bilmes, J.A.: Optimal selection of limited vocabulary speech corpora. In: INTERSPEECH, pp. 1489–1492, August 2011
13. Lovász, L., Grötschel, M., Schrijver, A.: Geometric Algorithms and Combinatorial Optimization. Springer, Heidelberg (1988). doi:10.1007/978-3-642-97881-4
14. Nagamochi, H., Ibaraki, T.: Algorithmic Aspects of Graph Connectivity. Cambridge University Press, New York (2008)
15. Nagamochi, H., Ibaraki, T.: Computing edge-connectivity in multigraphs and capacitated graphs. SIAM J. Discrete Math. **5**(1), 54–66 (1992)
16. Orlin, J.B.: A faster strongly polynomial time algorithm for submodular function minimization. In: Fischetti, M., Williamson, D.P. (eds.) IPCO 2007. LNCS, vol. 4513, pp. 240–251. Springer, Heidelberg (2007). doi:10.1007/978-3-540-72792-7_19
17. Queyranne, M.: Minimizing symmetric submodular functions. Math. Program. **82**(1–2), 3–12 (1998)
18. Schrijver, A.: A combinatorial algorithm minimizing submodular functions in strongly polynomial time. J. Comb. Theor. Ser. B **80**(2), 346–355 (2000)
19. Stoer, M., Wagner, F.: A simple min-cut algorithm. J. ACM (JACM) **44**(4), 585–591 (1997)
20. Wan, P.J., Clinescu, G., Li, X.Y., Frieder, O.: Minimum-energy broadcasting in static ad hoc wireless networks. Wirel. Netw. **8**(6), 607–617 (2002)

Inverse Multi-objective Shortest Path Problem Under the Bottleneck Type Weighted Hamming Distance

Mobarakeh Karimi[1], Massoud Aman[1(✉)], and Ardeshir Dolati[2]

[1] Department of Mathematics, University of Birjand, Birjand, Iran
{mobarake.karimi,mamann}@birjand.ac.ir
[2] Department of Computer Science, Shahed University, Tehran, Iran
dolati@shahed.ac.ir

Abstract. Given a network $G(N,A,C)$ and a directed path P^0 from the source node s to the sink node t, an inverse multi-objective shortest path problem is to modify the cost matrix C so that P^0 becomes an efficient path and the modification is minimized. In this paper, the modification is measured by the bottleneck type weighted Hamming distance and is proposed an algorithm to solve the inverse problem. Our proposed algorithm can be applied for some other inverse multiobjective problem. As an example, we will mention how the algorithm is used to solve the inverse multi-objective minimum spanning tree problem under the bottleneck type weighted Hamming distance.

Keywords: Multi-objective optimization · Shortest path problem · Inverse problem · Hamming distance

1 Introduction

The invers shortest path problem(ISPP) is one of the most typical problems of the inverse optimization, which makes a predetermined solution to become an optimal solution after modifications. This problem has attracted many attentions recently due to its broad applications in practice such as the traffic modeling and the seismic tomography (see, e.g., [5,10]). For example, assume that in a road network, we would like to modify the costs of the crossing such that a special path between two given nodes becomes optimum in order that, for some reason, the users select this path. To do this, we need to solve an ISPP.

In 1992, Burton and Toint [2] first formulated the ISPP using the l_2 norm to measure the modification. Zhang et al. [13] showed that the ISPP is equivalent to solving a minimum weight circulation problem when the modifications are measured by the l_1 norm. In [12], a column generation scheme is developed to solve the ISPP under the l_1 norm. Ahuja and Orlin [1] showed that the

© IFIP International Federation for Information Processing 2017
Published by Springer International Publishing AG 2017. All Rights Reserved
M.R. Mousavi and J. Sgall (Eds.): TTCS 2017, LNCS 10608, pp. 34–40, 2017.
DOI: 10.1007/978-3-319-68953-1_4

ISPP under the l_1 norm can be solved by solving a new shortest path problem. For the l_∞ norm, they showed that the problem reduces to a minimum mean cycle problem. In [11], it is shown that all feasible solutions of the ISPP form a polyhedral cone and the relationship between this problem and the minimum cut problem is discussed. Duin and Volgenant [3] proposed an efficient algorithm based on the binary search technique to solve the ISPP under the bottleneck type Hamming distance (BWHD). In [9], Tayyebi and Aman extended their method to solve the inverse minimum cost flow problem and the inverse linear programming problem.

As with most real-world optimization problems, there is usually more than one objective that has to be taken into account, thus leading to multi-objective optimization problems (MOP) and inverse multi-objective optimization problems (IMOP). IMOP consists of finding a minimal adjustment of the objective functions coefficients such that a given feasible solution becomes efficient. Ronald et al. [7] proposed an algorithm to solve the inverse multi-objective combinatorial optimization problems under the l_∞ norm.

In this paper, we propose an algorithm to solve the inverse multi-objective shortest path problem under the BWHD. Our proposed algorithm can be used for solving the inverse of the multi-objective version of some problems under the BWHD. As an example, we apply the algorithm for the inverse multi-objective minimum spanning tree problem under the BWHD.

2   Preliminaries

The notations and definitions used in this paper are given in this section. Let $x, y \in \mathbb{R}^q$ be two vectors. $x \le y$ iff $x_k \le y_k$ for every $k \in \{1, \ldots, q\}$ and $x \ne y$. Let $G(N,A,C)$ be a directed network consisting of a set of nodes $N = \{1, 2, \ldots, n\}$, a set of arcs $A \subseteq N \times N$ with $|A| = m$ and a cost matrix $C \in \mathbb{R}^{m \times q}$. In the matrix C, we denote the row corresponding to the arc $a \in A$ by the vector $C(a)$. This vector is called the cost of the arc a. The element k of $C(a)$ is denoted by $C^k(a)$. For each $i_1, i_r \in N$ a directed path from i_1 to i_r in G is a sequence of nodes and arcs $i_1 - a_1 - i_2 - a_2 - \ldots - i_{r-1} - a_{r-1} - i_r$ satisfying the properties that for all $1 \le k \le r - 1$, $(i_k, i_{k+1}) \in A$ and for all $k, l \in \{1, \ldots, r\}$, $i_k \ne i_l$ if $k \ne l$. For each path P in G, the cost of P is defined as $C(P) = \sum_{a \in P} C(a)$. A path P from i to j is called an efficient path if there is no other path P' from i to j such that $C(P') \le C(P)$. Let $s, t \in N$ be two given nodes called the source and sink node, respectively. The multi-objective shortest path problem (MSPP) is to find all efficient directed paths from s to t.

Theorem 1 [8]. *The bicriterion shortest path problem is NP-complete.*

In [4] the multi-objective label setting algorithm is presented in the case that the cost of the arcs is nonnegative. Also the multi-objective label correcting algorithm is presented in the other case.

For a given path P^0 from s to t in G, The inverse multi-objective shortest path problem (IMSPP) is to find a matrix $D \in \mathbb{R}^{m \times q}$ such that

(a) P^0 is an efficient path in the network $G(N,A,D)$;
(b) For each $a \in A$ and $k \in \{1,\ldots,q\}$, $-L^k(a) \leq D^k(a) - C^k(a) \leq U^k(a)$,
    where $L^k(a), U^k(a) \geq 0$ are given bounds for modifying cost $C^k(a)$;
(c) The distance between C and D is minimized.

The distance between C and D can be measured by various matrix norms. Also these matrices can be converted to two vectors, by a vectorization method, and a vector norm is used. Let each arc a has an associated penalty $w(a) \in \mathbb{R}_{\geq}^q$. In this paper, we use the BWHD defined as follows:

$$H_w(C, D) = \max_{a \in A, k \in \{1,\ldots,q\}} w^k(a).H(C^k(a), D^k(a)), \tag{1}$$

where $H(C^k(a), D^k(a))$ is the Hamming distance, i.e.

$$H(C^k(a), D^k(a)) = \begin{cases} 1 & \text{if } C^k(a) \neq D^k(a), \\ 0 & \text{if } C^k(a) = D^k(a). \end{cases} \tag{2}$$

3   The IMSPP Under the BWHD

In this section, the IMSPP under the BWHD is considered and an algorithm is proposed to solve it. Let $G(N,A,C)$ be a network with a source node s and a sink node t. Assume that P^0 is a given directed path from s to t in G. We can write the IMSPP under the BWHD as follows:

$$\min \quad H_w(C, D), \tag{3}$$
$$\text{s.t.} \quad P^0 \text{ is an efficient path from } s \text{ to } t \text{ in } G(N,A,D),$$
$$- L^k(a) \leq D^k(a) - C^k(a) \leq U^k(a), \qquad \forall a \in A, \quad \forall k \in \{1,\ldots,q\}$$
$$D \in \mathbb{R}^{m \times q},$$

where $w : A \to \mathbb{R}^q$ is the arc penalties function and for each $a \in A$ and $k \in \{1, \cdots, q\}$, $L^k(a)$ and $U^k(a)$ are the bounds for modifying cost $C^k(a)$. Assume that $w_1 \leq w_2 \leq \ldots \leq w_{qm}$ denote the sorted list of the arc penalties. For each $k \in \{1,\ldots,q\}$ and $r \in \{1, 2, \ldots, qm\}$, we define $A_r^k = \{a \in A : w^k(a) \leq w_r\}$ and the matrix D_r with the following elements is defined:

$$D_r^k(a) = \begin{cases} C^k(a) & \text{if } a \in A \setminus A_r^k, \\ C^k(a) + U^k(a) & \text{if } a \in A_r^k \setminus P^0, \\ C^k(a) - L^k(a) & \text{if } a \in A_r^k \cap P^0. \end{cases} \tag{4}$$

The following theorem provides a helpful result for presenting our algorithm.

Theorem 2. *If D is a feasible solution to the problem (3) with the objective value w_r, then D_r defined in (4) is also feasible whose objective value is less than or equal to w_r.*

Proof. It is easily seen that D_r satisfies the bound constraints and its objective value is not greater than w_r. On the contrary, suppose that P^0 is not efficient in $G(N,A,D_r)$. This means that there exists a path P from s to t such that $D_r(P) \leq D_r(P^0)$. We prove that $D(P) \leq D(P^0)$. Hence P^0 is dominated by P in $G(N,A,D)$ which contradicts the feasibility of D for (3).

The inequality $D_r(P) - D_r(P^0) \leq 0$ implies that

$$D(P) - D(P^0) \leq D_r(P^0) - D_r(P) + D(P) - D(P^0)$$
$$= \sum_{a \in P^0} (D_r(a) - D(a)) + \sum_{a \in P} (D(a) - D_r(a))$$
$$= \sum_{a \in (P^0 \setminus P)} (D_r(a) - D(a)) + \sum_{a \in (P \setminus P^0)} (D(a) - D_r(a)). \qquad (5)$$

By the definition of D_r and feasibility of D for (3), all the phrases of the right hand side of (5) are nonpositive. Therefore $D(P) - D(P^0) \leq 0$, which completes the proof.

The following theorem is concluded immediately from Theorem 2.

Corollary 1. *If the optimal objective value of (3) is w_r, then D_r defined in (4) is an optimal solution to (3).*

The next theorem help us to find the optimal solution by a binary search on the set of the penalties.

Theorem 3. *If D_r is a feasible solution to the problem (3), then D_{r+1} is also feasible.*

Proof. On the contrary, suppose that D_{r+1} is not feasible to (3). Hence P^0 is not efficient in $G(N,A,D_{r+1})$. Thus there exists a path P from s to t such that $D_{r+1}(P) \leq D_{r+1}(P^0)$. Analysis similar to that in the proof of Theorem 2 shows that $D_r(P) \leq D_r(P^0)$ which contradicts the feasibility of D_r for (3).

Based on the previous results, we propose an algorithm to solve the IMSPP under the BWHD. We find the minimum value of $r \in \{1, \ldots, qm\}$ such that P^0 is an efficient path in $G(N,A,D_r)$. For checking this condition, we can use the proposed algorithm in [4] to find all efficient paths from s to t in $G(N,A,D_r)$. According to Theorem 3, the minimum value of r can be found by a binary search on the set of the penalties. We now state our proposed algorithm formally.

Algorithm 1

Step 1. Sort the arc penalties. Suppose $w_1 \leq w_2 \leq \ldots \leq w_{qm}$ is the sorted list

Step 2. Set $i = \lceil \frac{qm}{2} \rceil$ and $r = qm$

Step 3. construct the matrix D_r defined in (4)

Step 4. If P^0 is an efficient path in $G(N,A,D_r)$, then go to Step 5. Otherwise, go to Step 6

Step 5. If $i > 0$, then update $r = r - i$, $i = \lceil \frac{i}{2} \rceil$ and go to Step 3. Otherwise, go to Step 8

Step 6. If $r = qm$, then the problem (3) is infeasible and stop. Otherwise update $r = r + i$, $i = \lceil \frac{i}{2} \rceil$ and go to Step 7

Step 7. If $i > 0$ go to Step 3. Otherwise, go to Step 8

Step 8. Stop. D_r is an optimal solution to (3).

To analyze the complexity of the algorithm, note that the number of the iterations is $O(log(qm)) = O(log(qn))$ and in each iteration an MSPP is solved. Hence if an MSPP can be solved in T time, then the complexity of the algorithm is $O(Tlog(qn))$.

Theorem 4. *Algorithm 1 solves the IMSPP under the BWHD in $O(Tlog(qn))$ time.*

4   Inverse Multi-objective Minimum Spanning Tree Problem Under the BWHD

The algorithm proposed in the previous section can be used for the inverse of the others multi-objective combinatorial optimization problems under the BWHD. For instance, consider the inverse multi-objective minimum spanning tree problem (IMMSTP). Let $G(V,E,C)$ be a graph with $|V| = n$ nodes, $|E| = m$ edges and the cost matrix $C \in \mathbb{Z}^{m \times q}$. Assume that T^0 be a given spanning tree of G. The IMMSTP under the BWHD can be written as follows:

$$\min \quad H_w(C, D), \tag{6}$$

$$s.t. \quad T^0 \text{ is an efficient spanning tree of } G(V,E,D),$$

$$- L^k(a) \leq D^k(a) - C^k(a) \leq U^k(a), \qquad \forall a \in E, \quad \forall k \in \{1, \ldots, q\}$$

$$D \in \mathbb{Z}^{m \times q}.$$

For each $k \in \{1, ..., q\}$ and $r \in \{1, ..., qm\}$, the set A_r^k is exactly the same as the previous section and The matrix D_r is defined similar to (4) as follows:

$$D_r^k(a) = \begin{cases} C^k(a) & \text{if} \quad a \in E \setminus A_r^k, \\ C^k(a) + U^k(a) & \text{if} \quad a \in A_r^k \setminus T^0, \\ C^k(a) - L^k(a) & \text{if} \quad a \in A_r^k \cap T^0. \end{cases} \tag{7}$$

Similarly, Theorem 2, Corollary 1 and Theorem 3 can be concluded for the problem (6). Consequently, Algorithm 1 can be applied for IMMSTP under the BWHD with this difference that in Step 4 we must investigate the efficiency of the spanning tree T^0 for $G(V,E,D_r)$. It can be done by solving a multi-objective minimum spanning tree problem. We can use the Prim's spanning tree algorithm presented in [6].

5   Conclusion

In this article, the Inverse multi-objective shortest path problem under the bottleneck type weighted Hamming distance is considered. We proposed an algorithm based on the binary search technique to solve the inverse problem.

This work can be extended in different ways. For instance, other distances can be use. It is also possible to apply our proposed algorithm to solve the inverse of other problems.

Acknowledgments. The authors would like to thank the anonymous referees for their valuable comments to improve the paper.

References

1. Ahuja, R.K., Orlin, J.B.: Inverse optimization. Oper. Res. **49**, 771–783 (2001)
2. Burton, D., Toint, P.L.: On an instance of the inverse shortest paths problem. Math. Program. **53**, 45–61 (1992)
3. Duin, C.W., Volgenant, A.: Some inverse optimization problems under the Hamming distance. Eur. J. Oper. Res. **170**, 887–899 (2006)
4. Ehrgott, M.: Multicriteria Optimization. Springer, Heidelberg (2005). doi:10.1007/3-540-27659-9
5. Farago, A., Szentesi, A., Szviatovszki, B.: Inverse optimization in high-speed networks. Discr. Appl. Math. **129**, 83–98 (2003)
6. Prim, R.C.: Shortest connection networks and some generalizations. Bell Labs. Tech. J. **36**, 1389–1401 (1957)
7. Roland, J., Smet, Y.D., Figueira, J.R.: Inverse multi-objective combinatorial optimization. Discr. Appl. Math. **161**, 2764–2771 (2013)
8. Serafini, P.: Some considerations about computational complexity for multi objective combinatorial problems. In: Jahn, J., Krabs, W. (eds.) Recent Advances and Historical Development of Vector Optimization. Lecture Notes in Economics and Mathematical Systems, vol. 294. Springer, Heidelberg (1986). doi:10.1007/978-3-642-46618-2_15
9. Tayyebi, J., Aman, M.: On inverse linear programming problems under the bottleneck-type weighted Hamming distance. Discr. Appl. Math. (2016). doi:10.1016/j.dam.2015.12.017
10. Wei, D.C.: An optimized Floyd algorithm for the shortest path problem. J. Netw. **5**, 1496–1504 (2010)
11. Xu, S., Zhang, J.: An inverse problem of the weighted shortest path problem. Jpn. J. Ind. Appl. Math. **12**, 47–59 (1995)

12. Zhang, J.Z., Ma, Z., Yang, C.: A column generation method for inverse shortest path problems. Zeitschrift fo Oper. Res. **41**, 347–358 (1995)
13. Zhang, J.Z., Ma, Z.: A network flow method for solving some inverse combinatorial optimization problems. Optim. J. Math. Program. Oper. Res. **37**, 59–72 (1996)

Locality-Based Relaxation: An Efficient Method for GPU-Based Computation of Shortest Paths

Mohsen Safari[1] and Ali Ebnenasir[2(✉)]

[1] Department of Computer Engineering,
University of Zanjan, Zanjan, Iran
mohsen_safari@znu.ac.ir
[2] Department of Computer Science,
Michigan Technological University, Houghton, USA
aebnenas@mtu.edu

Abstract. This paper presents a novel parallel algorithm for solving the Single-Source Shortest Path (SSSP) problem on GPUs. The proposed algorithm is based on the idea of *locality-based relaxation*, where instead of updating just the distance of a single vertex v, we update the distances of v's neighboring vertices up to k steps. The proposed algorithm also implements a communication-efficient method (in the CUDA programming model) that minimizes the number of kernel launches, the number of atomic operations and the frequency of CPU-GPU communication without any need for thread synchronization. This is a significant contribution as most existing methods often minimize one at the expense of another. Our experimental results demonstrate that our approach outperforms most existing methods on real-world road networks of up to 6.3 million vertices and 15 million arcs (on weaker GPUs).

1 Introduction

Graph processing algorithms have a significant impact on several domains of applications as graphs are used to model conceptual networks, systems and natural phenomena. One of the most important problems in graph processing is the Single-Source Shortest Path (SSSP) problem that has applications in a variety of contexts (e.g., traffic routing [27], circuit design [22], formal analysis of computing systems [23]). Due to the significance of the time/space efficiency of solving SSSP on large graphs, researchers have proposed [7] parallel/distributed algorithms. Amongst these, the algorithms that harness the computational power of Graphical Processing Units (GPUs) using NVIDIA's Compute Unified Device Architecture (CUDA) have attracted noticeable attention in research community [10]. However, efficient utilization of the computational power of GPUs is a challenging (and problem-dependent) task. This paper presents a highly efficient method that solves SSSP on GPUs for road networks with large dimensions.

A CUDA program is parameterized in terms of thread IDs and its efficiency mostly depends on all threads performing useful work on the GPU. GPUs include

© IFIP International Federation for Information Processing 2017
Published by Springer International Publishing AG 2017. All Rights Reserved
M.R. Mousavi and J. Sgall (Eds.): TTCS 2017, LNCS 10608, pp. 41–56, 2017.
DOI: 10.1007/978-3-319-68953-1_5

a multi-threaded architecture containing several Multi-Processors (MPs), where each MP has some Streaming Processors (SPs). A CUDA program has a CPU part and a GPU part. The CPU part is called the *host* and the GPU part is called the *kernel*, capturing an array of threads. The threads are grouped in blocks and each block will run in one MP. A few threads (e.g., 32) can logically be grouped as a *warp*. The sequence of execution starts by copying data from host to device (GPU), and then invoking the kernel. Each thread executes the kernel code in parallel with all other threads. The results of kernel computations can be copied back from device to host. CUDA's memory model is hierarchical, starting from the fastest: registers, in-block shared memory and global memory. The communication between GPU and CPU can be done through shared variables allocated in the global memory. CUDA also supports *atomic* operations, where some operations (e.g., addition of a value to a memory location) are performed in a non-interruptible fashion. To optimize the utilization of computational resources of GPUs, a kernel must (i) ensure that all threads perform useful work and ideally no thread remains idle (i.e., work efficiency); (ii) have fewer atomic commands; (iii) use thread synchronization rarely (preferably not at all), and (iv) have little need for communication with the CPU. The *divergence* of a computation occurs when the number of idle threads of a warp increases.

Most existing GPU-based algorithms [5,12,13,15,25,26] for solving SSSP rely on methods that associate a group of vertices/arcs to thread blocks, and optimize a proper subset of the aforementioned factors, but not all. This is because in general it is hard to determine the workload of each kernel for optimum efficiency a priori. In the context of SSSP, each thread updates the distance of its associated vertex in a round-based fashion, called *relaxation*. For example, Harish *et al.* [12,13] present a GPU-based implementation of Dijkstra's shortest path algorithm [9] where they design two kernels; one for relaxing the recently updated vertices, called the *frontier*, and the second one for updating the list of frontier vertices. Singh *et al.* [26] improve Harish *et al.*'s algorithm by using memory efficiently and using just one kernel. They also present a parallelization of Bellman-Ford's algorithm [3,11], but use three atomic operations in the kernel. Kumar *et al.* [15] also present a parallelization of Bellman-Ford's algorithm in a two-kernel CUDA program. Busato *et al.* [5] exploit the new features of modern GPUs along with some algorithmic optimizations in order to enhance work efficiency. Meyer and Sanders [18] present the delta-stepping method where vertices are classified and relaxed in buckets based on their distance from the source. Davidson *et al.* [8] extend the idea of delta-stepping in a queue-based implementation of Bellman-Ford's algorithm where the queue contains the vertices whose outgoing arcs must be relaxed. There are several frameworks [14,28,29] for graph processing on GPUs whose main objective is to facilitate the formulation of graph problems on GPUs; nonetheless, the time efficiency of these approaches may not be competitive with hardcoded GPU programs.

In order to efficiently solve SSSP in large directed graphs, we present a GPU-based algorithm that minimizes the number of atomic operations, the number of kernel launches and CPU-GPU communication while increasing work efficiency.

The proposed algorithm is based on the novel idea of *locality-based relaxation*, where we relax the distance of a vertex up to a few steps in its vicinity. Figure 1 illustrates the proposed concept of *locality-based relaxation* where the thread associated with v and w not only updates the distance of v's (respectively, w's) immediate neighbors, but propagates the impact of this relaxation on the neighboring vertices that can be reached from v (respectively, w) in k steps. Moreover, we provide a mechanism for systematic (and dynamic) scheduling of threads using flag arrays where each bit represents whether a thread should execute in each kernel launch. The proposed scheduling approach significantly decreases the frequency of communication between CPU and GPU. We experimentally show that locality-based relaxation increases time efficiency up to 30% for $k < 5$. Furthermore, our locality-based relaxation method mitigates the divergence problem by increasing the workload of each thread systematically, thereby decreasing the number of kernel launches and the probability of divergence.

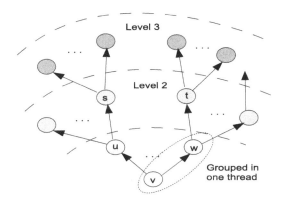

Fig. 1. Locality-based relaxation.

Our experimental results demonstrate that the proposed approach outperforms most existing methods (using a GeForce GT 630 with 96 cores). We conduct our experiments on the road network graphs of New York, Colorado, Pennsylvania, Northwest USA, California-Nevada and California with up to 1.9 million vertices and 5.5 million arcs, and Western USA with up to 6.3 million vertices and 15.3 million arcs. Our implementation and data sets are available at http://gpugraphprocessing.github.io/SSSP/. The proposed algorithm enables a computation and communication-efficient method by using (i) a single kernel launch per iteration of the host; (ii) only one atomic operation per kernel, and (iii) no thread synchronization.

Organization. Section 2 defines directed graphs, the shortest path problem and a classic GPU-based solution thereof. Section 3 introduces the idea of locality-based relaxation and presents our algorithm (implemented in CUDA) along with its associated experimental results. Section 4 discusses some important factors that could impact GPU-based solutions of SSSP. Finally, Sect. 5 makes concluding remarks and discusses future extensions of this work.

2 Preliminaries

In this section, we present some basic concepts about GPUs and CUDA's programming model. Moreover, we formulate the problem statement.

2.1 Synchronization Mechanisms in CUDA

In CUDA's programming model, programmers can define thread blocks in one, two or three dimensions; however, the GPU scheduler decides how to assign thread blocks to MPs; i.e., programmers have no control over the scheduling policy. Moreover, inter-block communications must be performed via the global memory. CUDA supports atomic operations to prevent data races, where a *data race* occurs when multiple threads access some shared data simultaneously and at least one of them performs a write. CUDA also provides a mechanism for barrier synchronization amongst the threads within a block, but there is no programming primitive for inter-block synchronization.

2.2 Directed Graphs and SSSP

Let $G = (V, A, w)$ be a weighted directed graph, where V denotes the set of vertices, A represents the set of arcs and the weight function $w : A \rightarrow \mathbb{Z}$ assigns a non-negative weight to each arc. A *simple path* from some vertex $s \in V$ to another vertex $t \in V$ is a sequence of vertices $v_0, \cdots, v_k$, where $s = v_0$ and $t = v_k$, each arc $(v_i, v_{i+1}) \in A$ and no vertex is repeated. A shortest path from s to t is a simple path whose summation of weights is minimum amongst all simple paths from s to t. The Single-Source Shortest Path (SSSP) problem is stated as follows:

- INPUT: A directed graph $G = (V, A, w)$ and a source vertex $s \in V$.
- OUTPUT: The weight of the shortest path from s to any vertex $v \in V$, where $v \neq s$.

2.3 Basic Functions

Two of the most famous algorithms for solving SSSP include Dijkstra's [9] and Bellman-Ford's [3,11] algorithms. These algorithms use a *Distance* array, denoted $d[]$. Initially, the distance of the source vertex is zero and that of other vertices is set to infinity. After termination, $d[v]$ includes the shortest distance of each vertex v from the source s. *Relaxation* is a core function in both algorithms where for each arc (u, v), if $d[v] > d[u] + w(u, v)$ then $d[v]$ is updated to $d[u] + w(u, v)$. We use the functions *notRelaxed* and *Relax* to respectively represent when an arc should be relaxed and performing the actual relaxation (see Algorithms 1 and 2). *atomicMin* is a built-in function in CUDA that assigns the minimum of its two parameters to its first parameter in an atomic step.

Algorithm 1. notRelaxed(u,v)

1: **if** $d[v] > d[u] + w(u, v)$ **then**
2:     return *true*;
3: **else**
4:     return *false*;

Algorithm 2. Relax(u,v)

1: *atomicMin*($d[v]$, $d[u] + w(u, v)$);

2.4 Harish *et al.*'s Algorithm

In this subsection, we represent Harish *et al.*'s [12,13] GPU-based algorithm for solving SSSP in CUDA. While their work belongs to almost 10 years ago, some researchers [26,29] have recently used Harish *et al.*'s method as a base for comparison due to its simplicity and efficiency. Moreover, our algorithm in this paper significantly extends their work. Harish *et al.* use the Compressed Sparse Row (CSR) representation of a graph where they store vertices in an array *startV* and the end vertices of arcs in an array *endV* (see Fig. 2). Each entry in *startV* points to the starting index of its adjacency list in array *endV*. Harish *et al.* use the following arrays: fa as a boolean array of size $|V|$, the weight array w of size $|A|$, the distance array d of size $|V|$ and the update array up of size $|V|$. They assign a thread to each vertex. Their algorithm in [13] invokes two kernels in each iteration of the host (see Algorithm 3). The first kernel (see Algorithm 4) relaxes each vertex u whose corresponding bit $fa[u]$ is equal to *true* indicating that u needs to be relaxed. Initially, only $fa[s]$ is set to *true*, where s denotes the source vertex. The distance of any neighbor of a vertex u that is updated is kept in the array up, and $fa[u]$ is set to *false*. After the execution of the first kernel, the second kernel (see Algorithm 5) assigns the minimum of $d[v]$ and $up[v]$ to $d[v]$ for each vertex v, and sets $fa[v]$ to *true*. Harish *et al.* [12] use two kernels in order to avoid read-write inconsistencies. Their algorithm terminates if there are no more distance value changes (indicated by flag variable f remaining false).

3 Locality-Based Relaxation

In this section, we present an efficient GPU-based algorithm centered on the idea of locality-based relaxation. Subsect. 3.1 discusses the idea behind our algorithm and Subsect. 3.2 presents our algorithm. Subsection 3.3 explains the data set we use in our experiments. Subsection 3.4 demonstrates our experimental results and shows how our algorithm outperforms most existing methods on large graphs representing road networks. Finally, Subsection 3.5 analyzes the impact of locality-based relaxation on time efficiency.

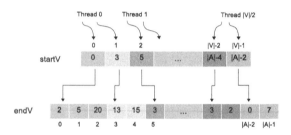

Fig. 2. Compressed Sparse Row (CSR) graph representation.

3.1   Basic Idea

Harish *et al.*'s [12] algorithm can potentially be improved in three directions. First, the for-loop in Lines 2–5 of the host Algorithm 3 requires a data exchange between the GPU and CPU in each iteration of the host through flag f. Second, their algorithm launches two kernels in each iteration of the host. Third, the kernels in Algorithms 4 and 5 contribute to propagating the wave of relaxation for just one step. We pose the hypothesis that *allocating more load to threads by (1) relaxing a few steps instead of just one, and/or (2) associating a few vertices to each thread can increase work/time efficiency.* Moreover, we claim that *a repetitive launch of kernels for some fixed number of times without any communication with the CPU can decrease the communication costs.*

Algorithm 3. Harish's algorithm: Host

1: $d[s] := 0$, $d[V - \{s\}] := \infty$, $up[s] := 0$, $up[V - \{s\}] := \infty$, $fa[s] := true$, $fa[V - \{s\}] := false$, $f := true$
2: **while** $f = true$ **do**
3:     $f := false$
4:     CUDA_Kernel1
5:     CUDA_Kernel2

Data structure. We use the CSR data structure (see Fig. 2) to store a directed graph in the global memory of GPUs, where vertices of the graph get unique IDs in $\{0, 1, \cdots, |V| - 1\}$.

Thread-Vertex affinity. In contrast to Harish *et al.* [12], we assign two vertices to each thread. (Our experiments show that assigning more than 2 vertices to each thread does not improve time efficiency significantly.) That is, thread t is responsible for the vertices whose IDs are stored in $startV[2t]$ and $startV[2t+1]$, where $0 \leq t < \lceil |V|/2 \rceil$ (see Fig. 2), and $|V|$ is even. If $|V|$ is odd, then the last thread will have only one vertex. There are two important rationales behind this idea. First, we plan to decrease the number of threads by half, but increase their load and investigate its impact on time efficiency. Second, we wish to ensure *data locality* for threads so that when a thread reads $startV[2t]$ it can read its neighboring memory cell too, hence potentially decreasing data access time.

Algorithm 4. Device: CUDA_Kernel1

1: For each thread assigned to vertices u
2: **if** $fa[u] = true$ **then**
3:     $fa[u] := false$
4:     **for** each neighbor vertex v of u **do**
5:         Begin Atomic
6:             **if** $up[v] > d[u] + w(u, v)$ **then**
7:                 $up[v] := d[u] + w(u, v)$
8:         End Atomic

Algorithm 5. Device: CUDA_Kernel2

1: For each thread assigned to vertices v
2: **if** $d[v] > up[v]$ **then**
3:     $d[v] := up[v]$
4:     $fa[v] := true$
5:     $f := true$
6: $up[v] := d[v]$

3.2   Algorithm

The algorithm proposed in this section includes two kernels (illustrated in Algorithms 8 and 9), but launches only one kernel per iteration. The host (Algorithm 6) initializes the distance array and an array of Boolean flags, called *FlagArray*, where $FlagArray[v] = true$ indicates that the neighbors of vertex v can be relaxed (up to k steps). Then, the host launches Kernel_1(i) for a fixed number of times, denoted N (see the for-loop), where $i \in \{0, 1\}$. We determine the value of N experimentally in an offline fashion. That is, before running our algorithm, we run existing algorithms on the graphs we use and compute the number of iterations for several runs. For example, we run Harish *et al.*'s algorithm on New York's road network for 100 random source vertices and observe that the minimum number of iterations in which this algorithm terminates is about 440. Thus, we set the value of N to $440/k$, where k is the distance up to which each thread performs locality-based relaxation. The objective is to reduce the frequency of CPU-GPU communications because no communication takes place between CPU and GPU in the for-loop in Lines 4–6 of Algorithm 6. While the repeat-until loop in Algorithm 6 might have fewer number of iterations compared with the total number of iterations of the for-loop, the device (i.e., GPU) communicates with the host by updating the value of *Flag* in each iteration of the repeat-until loop.

Algorithm 7 forms the core of the kernel Algorithms 8 and 9. Specifically, it generates a wave of relaxation from a vertex u that can propagate up to k steps, where k is a predetermined value (often less than 5 in our experiments). Lines

4–10 of Algorithm 7 update the distance of each vertex v that is reachable from u in at most k steps. The relaxation wave propagates in a Depth First Search (DFS) fashion up to depth k (see Lines 8–10 of Algorithm 7). Upon visiting each vertex v via its parent w in the DFS tree, we check if the arc (w, v) is already relaxed. If so, we backtrack to w. Otherwise, we relax (w, v) and check if v is at depth k. If so, then we set the flag array cell corresponding to v in order to indicate that relaxation should be picked up from the frontier vertex v in the next kernel iteration. The impact of a wave of relaxation that starts from u is multiple waves of relaxation starting from current frontier vertices in the next iteration of the for-loop (respectively, repeat-until loop) in Algorithm 6. Thus, we conjecture that the total number of iterations of both loops in the host Algorithm 6 should not go beyond the length of the graph diameter divided by k, where the *diameter* is the longest shortest path between any pair of vertices.

Algorithm 6. Host

1: $d[s] := 0$, $d[V − \{s\}] := \infty$,
2: $FlagArray[0][s] := true$, $FlagArray[0][V − \{s\}] := false$, $FlagArray[1][V] := false$, $i \in \{0, 1\}$, $Flag := false$
3: $i := 0$
4: **for** $j := 1$ to N **do**
5:     Launch Kernel_1($i \bmod 2$)
6:     $i := i + 1$;
7: **repeat** {
8:     $Flag := false$ // GPU and CPU communicate through $Flag$ variable.
9:     Launch Kernel_2($i \bmod 2$)
10:    $i := i + 1$
11: } **until** ($Flag = false$)

Algorithm 7 uses a two-dimensional flag array in order to ensure Lines 2–3 and 9 of Algorithm 7 will not be executed simultaneously on the same array cell; hence data race-freedom. Consider the case where Algorithm 7 used a single-dimensional flag array. Let u be a frontier vertex of the previous kernel launch (i.e., $FlagArray[u]$ is $true$) and t_1 be the thread associated with u. Moreover, let t_2 be another thread whose DFS search reaches u at depth k. As a result, there is a possibility that thread t_2 assigns $true$ to $FlagArray[u]$ in Line 9 of Algorithm 7 exactly at the same time that thread t_1 is reading/writing $FlagArray[u]$ at Line 2 or 3; hence a data race. Since we would like to have no inter-thread synchronization (for efficiency purposes) and yet ensure data race-freedom, we propose a scheme with two flag arrays where in each kernel launch one of them plays the role of the array from which threads read (i.e., $FlagArray[i][u]$) and the other one is the array that holds the frontier vertices (i.e., $FlagArray[i \oplus 1][u]$). Thus, in each iteration of the host where Algorithm 7 is invoked through one of the kernels, $FlagArray[i][u]$ and $FlagArray[i \oplus 1][v]$ cannot point to the same memory cell because i and $i \oplus 1$ cannot be equal in modulo 2.

To increase resource utilization, each thread t, where $0 \le t < \lceil |V|/2 \rceil$, in the kernel Algorithms 8 and 9 simultaneously performs locality-based relaxation on two vertices $u := startV[2t]$ and $u' := startV[2t+1]$. If vertex u is flagged for relaxation (Line 2 in Algorithm 7), then thread t resets its flag and starts relaxing the neighbors of u that are reachable from u by up to k steps. We invoke Kernel_1(i) repeatedly (in the for-loop in Algorithm 6) in order to propagate the wave of relaxation in the graph for N times without communicating the results with the CPU. After exiting from the for-loop in the host (Algorithm 6), we expect to have updated the distances of majority of vertices. To finalize the relaxation, the repeat-until loop in the host repeatedly invokes Kernel_2(i) until no more updates take place. Kernel_2(i) (Algorithm 9) is similar to Kernel_1(i) (Algorithm 8) except that it communicates the result of locality-based relaxation with the CPU in each iteration via the *Flag* variable.

Algorithm 7. RelaxLocalityAndSetFrontier(u, k, i)

1: $localFlag := false$
2: **if** $FlagArray[i][u] = true$ **then**
3:     $FlagArray[i][u] := false$
4:     Launch an iterative DFS traversal starting at u
5:         Upon visiting any vertex v via another vertex w, do the following:
6:         **if** (w, v) is already relaxed **then** backtrack to w.
7:         **else** $Relax(w, v)$
8:         **if** (v is at depth k from u) **then**
9:             $FlagArray[i \oplus 1][v] := true$ $// \oplus$ denotes addition modulo 2
10:             $localFlag := true$
11: **return** $localFlag$;

Algorithm 8. Device: Kernel_1(i)

1: For each thread t assigned to vertices $u := startV[2t]$ and $u' := startV[2t+1]$
2:     RelaxLocalityAndSetFrontier(u, k, i)
3:     RelaxLocalityAndSetFrontier(u', k, i)

Algorithm 9. Device: Kernel_2(i)

1: For each thread t assigned to vertices $u := startV[2t]$ and $u' := startV[2t+1]$
2:     $Flag := Flag \lor$ RelaxLocalityAndSetFrontier(u, k, i)
3:     $Flag := Flag \lor$ RelaxLocalityAndSetFrontier(u', k, i)

Theorem 1. *The proposed algorithm terminates and correctly calculates the distance of each vertex from the source. (Proof omitted due to space constraints.)*

3.3   Data Set

In our experiments, we use real-world road network graphs. Table 1 summarizes these graphs along with the names we use to refer to them throughout the paper. These graphs represent real-world road networks taken from [1,2], and they are practical examples of sparse graphs with a low max outdegree, low median outdegree and low standard deviation of outdegrees.

3.4   Experimental Results

In this section, we present our experimental results in addition to comparing them with related work (see Table 2). We conduct our experiments with 100 random sources in each graph and take an average of the time cost over these 100 experiments.

Platform. We use a workstation with 16 GB RAM, Intel Core i7 3.50 GHz processor running Linux Ubuntu and a single NVIDIA GeForce GT 630 GPU with 96 cores. The graphics card has a total of 4095 MB RAM, but 2048 MB is dedicated to video. We implement our algorithm in CUDA version 7.5.

Table 1. Graphs used in our experiments (All graphs have an average outdegree of 2).

Graphs	Name	♯ of vertices	♯ of arcs	Maximum outdegree	Standard deviation of outdegree	Median of outdegree
New York City [1]	New York	264,346	733,846	8	1.24	3
Colorado [1]	Colorado	435,666	1,057,066	8	1.02	2
roadNet-PA [2]	Pennsylvania	1,090,903	3,083,796	20	1.31	3
Northwest USA [1]	Northwest	1,207,945	2,840,208	9	1.00	2
California and Nevada [1]	CalNev	1,890,815	4,657,742	8	1.05	3
roadNet-CA [2]	California	1,971,278	5,533,214	12	1.28	3
Western USA [1]	Western	6,262,104	15,248,146	9	1.02	3

Results. Table 2 compares our algorithm with some related work in terms of space complexity, number of kernel launches, frequency of CPU-GPU communication, the number of atomic statements and speed up over Harish *et al.*'s algorithm. Notice that our approach provides the best speed up while minimizing other factors. The most recent approaches that outperform Harish *et al.*'s algorithm belong to [16,25,26] with a speed up of at most 2.6 (see Table 2). Figure 3 illustrates our experimental results in comparison with Harish *et al.*'s. We have run both algorithms on the same platform and same graphs. Observe that in all graphs our algorithm outperforms Harish *et al.*'s algorithm significantly. Specifically, we get a speed up from 3.36 for CalNev to 5.77 for California. Notice that Western (see Fig. 3) is the largest sparse graph in our experiments with 6.2 million vertices and more than 15 million arcs. Our algorithm solved SSSP for Western in about 4.9 s, whereas Harish *et al.*'s algorithm took 24.7 s! Moreover, for the road networks of California and Nevada, our implementation solves SSSP in almost 3.5 s on an NVIDIA GeForce GT 630 GPU, whereas (1) Davidson *et al.*'s [8] method takes almost 4 s on an NVIDAI GTX 680 GPU; (2) Boost library [24] takes 588 ms; (3) LoneSatr [4] takes 3.9 s, and (4) H-BF [5] takes 720 ms on an NVIDIA (Kepler) GeForce GTX 780. Observe that given the weak GPU available to us, our implementation performs well and outperforms some of the aforementioned approaches.

Table 2. Comparison with related work

Summarizing all related works					
Methods/criteria	Space complexity	♯ of kernel launches	CPU-GPU communication (# per host iteration)	♯ of atomic stmts	Speed up over Harish
Harish *et al.* [12,13]	$4V + 2A$	2	≥ 1	1	–
Chaibou *et al.* [6]	$V^2 + 3V$	2	≥ 1	1	–
Singh *et al.* [26]	$3V + 2A$	1	≥ 1	1	2.5×
Singh *et al.* [25]	$4V + 2A$	2	≥ 1	2	1.9×–2.6×
Busato *et al.* [5]	$4V + 2A$	2	≥ 1	2	–
Ortega *et al.* [20,21]	$5V + 2A$	3	≥ 1	1	–
Proposed algorithm	$4V + 2A$	1	< 1	1	3.36×–5.77×

Number of kernel launches. The number of kernel launches in each iteration of the host algorithm has a direct impact on time efficiency; the lower the number of kernel launches, the better. Observe that our algorithm and that of Singh *et al.* [26] outperform the rest.

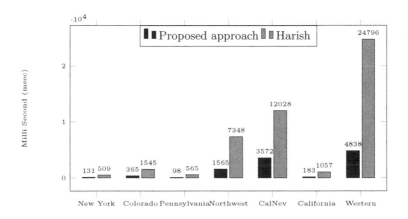

Fig. 3. Time efficiency of the proposed approach vs. Harish *et al.*'s [12,13].

Number of atomic statements. While the use of atomic statements helps in data race-freedom, they are considered heavy-weight instructions. As such, we would like to minimize the number of atomic statements. In addition to our algorithm and Harish *et al.*'s [12,13], Singh *et al.* [26], Chaibou *et al.* [6] and Ortega *et al.* [20,21] present algorithms with just one atomic statement. Chaibou *et al.* [6] evaluate the cost of memory copy between CPU and GPU. Ortega *et al.*

[20,21] propose an algorithm based on Dijkstra's algorithm to find SSSP. Their method extends Martin *et al.*'s [17] and Crauser *et al.*'s [7]. To increase the degree of parallelism in Dijkstra's algorithm, Martin *et al.* [17] consider all vertices from frontier with minimum distances to do the relaxation simultaneously. Crauser *et al.* [7] improve this method by proposing a threshold. Their idea is based on maximizing the number of relaxations in each iteration while preserving the correctness of Dijkstra's algorithm. Ortega *et al.* [20,21] implement these two ideas on GPUs. Nasre *et al.* [19] claim that atomic-free algorithms perform more efficiently than the algorithms that use atomic statements. Their results show a small time improvement for SSSP.

Speed up over Harish's. We include a column in Table 2 to illustrate how much speed up our algorithms provide compared with Harish *et al.*'s work. Notice that our algorithm improves time efficiency in comparison to other methods.

3.5   Locality-Based Relaxation

This section analyzes the impact of locality-based relaxation on time efficiency. To validate the proposed hypotheses in Sect. 3.1, we have conducted a few comparative experiments on graphs NY, CN and WUS in Table 3. We consider two criteria: one is the value of k that determines how far relaxations would go when updating $d[v]$ for some vertex v, and the other one is the impact of thread-vertex affinity. As such, we replace the original weights in the road network graphs of New York City, California-Nevada and Western USA with random values in the interval $[1..10]$; the actual weights are irrelevant for this experiment. This change enables faster runs of our algorithm on the aforementioned graphs.

Figure 4 illustrates the results of our experiments. Observe that as the value of k is increased from $k = 1$ the time costs decrease until we reach $k = 4$. From $k = 4$ to $k = 5$ we do not observe a significant decrease in time costs since the threads get saturated in terms of their workload. Moreover, determining the best value of k seems to be dependent on a few factors such as (i) the graph being processed; (ii) the algorithm, and (iii) the platform. In the context of our setting, $k = 4$ seems to be the best value. Moreover, we notice that assigning two vertices to one thread increases the workload of each thread and decreases the execution time (see Fig. 4), but assigning more than 2 vertices does not result in a significant performance improvement.

Table 3. Revised graphs used in our experiments.

Graphs	Acronym	Description
New York City [1]	NY	Replaced the original arc weights with some random value between 1 and 10 (inclusive)
California and Nevada [1]	CN	Same as above
Western USA [1]	WUS	Same as above

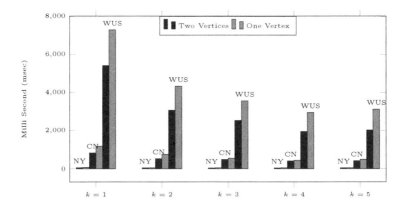

Fig. 4. Impact of locality-based relaxation and association of threads to vertices on execution time.

4 Discussion

In this section, we discuss some ideas that can potentially result in a more efficient GPU implementation that solves SSSP and its variants. In our experience, there are a few factors that have a direct impact on the time/space/work efficiency of a GPU implementation for SSSP. First, minimizing **CPU-GPU communication** can have a significant impact on time efficiency of CUDA programs. For this reason, we design our algorithm in a way that for N iterations of the host there is no communication between the GPU and the CPU. We experimentally observe that this design decision made a significant difference in decreasing the overall execution time. Second, the **data structure** that keeps the frontier vertices, has a noticeable impact on both space and time efficiency. Most existing methods use a queue. The operations performed on queues include enqueue, dequeue and extractMin, which may become costly depending on the graph being processed. A flag array keeps track of the frontier by a bit pattern, where each vertex v has a corresponding bit indicating whether v's distance got updated in the last round. The use of queues may cause another problem where two different threads update the same vertex v at different times and enqueue v, called *vertex duplication* (addressed by Davidson *et al.* [8]). Moreover, using flag arrays allows programmers to devise a well-thought schedule for threads towards avoiding data races; hence decreasing the number of required atomic statements. Third, the **number of kernel launches** and the way we launch them is influential. We observe that having fewer number of kernel launches in each iteration of the host is useful, but on-demand kernel launches do not help; rather it is better to have a fixed number of threads that are loaded with useful work in each launch. Thus, it is important to design algorithms in which all threads perform useful work in each launch (see Sect. 3.5). We also note that, in the context of our work, replacing atomic operations with busy waiting (as suggested by Nasre *et al.* [19]) does not improve the efficiency of our implementation. Finally, the

scalability of the proposed algorithm is a challenge in that the GPU memory is limited but there is a constant need for solving SSSP in larger graphs.

5   Conclusions and Future Work

This paper presented an efficient GPU-based algorithm for solving the SSSP problem based on a novel idea of *locality-based relaxation*, where we allow a thread to relax all vertices up to k steps away from the current vertex. We also devised a mechanism for systematic scheduling of threads using flag arrays where each bit represents whether a thread should execute in a kernel launch. The proposed scheduling approach enables a communication-efficient method (in the CUDA programming model) that minimizes the number of kernel launches, the number of atomic operations and the frequency of CPU-GPU communication without any need for thread synchronization. The proposed algorithm solves the SSSP problem on large graphs (representing road networks) with up to 6.2 million vertices and 15 million arcs in a few seconds, outperforming existing methods. As for the extensions of this work, we would like to leverage our proposed technique in solving search problems (e.g., DFS, BFS) on large graphs. We also plan to investigate the application of our GPU-based implementation in devising efficient model checking algorithms. Finally, we will study a multi-GPU implementation of our algorithm towards processing even larger graphs.

References

1. 9th DIMACS implementation challenge-shortest paths. http://www.dis.uniroma1.it/challenge9/download.shtml
2. Stanford Network Analysis Project. http://snap.stanford.edu/
3. Bellman, R.: On a routing problem. Q. Appl. Math. 87–90 (1958)
4. Burtscher, M., Nasre, R., Pingali, K.: A quantitative study of irregular programs on GPUs. In: IEEE International Symposium on Workload Characterization (IISWC), pp. 141–151. IEEE (2012)
5. Busato, F., Bombieri, N.: An efficient implementation of the Bellman-Ford algorithm for Kepler GPU architectures. IEEE Trans. Parallel Distrib. Syst. **27**(8), 2222–2233 (2016)
6. Chaibou, A., Sie, O.: Improving global performance on GPU for algorithms with main loop containing a reduction operation: case of Dijkstra's algorithm. J. Comput. Commun. **3**(08), 41 (2015)
7. Crauser, A., Mehlhorn, K., Meyer, U., Sanders, P.: A parallelization of Dijkstra's shortest path algorithm. In: Brim, L., Gruska, J., Zlatuška, J. (eds.) MFCS 1998. LNCS, vol. 1450, pp. 722–731. Springer, Heidelberg (1998). doi:10.1007/BFb0055823
8. Davidson, A., Baxter, S., Garland, M., Owens, J.D.: Work-efficient parallel GPU methods for single-source shortest paths. In: Proceedings of the IEEE 28th International Parallel and Distributed Processing Symposium (IPDPS 2014), pp. 349–359 (2014)
9. Dijkstra, E.W.: A note on two problems in connexion with graphs. Numerische mathematik **1**(1), 269–271 (1959)

10. Farber, R.: CUDA Application Design and Development. Elsevier, Oxford (2011)
11. Ford Jr., L.R.: Network flow theory. Technical report, DTIC Document (1956)
12. Harish, P., Narayanan, P.J.: Accelerating large graph algorithms on the GPU using CUDA. In: Aluru, S., Parashar, M., Badrinath, R., Prasanna, V.K. (eds.) HiPC 2007. LNCS, vol. 4873, pp. 197–208. Springer, Heidelberg (2007). doi:10.1007/978-3-540-77220-0_21
13. Harish, P., Vineet, V., Narayanan, P.: Large graph algorithms for massively multi-threaded architectures. International Institute of Information Technology Hyderabad, Technical report IIIT/TR/2009/74 (2009)
14. Khorasani, F., Vora, K., Gupta, R., Bhuyan, L.N.: CuSha: vertex-centric graph processing on GPUs. In: Proceedings of the 23rd International Symposium on High-Performance Parallel and Distributed Computing, pp. 239–252 (2014)
15. Kumar, S., Misra, A., Tomar, R.S.: A modified parallel approach to single source shortest path problem for massively dense graphs using CUDA. In: 2nd International Conference on Computer and Communication Technology (ICCCT), pp. 635–639. IEEE (2011)
16. Li, D., Becchi, M.: Deploying graph algorithms on GPUs: an adaptive solution. In: IEEE 27th International Symposium on Parallel & Distributed Processing (IPDPS), pp. 1013–1024. IEEE (2013)
17. Martín, P.J., Torres, R., Gavilanes, A.: CUDA solutions for the SSSP problem. In: Allen, G., Nabrzyski, J., Seidel, E., van Albada, G.D., Dongarra, J., Sloot, P.M.A. (eds.) ICCS 2009. LNCS, vol. 5544, pp. 904–913. Springer, Heidelberg (2009). doi:10.1007/978-3-642-01970-8_91
18. Meyer, U., Sanders, P.: Δ-stepping : a parallel single source shortest path algorithm. In: Bilardi, G., Italiano, G.F., Pietracaprina, A., Pucci, G. (eds.) ESA 1998. LNCS, vol. 1461, pp. 393–404. Springer, Heidelberg (1998). doi:10.1007/3-540-68530-8_33
19. Nasre, R., Burtscher, M., Pingali, K.: Atomic-free irregular computations on GPUs. In: Proceedings of the 6th Workshop on General Purpose Processor Using Graphics Processing Units, pp. 96–107. ACM (2013)
20. Ortega-Arranz, H., Torres, Y., Gonzalez-Escribano, A., Llanos, D.R.: Comprehensive evaluation of a new GPU-based approach to the shortest path problem. Int. J. Parallel Program. **43**(5), 918–938 (2015)
21. Ortega-Arranz, H., Torres, Y., Llanos, D., Gonzalez-Escribano, A.: A new GPU-based approach to the shortest path problem. In: High Performance Computing and Simulation (HPCS), pp. 505–511. IEEE (2013)
22. Sherwani, N.A.: Algorithms for VLSI Physical Design Automation. Springer (2012)
23. Shirinivas, S., Vetrivel, S., Elango, N.: Applications of graph theory in computer science an overview. Int. J. Eng. Sci. Technol. **2**(9), 4610–4621 (2010)
24. Siek, J.G., Lee, L.-Q., Lumsdaine, A.: The Boost Graph Library: User Guide and Reference Manual, Portable Documents. Pearson Education (2001)
25. Singh, D.P., Khare, N.: Modified Dijkstra's algorithm for dense graphs on GPU using CUDA. Indian J. Sci. Technol. **9**(33) (2016)
26. Singh, D.P., Khare, N., Rasool, A.: Efficient parallel implementation of single source shortest path algorithm on GPU using CUDA. Int. J. Appl. Eng. Res. **11**(4), 2560–2567 (2016)
27. Sommer, C.: Shortest-path queries in static networks. ACM Comput. Surv. (CSUR) **46**(4), 45 (2014)

28. Wang, Y., Davidson, A., Pan, Y., Wu, Y., Riffel, A., Owens, J.D.: Gunrock: a high-performance graph processing library on the GPU. In: Proceedings of the 21st ACM SIGPLAN Symposium on Principles and Practice of Parallel Programming (PPoPP 2016), pp. 11:1–11:12 (2016)
29. Zhong, J., He, B.: Medusa: simplified graph processing on GPUs. IEEE Trans. Parallel Distrib. Syst. **25**(6), 1543–1552 (2014)

Logic, Semantics, and Programming Theory

Exposing Latent Mutual Exclusion
by Work Automata

Kasper Dokter$^{(\boxtimes)}$ and Farhad Arbab

Centrum Wiskunde & Informatica, Amsterdam, Netherlands
{K.P.C.Dokter,Farhad.Arbab}@cwi.nl

Abstract. A concurrent application consists of a set of concurrently executing interacting processes. Although earlier we proposed work automata to specify both computation and interaction of such a set of executing processes, a detailed formal semantics for them was left implicit. In this paper, we provide a formal semantics for work automata, based on which we introduce equivalences such as weak simulation and weak language inclusion. Subsequently, we define operations on work automata that simplify them while preserving these equivalences. Where applicable, these operations simplify a work automaton by merging its different states into a state with a 'more inclusive' state-invariant. The resulting state-invariant defines a region in a multidimensional real vector space that potentially contains holes, which in turn expose mutual exclusion among processes. Such exposed dependencies provide additional insight in the behavior of an application, which can enhance scheduling. Our operations, therefore, potentially expose implicit dependencies among processes that otherwise may not be evident to exploit.

1 Introduction

Shared resources in a concurrent application must be protected against concurrent access. Mutual exclusion protocols offer such protection by granting access to a resource only if no other process has access. Moreover, concurrent applications often require some of their tasks to execute in some specific order. It is customary to implement both mutual exclusion and execution order among (sub-)tasks by means of locks. This practice suffers from two main drawbacks: First, contention on the shared resources results in blocked processes, which may lead to idle processors. Second, lock implementations introduce overhead that can become significant when executed repeatedly.

Alternatively, smart scheduling of processes can also offer protection against concurrent access, without suffering from drawbacks of locks. Suppose we have a crystal ball that accurately reveals when each process accesses its resources and their proper order of execution. We can then use this information to synthesize a scheduler that executes the processes in the correct order and prevents concurrent access to shared resources by speeding up or slowing down the execution of each process. Locks now become redundant, and their overhead can be avoided.

© IFIP International Federation for Information Processing 2017
Published by Springer International Publishing AG 2017. All Rights Reserved
M.R. Mousavi and J. Sgall (Eds.): TTCS 2017, LNCS 10608, pp. 59–73, 2017.
DOI: 10.1007/978-3-319-68953-1_6

In practice we have no such crystal ball for such accurate predictions. We can, however, take a step in the right direction by imagining the picture that we would see, if we had one. In our previous paper, we formalized such picture by introducing *work automata* [4]. A work automaton consists of states and transitions. Variables, called *jobs*, measure progress of all processes in a concurrent application. Each state admits a boolean constraint over jobs, called a *state-invariant*, that defines the amount of work that can be done before a process blocks. Each transition consists of three parts: (1) a set of ports, called a *synchronization constraint*, that defines access to resources; (2) a boolean constraint over jobs, called a *guard*, that defines the amount of work that must be done before a transition can be fired; and (3) a set of jobs, called a *reset*, that identifies the jobs whose progress must be reset to zero.

The original definition of work automata in [4] left state-invariants, resets, and the formal semantics of work automata implicit, as this simpler model adequately served the purpose of that paper. In the current work (Sect. 2), however, we extend the generality of the work automata model by introducing state-invariants and explicit reset of jobs. We define the formal semantics of work automata by means of labeled transition systems.

Compositionality is one of the most important features of work automata. Many small work automata compose into a single large automaton that models the behavior of the complete application. In view of state space explosion, a large number of states in a work automaton complicates its analysis. In Sect. 3, we show by means of an example that some large work automata can be simplified to their respectively "equivalent" single state work automata. The state-invariant of the single state of such a resulting automaton defines a region in a multidimensional real vector space. Geometric features of this region reveal interesting behavioral properties of the corresponding concurrent application. For example, (explicit or implied) mutual exclusion in an application corresponds to a hole in its respective region, and non-blocking executions correspond to straight lines through this region. Since straight lines are easier to detect than non-blocking executions, the geometric perspective provides additional insight into the behavior of an application. We postulate that such information may be used to develop a smart scheduler that avoids the drawbacks of locks.

Motivated by our example, we define in Sect. 3 two procedures, called *translation* and *contraction*, that simplify a given work automaton by minimizing its number of states. We define weak simulation of work automata, and provide conditions (Theorems 1 and 2) under which translation and contraction preserve weak simulation. In Sect. 4, we discuss related work, and in Sect. 5 we conclude and point out future work.

2   Work Automata

Work automata, introduced in [4], originate from the need to represent progressing parallel tasks as a single automaton. In this section, we define work automata, their semantics, and operators such as composition and hiding. Our current definition of work automata differs from the original definition in [4] in two ways.

First, our current definition of work automata includes explicit resets, while the original definition left this implicit. In Sect. 3.2, we use explicit resets to define a *shifting* operator that simplifies work automata. Second, our current definition of work automata includes state-invariants, while the original definition left them implicit. We use our explicit state-invariants to simplify the semantics of work automata, to simplify the composition of work automata, and, in Sect. 3.1, to allow for more compact representations of an automaton.

2.1   Syntax

Consider an application A that consists of $n \geq 1$ concurrently executing processes $X_1, \ldots, X_n$. We measure the progress of each process X_i in A by a positive real variable $x_i \in \mathbb{R}_+$, called a *job*, and represent the current *progress of application* A by a map $p : J \to \mathbb{R}_+$, where $J = \{x_1, \ldots, x_n\}$ is the set of all jobs in A. We regulate the progress using boolean constraints $\phi \in B(J)$ over jobs:

$$\phi ::= \top \mid \bot \mid x \sim n \mid \phi_0 \wedge \phi_1 \mid \phi_0 \vee \phi_1, \tag{1}$$

with $\sim \in \{\leq, \geq, =\}$, $x \in J$ a job and $n \in \mathbb{N}_0 \cup \{\infty\}$. We define *satisfaction* $p \models \phi$ of a progress $p : J \to \mathbb{R}_+$ and a constraint $\phi \in B(J)$ by the following rules: $p \models x \sim n$, if $p(x) \sim n$; $p \models \phi_0 \wedge \phi_1$, if $p \models \phi_0$ and $p \models \phi_1$; $p \models \phi_0 \vee \phi_1$, if $p \models \phi_0$ or $p \models \phi_1$. The *interface* of application A consists of a set of ports through which A interacts with its environment via synchronous operations, each one involving a subset $N \subseteq P$ of its ports.

We define the exact behavior of a set of processes as a labeled transition system called a *work automaton*. The progress value $p(x)$ of job x may increase in a state q of a work automaton, as long as the *state-invariant* $I(q) \in B(J)$ is satisfied. A state-invariant $I(q)$ defines the amount of work that each process can do in state q before it blocks. A transition $\tau = (q, N, w, R, q')$ allows the work automaton to reset the progress of each job $x \in R \subseteq J$ to zero and change to state q', provided that the *guard*, defined as *synchronization constraint* $N \subseteq P$ together with the *job constraint* $w \in B(J)$, is satisfied. That is, the transition can be fired, if the environment is able to synchronize on the ports N and the current progress $p : J \to \mathbb{R}_+$ of A satisfies job constraint w.

Definition 1 (Work automata). *A work automaton is a tuple $(Q, P, J, I, \to, \phi_0, q_0)$ that consists of a set of states Q, a set of ports P, a set of jobs J, a state invariant $I : Q \to B(J)$, a transition relation $\to\, \subseteq Q \times 2^P \times B(J) \times 2^J \times Q$, an initial progress $\phi_0 \in B(J)$, and an initial state $q_0 \in Q$.*

Example 1 (Mutual exclusion). Figure 1 shows the work automata of two identical processes A_1 and A_2 that achieve mutual exclusion by means of a global lock L. The progress of process A_i is recorded by its associated job x_i, and the interface of each process A_i consists of two ports a_i and b_i. Suppose we ignore the overhead of the mutual exclusion protocol. Then, lock L does not need a job and its interface consists of ports a_1, a_2, b_1, and b_2. Each process A_i starts in

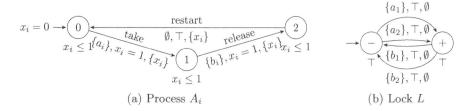

(a) Process A_i (b) Lock L

Fig. 1. Mutual exclusion of processes A_1 and A_2 by means of a lock L.

state 0 with $\phi_0 := x_i = 0$ and is allowed to execute at most one unit of work, as witnessed by the state-invariant $x_i \leq 1$. After finishing one unit of work, A_i starts to compete for the global lock L by synchronizing on port a_i of lock L. When A_i succeeds in taking the lock, then lock L changes its state from $-$ to $+$ and process A_i moves to state 1, its critical section, and resets the progress value of job x_i to zero. Next, process A_i executes one unit of work in its critical section. Finally, A_i releases lock L by synchronizing on port b_i, executes asynchronously its last unit of work in state 2, and resets to state 0.   ♣

2.2 Semantics

We define the semantics of a work automaton $A = (Q, P, J, I, \rightarrow, \phi_0, q_0)$ by means of a finer grained labeled transition system $[\![A]\!]$ whose states are configurations:

Definition 2 (Configurations). *A configuration of a work automaton A is a pair $(p, q) \in \mathbb{R}_+^J \times Q$, where $p : J \rightarrow \mathbb{R}_+$ is a state of progress, and $q \in Q$ a state.*

The transitions of $[\![A]\!]$ are labeled by two kinds of labels: one for advancing progress of A and one for changing the current state of A. To model advance of progress of A, we use a map $d : J \rightarrow \mathbb{R}_+$ representing that $d(x)$ units of work has been done on job x. Such a map induces a transition

$$(p, q) \xrightarrow{d} (p + d, q), \qquad (2)$$

where $+$ is component-wise addition of maps (i.e., $(p + d)(x) = p(x) + d(x)$, for all $x \in J$). Figure 2(a) shows a graphical representation of transition (2). A state of progress p of A corresponds to a point in the plane.

In practice, the value of each job $x \in J$ continuously evolves from $p(x)$ to $p(x) + d(x)$. We assume that, during transition (2), each job makes progress at a constant speed. This allows us to view the actual execution as a path $\gamma : [0, 1] \rightarrow \mathbb{R}_+^J$ defined by $\gamma(c) = p + c \cdot d$, where $\mathbb{R}_+^J$ is the set of maps from J to $\mathbb{R}_+$ and $\cdot$ is component-wise scalar multiplication (i.e., $(p + c \cdot d)(x) = p(x) + c \cdot d(x)$, for all $x \in J$). At any instant $c \in [0, 1]$, the state of progress $p + c \cdot d$ must satisfy the current state-invariant $I(q)$. Figure 2(a) shows execution γ as the straight line connecting p and $p + d$. For every $c \in [0, 1]$, state of progress $\gamma(c) = p + c \cdot d$ corresponds to a point on the line from p to $p + d$. Note that, since we have a transition from p to $p + c \cdot d$ in $[\![A]\!]$ for all $c \in [0, 1]$, Fig. 2(a) provides essentially a finite representation of an infinite semantics, i.e., one with an infinite number of transitions through intermediate configurations between (p, q) and $(p + d, q)$. In Sect. 3.1, we use this perspective to motivate our gluing procedure.

The transition in (2) is possible only if the execution does not block between p and $p + d$, i.e., state of progress $p + c \cdot d$ satisfies the state-invariant $I(q)$ of q, for all $c \in [0, 1]$. Since $I(q)$ defines a region $\{p \in \mathbb{R}_+^J \mid p \models I(q)\}$ of a $|J|$-dimensional real vector space, the non-blocking condition just states that the straight line γ between p and $p + d$ is contained in the region defined by $I(q)$ (see Fig. 2(a)).

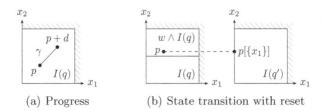

(a) Progress   (b) State transition with reset

Fig. 2. Progress (a) of the application along the path γ in $I(q)$ from p to $p + d$, and (b) transition from state q to q' with reset of job x_1.

A transition $\tau = (q, N, w, R, q')$ changes the state of the current configuration from q to q', if the environment allows interaction via N and the current state of progress p satisfies job constraint w. As a side effect, the progress of each job $x \in R$ resets to zero. Such state changes occur on transitions of the form

$$(p, q) \xrightarrow{N} (p[R], q'), \tag{3}$$

where $p[R](x) = 0$, if $x \in R$, and $p[R](x) = p(x)$ otherwise. Figure 2(b) shows a graphical representation of transition (3). The current state of progress satisfies both the current state-invariant and the guard of the transition, which allows to change to state q' and reset the value of x_1 to zero. For convenience, we allow at every configuration (p, q) an $\emptyset$-labeled self loop which models idling.

Definition 3 (Operational semantics). *The semantics of a given work automaton $A = (Q, P, J, I, \rightarrow, \phi_0, q_0)$ is the labeled transition system $[\![A]\!]$ with states $(p, q) \in \mathbb{R}_+^J \times Q$, labels $\mathbb{R}_+^J \cup 2^P$, and transitions defined by the rules:*

$$\frac{d : J \rightarrow \mathbb{R}_+, \quad \forall c \in [0, 1] : p + c \cdot d \models I(q)}{(p, q) \xrightarrow{d} (p + d, q)} \tag{S1}$$

$$\frac{\tau = (q, N, w, R, q') \in \rightarrow, \quad p \models w \wedge I(q), \quad p[R] \models I(q')}{(p, q) \xrightarrow{N} (p[R], q')} \tag{S2}$$

$$\frac{}{(p, q) \xrightarrow{\emptyset} (p, q)} \tag{S3}$$

where $p[R](x) = 0$, if $x \in R$, and $p[R](x) = p(x)$ otherwise.

Based on the operational semantics $[\![A]\!]$ of a work automaton A, we define the *trace semantics* of a work automaton. The trace semantics defines all finite sequences of observable behavior that are *accepted* by the work automaton.

Definition 4 (Actions, words). *Let P be a set of ports and J a set of jobs. An action is a pair $[N, d]$ that consist of a set of ports $N \subseteq P$ and a progress $d : J \to \mathbb{R}_+$. We write $\Sigma_{P,J}$ for the set of all actions over ports P and jobs J. We call the action $[\emptyset, \mathbf{0}]$, with $\mathbf{0}(x) = 0$ for all $x \in J$, the silent action. A word over P and J is a finite sequence $u \in \Sigma_{P,J}^*$ of actions over P and J.*

Definition 5 (Trace semantics). *Let $A = (Q, P, J, I, \to, \phi_0, q_0)$ be a work automaton. A run r of A over a word $([N_i, d_i])_{i=1}^n \in \Sigma_{P,J}^*$ is a path*

$$r \; : \; (p_0, q_0) \xrightarrow{N_1 \; d_1} s_1 \quad \cdots \quad s_{n-1} \xrightarrow{N_n \; d_n} s_n$$

in $[\![A]\!]$, with $p_0 \models \phi_0 \wedge I(q_0)$. The language $L(A) \subseteq \Sigma_{P,J}^*$ of A is the set of all words u for which there exists a run of A over u.

Example 2. The language of the process A_i in Fig. 1(a) trivially contains the empty word, and the word $u = [\emptyset, \mathbf{1}][\{a\}, \mathbf{1}][\{b\}, \mathbf{1}]$, where $\mathbf{1}(x_i) = 1$. Using Definitions 3 and 5, we conclude that $v = [\emptyset, \mathbf{1}][\{a\}, \mathbf{1}][\{b\}, \mathbf{0.5}][\emptyset, \mathbf{0.5}]$, with $\mathbf{0.5}(x_i) = 0.5$, is also accepted by A_i. Note that we can obtain v from u by splitting $[\{b\}, \mathbf{1}]$ into $[\{b\}, \mathbf{0.5}][\emptyset, \mathbf{0.5}]$. ♣

2.3 Weak Simulation

Different work automata may have similar observable behavior. In this section, we define *weak simulation* as a formal tool to show their similarity. Intuitively, a weak simulation between two work automata A and B can be seen as a map that transforms any run of A into a run of B with identical observable behavior.

Following Milner [13], we define a new transition relation, $\Rightarrow$, on the operational semantics $[\![A]\!]$ of a work automaton A that 'skips' silent steps.

Definition 6 (Weak transition relation). *For any two configurations s and t in $[\![A]\!]$, and any $a \in \mathbb{R}_+^J \cup 2^P$ we define $s \xRightarrow{a} t$ if and only if either*

1. *$a = \emptyset$ and $s \; (\xrightarrow{\emptyset})^* \; t$; or*
2. *$a \in 2^P \setminus \{\emptyset\}$ and $s \xRightarrow{\emptyset} s' \xrightarrow{a} s'' \xRightarrow{\emptyset} t$; or*
3. *$a \in \mathbb{R}_+^J$, $s \xRightarrow{\emptyset} s_1 \xrightarrow{c_1 \cdot a} t_1 \xRightarrow{\emptyset} s_2 \cdots t_{n-1} \xRightarrow{\emptyset} s_n \xrightarrow{c_n \cdot a} t_n \xRightarrow{\emptyset} t$, and $\sum_{i=1}^n c_i = 1$,*

with $n \geq 1$, s_i, t_i configurations in $[\![A]\!]$, $c_i \in [0, 1]$, $(c_i \cdot a)(x) = c_i \cdot a(x)$, for all $x \in J$ and all $1 \leq i \leq n$.

Definition 7 (Weak simulation). *Let $A_i = (Q_i, P, J, I_i, \to_i, \phi_{0i}, q_{0i})$, for $i \in \{0, 1\}$ be two work automata, and let $\preceq \subseteq (\mathbb{R}_+^J \times Q_0) \times (\mathbb{R}_+^J \times Q_1)$ be a binary relation over configurations of A_0 and A_1. Then, $\preceq$ is a weak simulation of A_0 in A_1 (denoted as $A_0 \preceq A_1$) if and only if*

1. $p_{00} \models \phi_{00} \wedge I_0(q_{00})$ *implies* $(p_{00}, q_{00}) \preceq (p_{01}, q_{01})$, *with* $p_{01} \models \phi_{01} \wedge I_1(q_{01})$;
2. $s \preceq t$ *and* $s \xrightarrow{a} s'$, *with* $a \in \mathbb{R}_+^J \cup 2^P$, *implies* $t \xRightarrow{a} t'$ *and* $s' \preceq t'$, *for some* t'.

We call $\preceq$ *a weak bisimulation if and only if* $\preceq$ *and its inverse* $\preceq^{-1} = \{(t, s) \mid s \preceq t\}$ *are weak simulations. We call* A_0 *and* A_1 *weakly bisimilar (denoted as* $A_0 \approx A_1$*) if and only if there exists a weak bisimulation between them.*

2.4   Composition

Thus far, our examples used work automata to define the exact behavior of a single job (or just a protocol L in Fig. 1(b)). We now show that work automata are expressive enough to define the behavior of multiple jobs simultaneously. To this end, we define a product operator $\times$ on the class of all work automata. Before we turn to the definition, we first introduce some notation. For $i \in \{0, 1\}$, let $A_i = (Q_i, P_i, J_i, I_i, \rightarrow_i, \phi_{0i}, q_{0i})$ be a work automaton and let $\tau_i = (q_i, N_i, w_i, R_i, q_i') \in \rightarrow_i$ be a transition in A_i. We say that τ_0 and τ_1 are *composable* (denoted as $\tau_0 \frown \tau_1$) if and only if $N_0 \cap P_1 = N_1 \cap P_0$. If $\tau_0 \frown \tau_1$, then we write $\tau_0 \mid \tau_1 = ((q_0, q_1), N_0 \cup N_1, w_0 \wedge w_1, R_0 \cup R_1, (q_0', q_1'))$ for the *composition* of τ_0 and τ_1.

Definition 8 (Composition). *Let* $A_i = (Q_i, P_i, J_i, I_i, \rightarrow_i, \phi_{0i}, q_{0i})$, $i \in \{0, 1\}$, *be two work automata. We define the composition* $A_0 \times A_1$ *of* A_0 *and* A_1 *as the work automaton* $(Q_0 \times Q_1, P_0 \cup P_1, J_0 \cup J_1, I_0 \wedge I_1, \rightarrow, \phi_{00} \wedge \phi_{01}, (q_{00}, q_{01}))$, *where* $\rightarrow$ *is the smallest relation that satisfies:*

$$\frac{i \in \{0,1\}, \ \tau_i \in \rightarrow_i, \ \tau_{1-i} \in \rightarrow_{1-i} \cup \{(q, \emptyset, \top, \emptyset, q) \mid q \in Q_{1-i}\}, \ \tau_0 \frown \tau_1}{\tau_0 \mid \tau_1 \in \rightarrow}$$

By means of the composition operator in Definition 8, we can construct large work automata by composing smaller ones. The following lemma shows that the composite work automaton does not depend on the order of construction.

Lemma 1. $(A_0 \times A_1) \times A_2 \approx A_0 \times (A_1 \times A_2)$, $A_0 \times A_1 \approx A_1 \times A_0$, *and* $A_0 \times A_0 \approx A_0$, *for any three work automata* A_0, A_1, *and* A_2.

Example 3. Consider the work automata from Example 1. The behavior of the application is the composition M of the two processes A_1 and A_2 and the lock L. Figure 3 shows the work automaton $M = L \times A_1 \times A_1$. Each state-invariant equals $\top \wedge x_1 \leq 1 \wedge x_2 \leq 1$. The competition for the lock is visualized by the branching at the initial state 00.   ♣

2.5   Hiding

Given a work automaton A and a port a in the interface of A, the *hiding* operator $A \setminus \{a\}$ removes port a from the interface of A. As a consequence, the hiding operator removes every occurrence of a from the synchronization constraint N of every transition $(q, N, w, R, q') \in \rightarrow$ by transforming N to $N \setminus \{a\}$. In case N becomes empty, the resulting transition becomes *silent*. If, moreover, the source and the target states of a transition are identical, we call the transition *idling*.

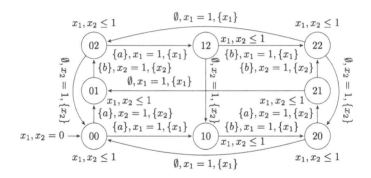

Fig. 3. The complete application $M = L \times A_1 \times A_2$. In state $q_1 q_2$, lock L is in state $(-1)^{q_1 + q_2 + 1}$ and process A_i is in state q_i.

Definition 9 (Hiding). *Let $A = (Q, P, J, I, \rightarrow, \phi_0, q_0)$ be a work automaton, and $M \subseteq P$ a set of ports. We define $A \setminus M$ as the work automaton $(Q, P \setminus M, J, \rightarrow_M, \phi_0, q_0)$, with $\rightarrow_M = \{(q, N \setminus M, w, R, q') \mid (q, N, w, R, q') \in \rightarrow\}$.*

Lemma 2. *Hiding partially distributes over composition: $M \cap P_0 \cap P_1 = \emptyset$ implies $(A_0 \times A_1) \setminus M \approx (A_0 \setminus M) \times (A_1 \setminus M)$, for any two work automata A_0 and A_1 with interfaces P_0 and P_1, respectively.*

Example 4. Consider the work automaton M in Fig. 3. Work automaton $M' = M \setminus \{a, b\}$ is M where every occurrence of $\{a\}$ or $\{b\}$ is substituted by $\emptyset$.   ♣

3   State Space Minimization

The composition operator from Definition 8 may produce a large complex work automaton with many different states. In this section, we investigate if, and how, a set of states in a work automaton can be merged into a single state, without breaking its semantics. In Sect. 3.1, we present by means of an example the basic idea for our simplification procedures. We define in Sect. 3.2 a *translation* operator that removes unnecessary resets from transitions. We define in Sect. 3.3 a *contraction* operator that identifies different states in a work automaton. We show that translation and contraction are correct by providing weak simulations between their pre- and post-operation automata.

3.1   Gluing

The following example illustrates an intuitive *gluing procedure* that relates the product work automaton M in Fig. 3 to the punctured square in Fig. 4(b). Formally, we define the gluing procedure as the composition of translation (Sect. 3.2) and contraction (Sect. 3.3).

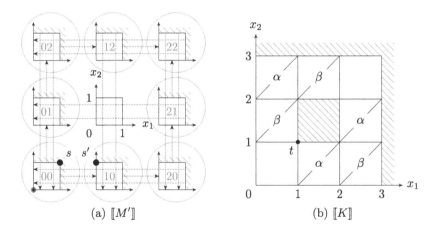

(a) $[\![M']\!]$ (b) $[\![K]\!]$

Fig. 4. Graphical representation (a) of semantics $[\![M']\!]$ of the work automaton M' in Example 4, where white regions represent state-invariants, and (b) result after gluing the regions in (a). Starting in a configuration below line α and above line β, parallel execution of x_1 and x_2 never blocks on lock L.

Example 5 (Gluing).   Consider the work automaton M' in Example 4 that describes the mutual exclusion protocol for two processes. Our goal is to simplify M' to a work automaton K that simulates M'. To this end, we introduce in Fig. 4(a) a finite representation of the infinite semantics $[\![M']\!]$ of M', based on the geometric interpretation of progress discussed in Sect. 2.2. For any given state q of M', the state-invariant $I(q) = x_1 \leq 1 \wedge x_2 \leq 1$ is depicted in Fig. 4(a) as a region in the first quadrant of the plane. Each configuration (p, q) of M' corresponds to a point in one of these regions: q determines its corresponding region wherein point p resides. Each transition of M' is shown in Fig. 4(a) as a dotted arrow from the border of one region to that of another region. We refer to these dotted arrows as *jumps*. A jump λ from a region R of state q to another region R' of state q' represents infinitely many transitions from configurations (p, q) to configurations (p', q'), for all p and p', as permitted by the semantics $[\![M']\!]$. By the job constraint of the transition corresponding to λ, p and p' must lie on the borders of R and R', respectively, that are connected by λ.

From a topological perspective, a jump from one region to another can be viewed as 'gluing' the source and target configuration of that jump. We can glue any two regions in Fig. 4(a) together by putting regions (i.e., state-invariants) of the source and the target states side by side to form a single state with a larger region. Each jump in Fig. 4(a) from a source to a target state corresponds to an idling transition (c.f., rule (S3) in Definition 3) within a single state. When we apply this gluing procedure in a consistent way to every jump in Fig. 4(a), we obtain a single state work automaton K that is defined by a single large region, as shown in Fig. 4(b). Figure 5 shows the actual work automaton that corresponds to this region. Note that the restart transition allows the state of progress to jump in Fig. 4(a) from configuration $((x, 1), i2)$ to $((x, 0), i0)$ and

$$\emptyset, x_2 = 3, \{x_2\} \qquad \emptyset, x_1 = 3, \{x_1\}$$

$$x_1 = 0 \wedge x_2 = 0 \rightarrow \boxed{0} \quad (x_1 \leq 1 \vee x_1 \geq 2 \vee x_2 \leq 1 \vee x_2 \geq 2) \wedge x_1 \leq 3 \wedge x_2 \leq 3$$

Fig. 5. Work automaton K that corresponds to Fig. 4(b).

from configuration $((1, y), 2j)$ to $((0, y), 0j)$, for all $x, y \in [0, 1]$ and $i, j \in \{0, 1, 2\}$. Thus, the restart transition identifies opposite boundaries in Fig. 4(b), turning the punctured square into a torus. ♣

The next example shows that the geometric view of the semantics of the work automaton in Example 5 reveals some interesting behavioral properties of M'.

Example 6. Consider the mutual exclusion protocol in Example 1. Is it possible to find a configuration such that parallel execution of jobs x_1 and x_2 (at identical speeds) never blocks, even temporarily, on lock L? It is not clear from the work automata in Fig. 1 (or in their product automaton as, e.g., in Fig. 3) whether such a non-blocking execution exists. Since only one process can acquire lock L, the execution that starts from the initial configuration blocks after one unit of work. However, using the geometric perspective offered by Fig. 4(b) and the fact that a parallel execution of jobs x_1 and x_2 at identical speeds correspond to a diagonal line in this representation, it is not hard to see that any execution path below line α and above line β is non-blocking. ♣

Regions of lock-free execution paths as revealed in Example 6 are interesting: if some mechanism (e.g., higher-level semantics of the application or tailor-made scheduling) can guarantee that execution paths of an application remains contained within such lock-free regions, then their respective locks can be safely removed from the application code. With or without such locks in an application code, a scheduler cognizant of such lock-free regions can improve resource utilization and performance by regulating the execution of the application such that its execution path remains in a lock-free region.

Example 7 (Correctness). Let M' be the work automaton in Example 4, and K the work automaton in Fig. 5. We denote a configuration of M' as a tuple $(p_1, p_2, q_0, q_1, q_2)$, where $p_i \in \mathbb{R}_+$ is the state of progress of job x_i, for $i \in \{0, 1\}$, and $(q_0, q_1, q_2) \in \{-, +\} \times \{0, 1, 2\}^2$ is the state of M'. We denote a configuration of K as a tuple $(p_1, p_2, 0)$, where $p_i \in \mathbb{R}_+$ is the state of progress of job x_i, for $i \in \{0, 1\}$. The binary relation $\preceq$ over configurations of M' and K defined by $(p_1, p_2, q_0, q_1, q_2) \preceq (q_1 + p_1, q_2 + p_2, 0)$, for all $0 \leq p_i \leq 1$ and $(q_0, q_1, q_2) \in \{-, +\} \times \{0, 1, 2\}^2$, is a weak simulation of M' in K.

Note that $\preceq^{-1}$ is not a weak simulation of K in M' due to branching. Consider the configurations $s = (1, 1, -, 0, 0)$ and $s' = (0, 1, +, 1, 0)$ of M', and $t = (1, 1, 0)$ of K (cf., Figs. 4(a) and (b)). While in configuration t job x_2 can make progress, execution of x_2 is blocked at s' because process A_1 has obtained the lock. Since $s' \preceq t$, we conclude that $\preceq^{-1}$ is not a weak simulation of K in M'.

Fortunately, we can still prove that K is a correct simplification of M by transform $\preceq^{-1}$ into a weak simulation. Intuitively, such transformation remove pairs like $(t, s') \in \preceq^{-1}$. We make this argument formal in Sect. 3.3. ♣

As illustrated in Example 6, gluing can reveal interesting and useful properties of an application. To formalize the gluing procedure, we define two operators on work automata. The main idea is to transform a given work automaton A_1 into an equivalent automaton A_2, such that (almost) any step $(p_1, q_1) \xrightarrow{\emptyset} (p'_1, q'_1)$ in $[\![A_1]\!]$ corresponds with an *idling* step $(p_2, q_2) \xrightarrow{\emptyset} (p'_2, q'_2)$ in $[\![A_2]\!]$, i.e., a step with $p'_2 = p_2$ and $q'_2 = q_2$. To achieve this correspondence, we define a translation operator that ensures $p'_2 = p_2$, and a contraction operator that ensures $q'_2 = q_2$.

3.2 Translation

In this section, we define the translation operator that allows us to remove resets of jobs from transitions. The following example shows that removal of job resets can be compensated by shifting the state-invariant of the target state.

Example 8 (Shifting). Suppose we remove the reset of job x on the transition of work automaton A in Fig. 6(a). If we fire the transition at $x = a \leq 1$, then the state of progress of x in state 1 equals a instead of 0. We can correct this error by *shifting* the state-invariant of 1 by a, for every $a \leq 1$. We, therefore, transform the state-invariant of 1 into $x \leq 2$ (see Fig. 6(b)). ♣

The transformation of work automata in Example 8 suggests a general translation procedure that, intuitively, (1) shifts each state-invariant $I(q)$, $q \in Q$, along the solutions of some job constraint $\theta(q) \in B(J)$, and (2) removes for every transition $\tau = (q, N, w, R, q')$ some resets $\rho(\tau) \subseteq J$ from R.

Definition 10 (Shifts). *A shift on a work automaton* $(Q, P, J, I, \longrightarrow, \phi_0, q_0)$ *is a tuple* (θ, ρ) *consisting of a map* $\theta : Q \to B(J)$ *and a map* $\rho : \longrightarrow \to 2^J$.

We define how to shift state-invariants along the solutions of a job constraint.

Definition 11. *Let* $\phi, \theta \in B(J)$ *be two job constraints with free variables among* $\mathbf{x} = (x_1, \dots, x_n)$, $n \geq 0$. *We define the shift* $\phi \uparrow \theta$ *of* ϕ *along (the solutions of)* θ *as any job constraint equivalent to* $\exists \mathbf{t}(\phi(\mathbf{x} - \mathbf{t}) \wedge \theta(\mathbf{t}))$.

Lemma 3. $\uparrow$ *is well-defined: for all* $\phi, \theta \in B(J)$ *there exists* $\psi \in B(J)$ *such that* $\exists \mathbf{t}(\phi(\mathbf{x} - \mathbf{t}) \wedge \theta(\mathbf{t})) \equiv \psi$.

$$x = 0 \to \boxed{0} \xrightarrow{\emptyset, x \leq 1, \{x\}} \boxed{1} \qquad x = 0 \to \boxed{0} \xrightarrow{\emptyset, x \leq 1, \emptyset} \boxed{1}$$

$$x \leq 1 \qquad x \leq 1 \qquad\qquad x \leq 1 \qquad x \leq 2$$

$$\text{(a) } A \qquad\qquad\qquad \text{(b) } B$$

Fig. 6. Shifting state-invariant $x \leq 1$ of state 1 in A by one unit.

We use a shift (θ, ρ) to translate guards and invariants along the solutions of job constraint θ and to remove resets occurring in ρ:

Definition 12 (Translation). *Let $\sigma = (\theta, \rho)$ be a shift on a work automaton $A = (Q, P, J, I, \rightarrow, \phi_0, q_0)$. We define the translation $A \uparrow \sigma$ of A along the shift σ as the work automaton $(Q, P, J, I_\sigma, \rightarrow_\sigma, \phi_0 \uparrow \theta(q_0), q_0)$, with $I_\sigma(q) = I(q) \uparrow \theta(q)$ and $\rightarrow_\sigma = \{(q, N, w \uparrow \theta(q), R \setminus \rho(\tau), q') \mid \tau = (q, N, w, R, q') \in \rightarrow\}$.*

Lemma 4. *If $\theta \in B(J)$ has a unique solution $\delta \models \theta$, then $p + \delta \models \phi \uparrow \theta$ implies $p \models \phi$, for all $p \in \mathbb{R}_+^J$ and $\phi \in B(J)$.*

Theorem 1. *If $p \models w \wedge I(q)$ and $\delta \models \theta(q)$ implies $(p + \delta)[R \setminus \rho(\tau)] - p[R] \models \theta(q')$, for every transition $\tau = (q, N, w, R, q')$ and every $p, d \in \mathbb{R}_+^J$, then $A \preceq A \uparrow \sigma$. If, moreover, $\theta(q)$ has for every $q \in Q$ a unique solution, then $A \approx A \uparrow \sigma$.*

For at transition $\tau = (q, N, w, R, q')$, suppose $\theta(q)$ and $\theta(q')$ define unique solutions δ and δ', respectively. If σ eliminates job $x \in R$ (i.e., $x \in \rho(\tau)$), then $p(x) + \delta(x) = \delta'(x)$, for all $p \models w \wedge I(q)$. Thus, $w \wedge I(q)$ must imply $x = \delta'(x) - \delta(x)$, which seems a strong assumption. For a deterministic application, however, it makes sense to have only equalities in transition guards. In this case, a transition is enabled only when a job finishes some fixed amount of work, which corresponds to having only equalities in transition guards.

Example 9. Let M' be the work automata in Example 4, $\sigma = (\delta, \rho)$ the shift defined by $\theta(q) := x_1 = q_1 \wedge x_2 = q_2$, and $\rho(\tau) = R_\tau$. Theorem 1 shows that $M' \uparrow \sigma$ and M' are weakly bisimilar.   ♣

3.3 Contraction

In this section, we define a contraction operator that merges different states into a single state. To determine which states merge and which stay separate, we use an equivalence relation $\sim$ on the set of states Q.

Definition 13 (Kernel). *A kernel of a work automaton A is an equivalence relation $\sim \subseteq Q \times Q$ on the state space Q of A.*

Recall that an *equivalence class* of a state $q \in Q$ is defined as the set $[q] = \{q' \in Q \mid q \sim q'\}$ of all $q' \in Q$ related to q. The *quotient set* of Q by $\sim$ is defined as the set $Q/\sim = \{[q] \mid q \in Q\}$ of all equivalence classes of Q by $\sim$. By transitivity, distinct equivalence classes are disjoint and $Q/\sim$ partitions Q.

Definition 14 (Contraction). *The contraction $A/\sim$ of a work automaton $A = (Q, P, J, I, \rightarrow, \phi_0, q_0)$ by a kernel $\sim$ is defined as $(Q/\sim, P, J, I', \rightarrow', \phi_0, [q_0])$, where $\rightarrow' = \{([q], N, w, R, [q']) \mid (q, N, w, R, q') \in \rightarrow\}$ and $I'([q]) = \bigvee_{\tilde{q} \in [q]} I(\tilde{q})$.*

The following results provides sufficient conditions for preservation of weak simulation by contraction. The relation $\preceq$ defined by $(p, [q]) \preceq (p, q)$, for all $(p, q) \in \mathbb{R}_+^J \times Q$, is not a weak simulation of $A/\sim$ in A. As indicated in Example 7, we can restrict $\preceq$ and require only $(p, [q]) \preceq (p, \alpha(p, [q]))$, for some *section* α.

Definition 15 (Section). *A section is a map* $\alpha : \mathbb{R}_+^J \times Q/{\sim} \to Q$ *such that for all* $q, q' \in Q$ *and* $p, d \in \mathbb{R}_+^J$

1. $p \models I'([q])$ *implies* $p \models I(\alpha(p, [q]))$;
2. $q \sim \alpha(p, [q])$;
3. $p \models \phi_0 \wedge I(q_0)$ *implies* $\alpha(p, [q_0]) = q_0$;
4. $(p, [q]) \xrightarrow{N} (p', [q'])$ *implies* $(p, \alpha(p, [q])) \overset{N}{\Rightarrow} (p', \alpha(p', [q']))$;
5. $(p, q) \xrightarrow{d} (p + d, q)$ *implies* $(p, \alpha(p, [q])) \overset{d}{\Rightarrow} (p + d, \alpha(p + d, [q]))$.

In contrast with conditions (1), (2), and (3) in Definition 15, conditions (4) and (5) impose restrictions on the contraction $A/{\sim}$. These restrictions allow us to prove, with the help of the following lemma, weak simulation of $A/{\sim}$ in A.

Lemma 5. *If* $(p, [q]) \xrightarrow{d} (p+d, [q])$, *then there exist* $k \geq 1$, $0 = c_0 < \cdots < c_k = 1$ *and* $q_1, \ldots, q_k \in [q]$ *such that* $p+c \cdot d \models I(q_i)$, *for all* $c \in [c_{i-1}, c_i]$ *and* $1 \leq i \leq k$.

Theorem 2. $A \preceq A/{\sim}$; *and if there exists a section* α, *then* $A/{\sim} \preceq A$.

In our concluding example below, we revisit our intuitive gluing procedure motivated in Sect. 3.1 to show how the theory developed in Sects. 3.2 and 3.3 formally supports our derivation of the geometric representation of $[\![K]\!]$ from $[\![M']\!]$ and implies the existence of mutual weak simulations between K and M'.

Example 10. Consider the work automaton $M' \uparrow \sigma$ from Example 9, and let $\sim$ be the kernel that relates all states of $M' \uparrow \sigma$. The contraction $(M' \uparrow \sigma)/{\sim}$ results in K, as defined in Example 5 (modulo some irrelevant idling transitions). Define $\alpha(p, [(q_1, q_2)]) = \min H$, where $H = \{(q_1, q_2) \in \{0, 1, 2\}^2 \mid p \models I_\sigma(q_1, q_2)\}$ is ordered by $(q_1, q_2) \leq (q_1', q_2')$ iff $q_1 \leq q_1'$ and $q_2 \leq q_2'$. By Theorem 2, we have $M' \preceq K$ and $M \preceq M'$. By Example 7, M' and K are not weakly bisimilar. ♣

The work automaton in Fig. 3 and the geometric representation of its infinite semantics in Fig. 4(a), only indirectly define a mutual exclusion protocol in M'. By Example 10, we conclude that M' is weakly language equivalent to a much simpler work automaton K that explicitly defines a mutual exclusion protocol by means of its state-invariant. Having such an explicit dependency visible in a state-invariant, reveals interesting behavioral properties of M', such as existence of non-blocking paths. These observations may be used to generate schedulers that force the execution to proceed along these non-blocking paths, which would enable a lock-free implementation and/or execution.

4   Related Work

Work automata without jobs correspond to *port automata* [12], which is a data-agnostic variant of *constraint automata* [3]. In a constraint automaton, each synchronization constraint $N \subseteq P$ is accompanied with a data constraint that interrelates the observed data d_a, at every port $a \in N$. Although it is straightforward to extend our work automata with data constraints, we refrain from doing

so because our work focuses on synchronization rather then data-aware interaction. Hiding on constraint automata defined by Baier et al. in [3] essentially
combines our hiding operator in Definition 9 with contraction from Theorem 2.

The syntax of work automata is similar to the syntax of *timed automata*
[1]. Semantically, however, timed automata are different from work automata
because jobs in a work automaton may progress independently (depending on
whether or not they are scheduled to run on a processor), while clocks in a timed
automaton progress at identical speeds. For the same reason, work automata
differ semantically from *timed constraint automata* [2], which is introduced by
Arbab et al. for the specification of time-dependent connectors.

This semantic difference suggests that we may specify a concurrent application as a *hybrid automaton* [11], which can be seen as a timed automaton wherein
the speed of each clock, called a *variable*, is determined by a set of first order
differential equations. Instead of fixing the speed of each process beforehand,
via differential equations in hybrid automata, our scheduling approach aims to
determine the speed of each process only after careful analysis of the application.
Therefore, we do not use hybrid automata to specify a concurrent application.

Weighted automata [5] constitute another popular quantitative model for
concurrent applications. Transitions in a weighted automaton are labeled by a
weight from a given semiring. Although weights can define the workload of transitions, weighted automata do not show dependencies among different concurrent
transitions, such as mutual exclusion [8]. As a consequence, weighted automata
do not reveal dependencies induced by a protocol like work automata do.

A geometric perspective on concurrency has already been studied in the
context of *higher dimensional automata*, introduced by Pratt [14] and Van
Glabbeek [6]. This geometric perspective has been successfully applied in [8]
to find and explain an essential counterexample in the study of semantic equivalences [7], which shows the importance of their, and indirectly our, geometric
perspective. A higher dimensional automaton is a geometrical object that is
constructed by gluing hypercubes. Each hypercube represents parallel execution
of tasks associated with each dimension. This geometrical view on concurrency
allows inheritance of standard mathematical techniques, such as homology and
homotopy, which leads to new methods for studying concurrent applications
[9,10].

5   Conclusion

We extended work automata with state-invariants and resets and provided a
formal semantics for these work automata. We defined weak simulation of work
automata and presented translation and contraction operators that can simplify
work automata while preserving their semantics up to weak simulation. Although
translation is defined for any shift (θ, ρ), the conditions in Theorem 1 prove
bisimulation only if θ has a unique solution. In the future, we want to investigate
if this condition can be relaxed—and if so, at what cost—to enlarge the class of
applications whose work automata can be simplified using our transformations.

Our gluing procedure in Example 5 associates a work automaton with a geo-metrical object, and Example 6 shows that this geometric view reveals interesting behavioral properties of the application, such as mutual exclusion and existence of non-blocking execution paths. This observation suggests our results can lead to smart scheduling that yields lock-free implementation and/or executions.

State-invariants and guards in work automata model the exact amount of work that can be performed until a job blocks. In practice, however, these exact amounts of work are usually not known before-hand. This observation suggests that the 'crisp' subset of the multidimensional real vector space defined by the state-invariant may be replaced by a density function. We leave the formalization of such stochastic work automata as future work.

References

1. Alur, R., Dill, D.L.: A theory of timed automata. Theor. Comput. Sci. **126**, 183–235 (1994)
2. Arbab, F., Baier, C., de Boer, F.S., Rutten, J.: Models and temporal logics for timed component connectors. In: Proceedings of SEFM, pp. 198–207 (2004)
3. Baier, C., Sirjani, M., Arbab, F., Rutten, J.: Modeling component connectors in Reo by constraint automata. Sci. Comput. Program. **61**(2), 75–113 (2006)
4. Dokter, K., Jongmans, S.-S., Arbab, F.: Scheduling games for concurrent systems. In: Lluch Lafuente, A., Proença, J. (eds.) COORDINATION 2016. LNCS, vol. 9686, pp. 84–100. Springer, Cham (2016). doi:10.1007/978-3-319-39519-7_6
5. Droste, M., Kuich, W., Vogler, H.: Handbook of Weighted Automata. Springer Science & Business Media. Springer, Heidelberg (2009)
6. van Glabbeek, R.J.: Bisimulation semantics for higher dimensional automata. Email message, July 1991. http://theory.stanford.edu/~rvg/hda
7. van Glabbeek, R.J.: On the expressiveness of higher dimensional automata. Theor. Comput. Sci. **356**(3), 265–290 (2006)
8. van Glabbeek, R.J., Vaandrager, F.: The difference between splitting in n and $n+1$. Inform. Comput. **136**(2), 109–142 (1997)
9. Goubault, E., Jensen, T.P.: Homology of higher dimensional automata. In: Cleaveland, W.R. (ed.) CONCUR 1992. LNCS, vol. 630, pp. 254–268. Springer, Heidelberg (1992). doi:10.1007/BFb0084796
10. Gunawardena, J.: Homotopy and concurrency. In: Păun, B., Rozenberg, G., Salomaa, A. (eds.) Current Trends in Theoretical Computer Science, pp. 447–459. World Scientific (2001)
11. Henzinger, T.A.: The theory of hybrid automata. In: Inan, M.K., Kurshan, R.P. (eds.) Verification of Digital and Hybrid Systems, pp. 265–292. Springer, Heidelberg (2000)
12. Koehler, C., Clarke, D.: Decomposing port automata. In: Proceedings of SAC, pp. 1369–1373. ACM (2009)
13. Milner, R.: Communication and Concurrency, vol. 84. Prentice Hall, New York (1989)
14. Pratt, V.: Modeling concurrency with geometry. In: Proceedings of POPL, pp. 311–322. ACM (1991)

A Decidable Subtyping Logic for Intersection and Union Types

Luigi Liquori[✉] and Claude Stolze[✉]

Université Côte d'Azur, INRIA, Sophia Antipolis, France
{Luigi.Liquori,Claude.Stolze}@inria.fr

Abstract. Using Curry-Howard isomorphism, we extend the typed lambda-calculus with intersection and union types, and its corresponding proof-functional logic, previously defined by the authors, with subtyping and explicit coercions.

We show the extension of the lambda-calculus to be isomorphic to the Barbanera-Dezani-de'Liguoro type assignment system and we provide a sound interpretation of the proof-functional logic with the $\mathsf{NJ}(\beta)$ logic, using Mints' realizers.

We finally present a sound and complete algorithm for subtyping in presence of intersection and union types. The algorithm is conceived to work for the (sub)type theory Ξ.

Keywords: Logics and lambda-calculus · Type · Subtype systems

1 Introduction

This paper is a contribution to the study of typed lambda-calculi *à la* Church in presence of intersection, union types, and subtyping and their role in logical investigations; it is a natural follow up of a recent paper by the authors [DdLS16].

Intersection types were first introduced as a form of *ad hoc* polymorphism in (pure) lambda-calculi *à la* Curry. The paper by Barendregt, Coppo, and Dezani [BCDC83] is a classic reference, while [Bar13] is a definitive reference.

Union types were later introduced as a dual of intersection by MacQueen, Plotkin, and Sethi [MPS86]: Barbanera, Dezani, and de'Liguoro [BDCd95] is a definitive reference; Frisch, Castagna, and Benzaken [FCB08] designed a type system with intersection, union, and negation types whose semantics are loosely the corresponding set-theoretical constructs.

As intersection and union types had their classical development for (undecidable) type assignment systems, many papers moved from intersection and union type theories to (typed) lambda-calculi *à la* Church: the programming language Forsythe, by Reynolds [Rey96], is probably the first reference for intersection

---

Work supported by the COST Action CA15123 EUTYPES "The European research network on types for programming and verification".

M.R. Mousavi and J. Sgall (Eds.): TTCS 2017, LNCS 10608, pp. 74–90, 2017.
DOI: 10.1007/978-3-319-68953-1_7

types, while Pierce's PhD thesis combines also unions and intersections [Pie91]; a recent implementation of a typed programming language featuring intersection and union types is [Dun14].

Proof-functional logical connectives allow reasoning about the structure of logical proofs, in this way giving to the latter the status of first-class objects. This is in contrast with classical truth-functional connectives where the meaning of a compound formula is dependent only on the truth value of its subformulas. Following this approach, the logical relation between type assignment systems and typed systems featuring intersection and union types were studied in [LR07, DL10, DdLS16].

Proof-functional connectives represent evidence as a "polymorphic" construction, that is, the same evidence can be used as a proof for different sentences. Pottinger [Pot80] first introduced a conjunction, called strong conjunction $\cap$, requiring more than the existence of constructions proving the left and the right hand side of the conjuncts. According to Pottinger: *"The intuitive meaning of $\cap$ can be explained by saying that to assert $A \cap B$ is to assert that one has a reason for asserting A which is also a reason for asserting B"*. This interpretation makes inhabitants of $A \cap B$ as uniform evidences for both A and B. Later, Lopez-Escobar [LE85] presented the first proof-functional logic with strong conjunction as a special case of ordinary conjunction.

Mints [Min89] presented a logical interpretation of strong conjunction using *realizers*: the logical predicate $r_{A \cap B}[M]$ is true if the pure lambda-term M is a realizer (also read as "M is a method to assess $A \cap B$") for both the formula $r_A[M]$ and $r_B[M]$.

Inspired by this, Barbanera and Martini tried to answer the question of realizing other "proof-functional" connectives, like strong implication, Lopez-Escobar's strong equivalence, or Bruce, Di Cosmo, and Longo provable type isomorphism [BCL92].

Recently [DdLS16] extended the logical interpretation with union types as another proof-functional operator, the strong union $\cup$. Paraphrasing Pottinger's point of view, we could say that the intuitive meaning of $\cup$ is that if we have a reason to assert A (or B), then the same reason will also assert $A \cup B$. This interpretation makes inhabitants of $(A \cup B) \supset C$ be uniform evidences for both $A \supset C$ and $B \supset C$. Symmetrically to intersection, and extending Mints' logical interpretation, the logical predicate $r_{A \cup B}[M]$ succeeds if the pure lambda-term M is a realizer for either the formula $r_A[M]$ or $r_B[M]$.

1.1 Contributions

This paper focus on the logical and algorithmic aspects of subtyping in presence of intersection and union types: our interest is not only theoretical but also pragmatic since, in a dependent-type setting, it opens the door to logical frameworks and proof-assistants. We also inspect the relationship between pure and typed lambda-calculi and their corresponding proof-functional logics as dictated by the well-known Curry-Howard [How80] correspondence. We'll present and explore the relationships between the following four formal systems:

- $\Lambda_{u\leqslant}^{\cap\cup}$, the type assignment system with intersection and union types for pure lambda-calculus with subtyping with the (sub)type theory Ξ, as defined in [BDCd95]: a type assignment judgment have the shape $\Gamma \vdash M : \sigma$;
- $\Lambda_{t\leqslant}^{\cap\cup}$, an extension of the typed lambda-calculus with strong pairs and strong sums $\Lambda_t^{\cap\cup}$, as defined in [DL10], with subtyping and explicit coercions: a type judgment has the shape $\Gamma^{@} \vdash M@\Delta : \sigma$, where Δ is a typed lambda-term enriched with strong pairs and strong sums;
- $\mathcal{L}_{\leqslant}^{\cap\cup}$, an extension of the proof-functional logic $\mathcal{L}^{\cap\cup}$ of [DdLS16] with *ad hoc* formulas and inference rules for subtyping and explicit coercions: sequents have the shape $\Gamma \vdash \Delta : \sigma$;
- $\mathsf{NJ}(\beta)$, a natural deduction system for derivations in first-order intuitionistic logic with pure lambda-terms [Pra65].

Intuitively, Δ denotes a proof for a type assignment derivation for M; from an operational point of view, reductions in pure M and typed Δ must be synchronized by suitable parallel reduction rules in order to preserve parallel reduction of subjects. From a typing point of view, the type rules of $\Lambda_{t\leqslant}^{\cap\cup}$ should encode the proof-functional nature of strong intersection and strong union, *i.e.* the fact that in an intersection (resp. union) the two Δ relate to the same M.

Thanks to an erasing function $\wr-\wr$ translating typed Δ to pure M, we could reason only on a proof-functional logic $\mathcal{L}_{\leqslant}^{\cap\cup}$ assigning types to Δ. Therefore, the original contribution are as follows:

- to define the typed lambda-calculus $\Lambda_{t\leqslant}^{\cap\cup}$ obtained by extending the typed calculus of [DL10] with a subtyping relation and explicit coercions, keeping decidability of type checking, and showing the isomorphism with the type assignment system $\Lambda_{u\leqslant}^{\cap\cup}$ of [BDCd95]. Terms of $\Lambda_{t\leqslant}^{\cap\cup}$ have the form $M@\Delta$ where M is a pure lambda-term, while Δ is a typed lambda-term enriched with strong pairs and and strong sums;
- to define $\mathcal{L}_{\leqslant}^{\cap\cup}$ obtained by extending the proof-functional logic $\mathcal{L}^{\cap\cup}$ of [DdLS16]: we show that the extended $\mathcal{L}_{\leqslant}^{\cap\cup}$ logic of subtyping is sound with respect to the realizability logic $\mathsf{NJ}(\beta)$, using Mint's realizability arguments;
- to present an algorithm for subtyping in presence of intersection and union types. The algorithm (presented in functional style) is conceived to work for the (sub)type theory Ξ (*i.e.* axioms 1 to 14, as presented in [BDCd95]).

For lack of space, the full metatheoretical development can be found in [LS17].

1.2 Related Work

We shortly list the main research lines involving type (assignment) systems with intersection, union, and subtyping for (un)typed lambda-calculi, proof-functional logics containing "strong operators", and realizability.

The formal investigation of soundness and completeness for a notion of realizability was initiated by Lopez-Escobar [LE85] and subsequently refined by Mints [Min89].

Barbanera and Martini [BM94] studied three proof-functional operators, namely the strong conjunction, the relevant implication (related with Meyer-Routley's [MR72] system B^+), and the strong equivalence connective for double implication, relating those connectives with a suitable type assignment system, a realizability semantics, and a completeness theorem.

Dezani-Ciancaglini, Ghilezan, and Venneri [DCGV97] investigated a Curry-Howard interpretation of intersection and union types (for Combinatory Logic): using the well-understood relation between combinatory logic and lambda-calculus, they encode type-free lambda-terms into suitable combinatory logic formulas and then type them using intersection and union types. This is a complementary approach to the realizability-based one here and in [DdLS16].

Various authors defined lambda-calculi *à la* Church for intersection types with related logics: see [Bar13] (pp. 780–781) for a complete list.

As mentioned before, Barbanera, Dezani-Ciancaglini, and de'Liguoro [BDCd95] introduced a pure lambda-calculus $\Lambda_u^{\cap\cup}$ with a related type assignment system featuring intersection and union types, and a powerful subtyping relation.

The previous work [DL10] presented a typed calculus $\Lambda_t^{\cap\cup}$ (without subtyping) that explored the relationship between the proof-functional intersections and unions and the corresponding type assignment system (without subtyping).

In [DdLS16] we introduced an erasing function, called *essence* and denoted by $\wr\Delta\wr$, to understand the connection between pure terms and typed terms: we proved the isomorphism between $\Lambda_t^{\cap\cup}$ and $\Lambda_u^{\cap\cup}$, and we showed that $\mathcal{L}^{\cap\cup}$ can be thought of as a proof-functional logic. The present paper extends all the systems and logics of [DdLS16] and presents a comparative analysis of the (sub)type theories Ξ and Π of [BDCd95]: this motivates the use of the (sub)type theory Ξ with their natural correspondence with $\mathsf{NJ}(\beta)$.

Hindley gave first a subtyping algorithm for type intersection [Hin82]: there is a rich literature reducing the subtyping problem in presence of intersection and union to a set constraint problem: good references are [Dam94, Aik99, DP04, FCB08]. The closest work to the algorithm presented in this paper has been made by Aiken and Wimmers [AW93] who designed an algorithm whose input is a list of set constraints with unification variables, usual arrow types, intersection, complementation, and constructor types. Their algorithm first rewrites types in disjunctive normal form, then simplifies the constraints until it shows the system has no solution, or until it can safely unify the variables. The rewriting in disjunctive normal form makes this algorithm exponential in time and space in the worst case.

Pfenning work on Refinement Types [Pfe93] pioneered an extension of Edinburgh Logical Framework with subtyping and intersection types: our aim is to study extensions of LF featuring fully fledged proof-functional logical connectives like strong conjunction, strong disjunction in presence of subtyping and relevant implication.

2   System

The pseudo-syntax of σ, M, Δ, and the derived $M@\Delta$ are defined using the following three syntactic categories:

$$\sigma ::= \omega \mid \phi \mid \sigma \to \sigma \mid \sigma \cap \sigma \mid \sigma \cup \sigma$$
$$M ::= x \mid \lambda x.M \mid M\,M$$
$$\Delta ::= * \mid x \mid \lambda x{:}\sigma.\Delta \mid \Delta\,\Delta \mid \langle \Delta , \Delta \rangle \mid [\Delta , \Delta] \mid \mathsf{pr}_1\,\Delta \mid \mathsf{pr}_2\,\Delta \mid \mathsf{in}_1\,\Delta \mid \mathsf{in}_2\,\Delta \mid [\sigma]\Delta$$

where ϕ denotes arbitrary constant types and ω denotes a special type that is inhabited by all terms. The Δ-expression $\langle \Delta , \Delta \rangle$ denotes the strong pair while $[\Delta , \Delta]$ denotes the strong sum, with the respective projections and injections, respectively. Finally $[\sigma]\Delta$ denotes the explicit coercion of Δ with the type σ.

The untyped reduction semantics for the calculus *à la* Curry $\Lambda_{\mathsf{u}}^{\cap\cup}$ is ordinary β-reduction, even if subject reduction holds only in presence of the "Gross-Knuth" parallel reduction (Definition 13.2.7 in [Bar84]), where all redexes in M are contracted simultaneously. Reduction for the calculus *à la* Church $\Lambda_{\mathsf{t}}^{\cap\cup}$ is delicate because it must keep *synchronized* the untyped reduction of M with the typed reduction of Δ: it is defined in Sect. 5 of [DL10]. Reductions in $\mathcal{L}^{\cap\cup}$ is ordinary β-reduction plus the following four reduction rules:

$$\mathsf{pr}_i\,\langle \Delta_1 , \Delta_2 \rangle \longrightarrow_{\mathsf{pr}_i}\Delta_i \quad [\lambda x{:}\sigma_1.\Delta_1 , \lambda x{:}\sigma_2.\Delta_2]\,\mathsf{in}_i\,\Delta_3 \longrightarrow_{\mathsf{in}_i}\Delta_i\{\Delta_3/\iota\} \quad i \in \{1,2\}$$

Figure 1 presents the main rules of the type assignment system of [BDCd95]: note that the type inference rules are not syntax-directed. Figure 2 presents the main rules of the typed calculus $\Lambda_{\mathsf{t}}^{\cap\cup}$ of [DL10][1]; note that this type system is completely syntax directed.

$$\frac{\Gamma \vdash M : \sigma_1 \quad \Gamma \vdash M : \sigma_2}{\Gamma \vdash M : \sigma_1 \cap \sigma_2}\;(\cap I) \qquad \frac{\Gamma \vdash M : \sigma_1 \cap \sigma_2 \quad i = 1,2}{\Gamma \vdash M : \sigma_i}\;(\cap E_i)$$

$$\frac{\Gamma \vdash M : \sigma_i \quad i = 1,2}{\Gamma \vdash M : \sigma_1 \cup \sigma_2}\;(\cup I_i) \qquad \frac{\Gamma, x{:}\sigma_1 \vdash M : \sigma_3 \quad \Gamma, x{:}\sigma_2 \vdash M : \sigma_3 \quad \Gamma \vdash N : \sigma_1 \cup \sigma_2}{\Gamma \vdash M[N/x] : \sigma_3}\;(\cup E)$$

Fig. 1. Intersection and Union Type Assignment System $\Lambda_{\mathsf{u}}^{\cap\cup}$ [BDCd95] (main rules).

The next definition clarifies what we intend with "correspondence" between an untyped M and a typed Δ: the essence partial function shows the syntactic relation between type free and typed lambda-terms. Essence maps typed proof-terms (Δ's) into pure λ-terms: intuitively, two typed Δ-terms prove the same formula if they have the same proof-essence.

---

[1] Contexts $\Gamma^@$ contains assumptions of the shape $x@\iota_x{:}\sigma$: the present paper uses ordinary contexts Γ, since Γ can be easily obtained by erasing all the $\_@\iota_x$ in $\Gamma^@$.

$$\frac{\Gamma, x{:}\sigma_1 \vdash M@\Delta : \sigma_2}{\Gamma \vdash \lambda x.M@\lambda x{:}\sigma_1.\Delta : \sigma_1 \to \sigma_2} \ (\to I) \qquad \frac{\Gamma \vdash M@\Delta : \sigma_i \quad i \in \{1,2\}}{\Gamma \vdash M@\mathsf{in}_i\, \Delta : \sigma_1 \cup \sigma_2} \ (\cup I_i)$$

$$\frac{\Gamma \vdash M@\Delta_1 : \sigma_1 \quad \Gamma \vdash M@\Delta_2 : \sigma_2}{\Gamma \vdash M@\langle \Delta_1 , \Delta_2 \rangle : \sigma_1 \cap \sigma_2} \ (\cap I) \qquad \frac{\Gamma \vdash M@\Delta : \sigma_1 \cap \sigma_2 \quad i \in \{1,2\}}{\Gamma \vdash M@\mathsf{pr}_i\, \Delta : \sigma_i} \ (\cap E_i)$$

$$\frac{\Gamma, x{:}\sigma_1 \vdash M@\Delta_1 : \sigma_3 \quad \Gamma, x{:}\sigma_2 \vdash M@\Delta_2 : \sigma_3 \quad \Gamma \vdash N@\Delta_3 : \sigma_1 \cup \sigma_2}{\Gamma \vdash M[N/x]@[\lambda x{:}\sigma_1.\Delta_1 , \lambda x{:}\sigma_2.\Delta_2]\, \Delta_3 : \sigma_3} \ (\cup E)$$

Fig. 2. Typed Calculus $\Lambda_{\mathsf{t}}^{\cap\cup}$ [DL10] (main rules).

Definition 1 (Proof Essence). *The essence function between pure and typed lambda-terms is defined as follows:*

$$\langle x \rangle \triangleq x \qquad\qquad \langle \lambda x{:}\sigma.\Delta \rangle \triangleq \lambda x.\langle \Delta \rangle$$
$$\langle \Delta_1\, \Delta_2 \rangle \triangleq \langle \Delta_1 \rangle \langle \Delta_2 \rangle \qquad\qquad \langle [\sigma]\Delta \rangle \triangleq \langle \Delta \rangle$$
$$\langle \mathsf{pr}_i\, \Delta \rangle \triangleq \langle \Delta \rangle \qquad\qquad \langle \mathsf{in}_i\, \Delta \rangle \triangleq \langle \Delta \rangle$$
$$\langle \langle \Delta_1 , \Delta_2 \rangle \rangle \triangleq \langle \Delta_1 \rangle \qquad\qquad if\ \langle \Delta_1 \rangle \equiv \langle \Delta_2 \rangle$$
$$\langle [\lambda x{:}\sigma_1.\Delta_1 , \lambda x{:}\sigma_2.\Delta_2)]\, \Delta_3 \rangle \triangleq \langle \Delta_1 \rangle \{\langle \Delta_3 \rangle / x\} \qquad if\ \langle \Delta_1 \rangle \equiv \langle \Delta_2 \rangle$$

$$\frac{\Gamma, x{:}\sigma_1 \vdash \Delta : \sigma_2}{\Gamma \vdash \lambda x{:}\sigma_1.\Delta : \sigma_1 \to \sigma_2} \ (\to I) \qquad \frac{\Gamma \vdash \Delta_1 : \sigma_1 \to \sigma_2 \quad \Gamma \vdash \Delta_2 : \sigma_1}{\Gamma \vdash \Delta_1\, \Delta_2 : \sigma_2} \ (\to E)$$

$$\frac{\begin{array}{c}\Gamma \vdash \Delta_1 : \sigma_1 \\ \Gamma \vdash \Delta_2 : \sigma_2 \quad \langle \Delta_1 \rangle \equiv \langle \Delta_2 \rangle\end{array}}{\Gamma \vdash \langle \Delta_1 , \Delta_2 \rangle : \sigma_1 \cap \sigma_2} \ (\cap I) \qquad \frac{\Gamma \vdash \Delta : \sigma_1 \cap \sigma_2 \quad i \in \{1,2\}}{\Gamma \vdash \mathsf{pr}_i\, \Delta : \sigma_i} \ (\cap E_i)$$

$$\frac{\Gamma \vdash \Delta : \sigma_i \quad i \in \{1,2\}}{\Gamma \vdash \mathsf{in}_i\, \Delta : \sigma_1 \cup \sigma_2} \ (\cup I_i) \qquad \frac{\begin{array}{c}\Gamma, x{:}\sigma_1 \vdash \Delta_1 : \sigma_3 \quad \langle \Delta_1 \rangle \equiv \langle \Delta_2 \rangle \\ \Gamma, x{:}\sigma_2 \vdash \Delta_2 : \sigma_3 \quad \Gamma \vdash \Delta_3 : \sigma_1 \cup \sigma_2\end{array}}{\Gamma \vdash [\lambda x{:}\sigma_1.\Delta_1 , \lambda x{:}\sigma_2.\Delta_2]\, \Delta_3 : \sigma_3} \ (\cup E)$$

Fig. 3. Proof-functional logic $\mathcal{L}^{\cap\cup}$ (main rules).

Figure 3 presents the main rules of the proof-functional logic $\mathcal{L}^{\cap\cup}$ of [DdLS16]: that logic is *proof-functional*, in the sense of Pottinger [Pot80] and Lopez-Escobar [LE85]: formulas encode, using the Curry-Howard isomorphism, *derivations* $\mathcal{D} : \Gamma \vdash M : \sigma$ in the type assignment system $\Lambda_{\mathsf{u}}^{\cap\cup}$ which are, in turn, isomorphic to typed *judgments* $\Gamma \vdash M@\Delta : \sigma$ of $\Lambda_{\mathsf{t}}^{\cap\cup}$. It is worth noticing that if we drop the restriction concerning the "essence" in rules $(\cap I)$ and $(\cup E)$ in the system $\mathcal{L}^{\cap\cup}$ and replace $\sigma \cap \tau$ by $\sigma \times \tau$, and $\sigma \cup \tau$ by $\sigma + \tau$, we get a simply typed lambda-calculus with product and sums, namely a truth-functional intuitionistic propositional logic with implication, conjunction, and disjunction in disguise: the resulting logic loses its proof-functionality.

The whole picture is now ready to be extended with the subtyping relation, as introduced in [BCDC83] and extended in [BDCd95] with unions. Subtyping is a preorder over types, and it is written as $\sigma \leqslant \tau$; a (sub)type theory denotes any collection of inequalities between types satisfying natural closure conditions. The (sub)type theory, called Ξ (see Definition 3.6 of [BDCd95]), is defined by the subtyping axioms and inference rules defined as follows:

(1) $\sigma \leqslant \sigma \cap \sigma$

(2) $\sigma \cup \sigma \leqslant \sigma$

(3) $\sigma \cap \tau \leqslant \sigma, \sigma \cap \tau \leqslant \tau$

(4) $\sigma \leqslant \sigma \cup \tau, \tau \leqslant \sigma \cup \tau$

(5) $\sigma \leqslant \omega$

(6) $\sigma \leqslant \sigma$

(7) $\sigma_1 \leqslant \sigma_2, \tau_1 \leqslant \tau_2 \Rightarrow$
     $\sigma_1 \cap \tau_1 \leqslant \sigma_2 \cap \tau_2$

(8) $\sigma_1 \leqslant \sigma_2, \tau_1 \leqslant \tau_2 \Rightarrow \sigma_1 \cup \tau_1 \leqslant \sigma_2 \cup \tau_2$

(9) $\sigma \leqslant \tau, \tau \leqslant \rho \Rightarrow \sigma \leqslant \rho$

(10) $\sigma \cap (\tau \cup \rho) \leqslant (\sigma \cap \tau) \cup (\sigma \cap \rho)$

(11) $(\sigma \rightarrow \tau) \cap (\sigma \rightarrow \rho) \leqslant \sigma \rightarrow (\tau \cap \rho)$

(12) $(\sigma \rightarrow \rho) \cap (\tau \rightarrow \rho) \leqslant (\sigma \cup \tau) \rightarrow \rho$

(13) $\omega \leqslant \omega \rightarrow \omega$

(14) $\sigma_2 \leqslant \sigma_1, \tau_1 \leqslant \tau_2 \Rightarrow$
     $\sigma_1 \rightarrow \tau_1 \leqslant \sigma_2 \rightarrow \tau_2$

The (sub)theory Ξ suggests the interpretation of ω as the *set universe*, of $\cap$ as the *set intersection*, of $\cup$ as the *set union*, and of $\leqslant$ as a sound (but not complete) *subset relation*, respectively, in the spirit of [FCB08]. In the following, we write $\sigma \sim \tau$ iff $\sigma \leqslant \tau$ and $\tau \leqslant \sigma$. We note that distributivity of union over intersection and intersection over union, *i.e.* $\sigma \cup (\tau \cap \rho) \sim (\sigma \cup \tau) \cap (\sigma \cup \rho)$ and $\sigma \cap (\tau \cup \rho) \sim (\sigma \cap \tau) \cup (\sigma \cap \rho)$ are derivable (see, *e.g.* derivation in [BDCd95], p. 9).

Once the subtyping preorder has been defined, a classical subsumption (respectively an explicit coercion rule) can be defined as follows:

$$\frac{\Gamma \vdash M : \sigma \quad \sigma \leqslant \tau}{\Gamma \vdash M : \tau} \ (\leqslant) \qquad \frac{\Gamma \vdash M@\Delta : \sigma \quad \sigma \leqslant \tau}{\Gamma \vdash M@[\tau]\Delta : \tau} \ (\leqslant) \qquad \frac{\Gamma \vdash \Delta : \sigma \quad \sigma \leqslant \tau}{\Gamma \vdash [\tau]\Delta : \tau} \ (\leqslant)$$

This completes the reminder of the type assignment $\Lambda_{u\leqslant}^{\cap\cup}$ of [BDCd95], and the presentation of the typed system $\Lambda_{t\leqslant}^{\cap\cup}$, and of the proof-functional logic $\mathcal{L}_{\leqslant}^{\cap\cup}$, respectively.

The next theorem relates the three systems: the key concept is the essence partial map $\wr-\wr$ that allows to interpret union, intersection, and explicit coercions as proof-functional connectives.

Theorem 2 (Equivalence). *Let M and Δ and $\Gamma^{@}, \Gamma, B$ such that $\wr\Delta\wr \equiv M$. Then:*

1. $\Gamma \vdash M : \sigma$ *iff* $\Gamma^{@} \vdash M@\Delta : \sigma$;
2. $\Gamma^{@} \vdash M@\Delta : \sigma$ *iff* $\Gamma \vdash \Delta : \sigma$;
3. $\Gamma \vdash M : \sigma$ *iff* $\Gamma \vdash \Delta : \sigma$.

Proof. Point 1 by upgrading Theorem 10 of [DL10]; point 2 by induction on the structure of derivations, using Definition 1; point 3 by 1, 2. □

The next theorem states that adding subtyping as explicit coercions does not break the properties of the extended typed systems.

Theorem 3 (Conservativity). *The typed system $\Lambda_{t\leqslant}^{\cap\cup}$ and the proof-functional logic $\mathcal{L}_{\leqslant}^{\cap\cup}$, both obtained by extending with the (sub)type theory Ξ and with explicit coercions type rules ($\leqslant$), preserve subject reduction (parallel-synchronized β-reduction for $\Lambda_{t\leqslant}^{\cap\cup}$), Church-Rosser, strong normalization, unicity of typing, decidability of type reconstruction and of type checking, judgment decidability and isomorphism of typed-untyped derivations.*

Proof. For proving properties of $\Lambda_{t\leqslant}^{\cap\cup}$ we proceeds by upgrading results of Theorems 11, 12 and 19 of [DL10] with the subsumption rule ($\leqslant$). Properties of $\mathcal{L}_{\leqslant}^{\cap\cup}$ are mostly inherited by $\Lambda_{t\leqslant}^{\cap\cup}$ using Theorem 2 or, as for case of subject reduction for β-, pr_i- and in_i-reductions, is proved by induction on the structure of the derivation. Decidability of subtyping is proved in Theorems 18 and 19.   □

3   Realizers

We start this section by recalling the logic $\vdash_{\mathsf{NJ}}$, as sketched in Fig. 4. By NJ we mean the natural deduction presentation of the intuitionistic first-order predicate calculus [Pra65]. Derivations in NJ are trees of judgments $G \vdash_{\mathsf{NJ}} A$, where G is a set of undischarged assumptions, rather than trees of formulas, as in Gentzen's original formulation. Then we extend NJ as follows:

Definition 4 (Logic NJ(β)). *Let $\mathbf{P}_\phi(x)$ be a unary predicate for each atomic type ϕ: the natural deduction system for first-order intuitionistic logic NJ(β) extends NJ with untyped lambda-terms and predicates $\mathbf{P}_\phi(x)$, the latter being axiomatized via the two Post rules:*

$$\frac{G_\Gamma \vdash_{\mathsf{NJ}(\beta)} \mathbf{P}_\phi(M) \quad M =_{\beta\eta} N}{G_\Gamma \vdash_{\mathsf{NJ}(\beta)} \mathbf{P}_\phi(N)} \ (\beta) \qquad \frac{}{G_\Gamma \vdash_{\mathsf{NJ}(\beta)} \mathbf{P}_\omega(M)} \ (Ax_\omega)$$

For a given context $\Gamma \triangleq \{x_1{:}\sigma_1, \ldots, x_n{:}\sigma_n\}$, we associate a logical context $G_\Gamma \triangleq r_{\sigma_1}[x_1], \ldots, r_{\sigma_n}[x_n]$. Note that $G_{\Gamma, x:\sigma} \equiv G_\Gamma, r_\sigma[x]$ and $x \notin \mathsf{Fv}(G_\Gamma)$, since $x \notin \mathsf{Dom}(\Gamma)$, by context definition.

In [DdLS16], we provided a foundation for the proof-functional logic $\mathcal{L}^{\cap\cup}$ by extending Mints' provable realizability to cope with intersection and union types, but without subtyping. What follows scale up Mints' realizability to $\mathcal{L}_{\leqslant}^{\cap\cup}$. The next definition is a reminder of the notion of realizer, as first introduced for intersection types by Mints [Min89], and extended by the authors in [DdLS16].

$$\frac{G \vdash_{\mathsf{NJ}} A \quad G \vdash_{\mathsf{NJ}} B}{G \vdash_{\mathsf{NJ}} A \wedge B} \ (\wedge I) \qquad \frac{G \vdash_{\mathsf{NJ}} A_1 \wedge A_2 \quad i = 1, 2}{G \vdash_{\mathsf{NJ}} A_i} \ (\wedge E_i)$$

$$\frac{G \vdash_{\mathsf{NJ}} A_i \quad i = 1, 2}{G \vdash_{\mathsf{NJ}} A_1 \vee A_2} \ (\vee I_i) \qquad \frac{G, A \vdash_{\mathsf{NJ}} C \quad G, B \vdash_{\mathsf{NJ}} C \quad G \vdash_{\mathsf{NJ}} A \vee B}{G \vdash_{\mathsf{NJ}} C} \ (\vee E)$$

Fig. 4. The logic NJ (main rules)

Definition 5 (Mints' realizers in NJ(β)). *Let* $\mathbf{P}_\phi(x)$ *be a unary predicate for each atomic type* ϕ. *Then we define the predicates* $r_\sigma[x]$ *for each type* σ *by induction over* σ, *as follows:*

$$r_\phi[x] \triangleq \mathbf{P}_\phi(x) \qquad r_{\sigma_1 \to \sigma_2}[x] \triangleq \forall y.r_{\sigma_1}[y] \supset r_{\sigma_2}[x\,y]$$
$$r_\omega[x] \triangleq \top \qquad r_{\sigma_1 \cup \sigma_2}[x] \triangleq r_{\sigma_1}[x] \vee r_{\sigma_2}[x]$$
$$r_{\sigma_1 \cap \sigma_2}[x] \triangleq r_{\sigma_1}[x] \wedge r_{\sigma_2}[x]$$

where $\supset$ *denotes implication,* $\wedge$ *and* $\vee$ *are the logical connectives for conjunction and disjunction respectively, that must be kept distinct from* $\cap$ *and* $\cup$. *Formulas have the shape* $r_\sigma[M]$, *whose intended meaning is that* M *is a method for* σ *in the intersection-union type discipline with subtyping.*

Intuitively, we write $r_\sigma[M]$ to denote a formula in NJ(β), realized by the pure lambda-term M of type σ in $\Lambda^{\cap\cup}_{u\leqslant}$. Observe that M is "distilled" by applying the essence function to the typed proof-term Δ, which faithfully encodes the type assignment derivation $\Gamma \vdash \wr\Delta\wr : \sigma$ in $\Lambda^{\cap\cup}_{u\leqslant}$. The next theorem states that the proof-functional logic $\mathcal{L}^{\cap\cup}_\leqslant$ is sound *w.r.t.* Mints' realizers in NJ(β).

Lemma 6 ($\Lambda^{\cap\cup}_{u\leqslant}$ versus NJ(β)). *If* $\Gamma \vdash M : \sigma$, *then* $G_\Gamma \vdash_{\mathsf{NJ}(\beta)} r_\sigma[M]$.

Proof. By structural induction on the derivation tree of $B \vdash M : \sigma$:

- *rules* (Var), ($\cup I$), ($\cap I$), ($\cap E$) *correspond trivially to* (Hyp), ($\vee I$), ($\wedge I$), *and* ($\wedge E$);
- *rule* ($\cup E$) *is derivable from rule* ($\vee E$) *and a classical substitution lemma;*
- *it can be showed that all the subtyping rules are derivable in* NJ(β), *therefore* ($\leqslant$) *is derivable;*
- *rules* ($\to I$) *and* ($\to E$) *are derivable:*

$$\frac{\dfrac{G_\Gamma, r_\sigma[x] \vdash_{\mathsf{NJ}(\beta)} r_\tau[M]}{G_\Gamma \vdash_{\mathsf{NJ}(\beta)} r_\sigma[x] \supset r_\tau[M]} \ (\supset I)}{G_\Gamma \vdash_{\mathsf{NJ}(\beta)} r_{\sigma\to\tau}[\lambda x.M]} \ (\forall I)$$

$$\frac{\dfrac{G_\Gamma \vdash_{\mathsf{NJ}(\beta)} r_{\sigma\to\tau}[M]}{G_\Gamma \vdash_{\mathsf{NJ}(\beta)} r_\sigma[N] \supset r_\tau[MN]} \ (\forall E) \qquad G_\Gamma \vdash_{\mathsf{NJ}(\beta)} r_\sigma[N]}{G_\Gamma \vdash_{\mathsf{NJ}(\beta)} r_\tau[MN]} \ (\supset E) \qquad \square$$

Informally speaking, $r_\sigma[M]$ can be interpreted as "M is an element of the set σ", and the judgment $\sigma_1 \leqslant \sigma_2$ in the (sub)type theory Ξ can be interpreted as $r_{\sigma_1}[x] \vdash_{\mathsf{NJ}(\beta)} r_{\sigma_2}[x]$. As a simple consequence of Lemma 6, we can now state soundness:

Theorem 7 (Soundness of NJ(β) and $\mathcal{L}^{\cap\cup}_\leqslant$). *If* $\Gamma \vdash \Delta : \sigma$ *then* $G_\Gamma \vdash_{\mathsf{NJ}(\beta)}$ $r_\sigma[\wr\Delta\wr]$.

Proof. Trivial by Lemma 6 and Theorem 2 part 3. $\square$

The completeness result, *i.e.* If $G_\Gamma \vdash_{\mathsf{NJ}(\beta)} r_\sigma[M]$, then there exists Δ such that $\Gamma \vdash \Delta : \sigma$ and $\langle\Delta\rangle \equiv M$ is more tricky because of the presence of the union elimination rule ($\lor E$) in $\mathsf{NJ}(\beta)$. As an example, let $\phi \equiv (\sigma\cup\tau)\cap(\sigma\cup\rho) \to \sigma\cup(\tau\cap\rho)$: with a fairly complex derivation in $\mathsf{NJ}(\beta)$ we can realize $G_\emptyset \vdash_{\mathsf{NJ}(\beta)} r_\phi[\lambda x.x]$, and then by completeness the type assignment $\emptyset \vdash \lambda x.x : \phi$ should be derivable in [BDCd95], which is not the case without subtyping. We left completeness for a future work.

Remark 8. The type assignment system $\Lambda_{\mathsf{t}\leqslant}^{\cap\cup}$ of [BDCd95] was based on the (sub)type theory $\varXi$ (see Definition 3.6 of [BDCd95]): the paper also introduced a stronger (sub)type theory, called $\varPi$, by adding the extra axiom

$$(15) \qquad \mathbf{P}(\sigma) \Rightarrow \sigma \to \tau \cup \rho \leqslant (\sigma \to \tau) \cup (\sigma \to \rho),$$

where $\mathbf{P}(\sigma)$ is true if σ syntactically corresponds to an Harrop formula. However, in $\mathsf{NJ}(\beta)$, the judgment $r_{\sigma\to(\tau\cup\rho)}[x] \vdash_{\mathsf{NJ}(\beta)} r_{(\sigma\to\tau)\cup(\sigma\to\rho)}[x]$ is not derivable because the judgment $A \supset (B \lor C) \vdash_{\mathsf{NJ}(\beta)} (A \supset B) \lor (A \supset C)$ is not derivable in NJ. As such, the (sub)type theory $\varPi$ cannot be overlapped with an interpretation of (sub)types as (sub)sets, as the following example show. The identity function $\lambda x.x$ inhabits the function set $\{a,b\} \to \{a\}\cup\{b\}$ but, by axiom (15), it should also inhabit $\{a,b\} \to \{a\}$ or $\{a,b\} \to \{b\}$, which is clearly not the case.

4   Subtyping Algorithm

The previous section showed that the proof-functional logic $\mathcal{L}_{\leqslant}^{\cap\cup}$ is sound *w.r.t.* the logic $\mathsf{NJ}(\beta)$. The truth of the sequent "$\Gamma \vdash \Delta : \sigma$" complicates its decidability because of the presence of the predicate $\sigma \leqslant \tau$ as a premise in rule ($\leqslant$): in fact, the subtype system is not an algorithm because of the presence of reflexivity and transitivity rules that are not syntax-directed. The same subtyping premise can affect the decidability of type checking of $\Lambda_{\mathsf{t}\leqslant}^{\cap\cup}$. This section presents a sound and complete algorithm $\mathcal{A}$ for subtyping in the (sub)type theory $\varXi$. In what follows we use the following useful shorthands:

$$\cap_i(\cup_j\sigma_{i,j}) \triangleq \cap_1(\cup_1\sigma_{1,1}\ldots\cup_j\sigma_{1,j})\ldots\cap_i(\cup_1\sigma_{i,1}\ldots\cup_j\sigma_{i,j}), \text{and}$$

$$\cup_i(\cap_j\sigma_{i,j}) \triangleq \cup_1(\cap_1\sigma_{1,1}\ldots\cap_j\sigma_{1,j})\ldots\cup_i(\cap_1\sigma_{i,1}\ldots\cap_j\sigma_{i,j}).$$

Those shorthands can also apply to unions of unions, intersections of intersections, intersections of arrows, etc.

Algorithm $\mathcal{A}$ alone has a polynomial complexity, but it requires the types to be in some normal form that will be detailed later. We therefore have a preprocessing phase that is exponential in space. The preprocessing uses the following four subroutines:

- $\mathcal{R}_1$, to simplify the shape of types containing the ω type: its complexity is linear;

- $\mathcal{R}_2$ (well-known), to transform a type in its conjunctive normal form, denoted by CNF, *i.e.* types being, roughly, intersection of unions: its complexity is exponential in space;
- $\mathcal{R}_3$ (well-known), to transform a type in its disjunctive normal form, denoted by DNF, *i.e.* types being, roughly, union of intersections: its complexity is exponential in space;
- $\mathcal{R}_4$, to transform a type in its arrow normal form, denoted by ANF, *i.e.* types being, roughly, arrow types where all the domains are intersection of ANF and all the codomains are union of ANF: its complexity is exponential in space.

Definition 9 (Subroutine $\mathcal{R}_1$). *The term rewriting system $\mathcal{R}_1$ is defined as follows:*

- $\omega \cap \sigma$ *and* $\sigma \cap \omega$ *rewrite to* σ;
- $\omega \cup \sigma$ *and* $\sigma \cup \omega$ *rewrite to* ω;
- $\sigma \to \omega$ *rewrites to* ω.

It is easy to verify that $\mathcal{R}_1$ terminates and his complexity is linear. The next definition recall the usual conjunctive/disjunctive normal form with corresponding subroutines $\mathcal{R}_2$ and $\mathcal{R}_3$, and introduce the arrow normal form with his corresponding subroutine $\mathcal{R}_4$.

Definition 10 (Subroutines $\mathcal{R}_2$ and $\mathcal{R}_3$)

- *A type is in CNF if it has the form $\cap_i(\cup_j \sigma_{i,j})$, and all the $\sigma_{i,j}$ are either atomic types, arrow types, or ω;*
- *The term rewriting system $\mathcal{R}_2$ rewrites a type in its CNF; it is defined as follows:*
  - $\sigma \cup (\tau \cap \rho)$ *rewrites to* $(\sigma \cup \tau) \cap (\sigma \cup \rho)$;
  - $(\sigma \cap \tau) \cup \rho$ *rewrites to* $(\sigma \cup \rho) \cap (\tau \cup \rho)$;
- *A type is in DNF if it has the form $\cup_i(\cap_j \sigma_{i,j})$, and all the $\sigma_{i,j}$ are either atomic types, arrow types, or ω;*
- *The term rewriting system $\mathcal{R}_3$ rewrites a type in its DNF; it is defined as follows:*
  - $\sigma \cap (\tau \cup \rho)$ *rewrites to* $(\sigma \cap \tau) \cup (\sigma \cap \rho)$;
  - $(\sigma \cup \tau) \cap \rho$ *rewrites to* $(\sigma \cap \rho) \cup (\tau \cap \rho)$.

It is well documented in the literature that $\mathcal{R}_2$ and $\mathcal{R}_3$ terminate, and that the complexity of those algorithms is exponential.

As you can see in the (sub)type Ξ's rules (11) and (12), intersection and union interact with the arrow type; in order to simplify this, we define the following subroutine:

Definition 11 (Subroutine $\mathcal{R}_4$)

- *A type is in* arrow normal form *(ANF) if :*

- it is an atomic type or ω;
- it is an arrow type in the form $(\cap_i \sigma_i) \rightarrow (\cup_j \tau_j)$, where the σ_i and τ_j are ANFs;
- The term rewriting system $\mathcal{R}_4$ rewrites an arrow type into an intersection of ANF; it is defined as follows:
  - $\sigma \rightarrow \tau$ rewrites to $\mathcal{R}_3(\sigma) \rightarrow \mathcal{R}_2(\tau)$;
  - $\cup_i \sigma_i \rightarrow \cap_j \tau_j$ rewrites to $\cap_i(\cap_j(\sigma_i \rightarrow \tau_j))$.

Since $\mathcal{R}_2$ and $\mathcal{R}_3$ terminate, $\mathcal{R}_4$ terminates and its complexity is exponential. The next lemma ensures we can safely use the $\mathcal{R}_{1,2,3,4}$ subroutines in the pre-processing, because they preserve type equivalence, denoted by $\sim$. Let $\sigma \sim \tau$ iff $\sigma \leqslant \tau$ and $\tau \leqslant \sigma$.

Lemma 12. *For all the term rewriting systems $\mathcal{R}_{1,2,3,4}$ we have that $\mathcal{R}(\sigma) \sim \sigma$.*

Proof. Each rewriting rule rewrites a term into an equivalent ($\sim$) term. $\square$

We can now define how the types are being preprocessed before being fed to the algorithm $\mathcal{A}$.

Definition 13

- A type is in disjunctive arrow normal form (DANF) if it is in DNF and all the arrow type subterms are in ANF;
- A type is in conjunctive arrow normal form (CANF) if it is in CNF and all the arrow type subterms are in ANF.

Let $\sigma \leqslant \tau$ be an instance of the subtyping problem. The preprocessing algorithm rewrites σ into a DANF by applying $\mathcal{R}_3 \circ \mathcal{R}_4 \circ \mathcal{R}_1$, and τ into a CANF by applying $\mathcal{R}_2 \circ \mathcal{R}_4 \circ \mathcal{R}_1$.

4.1   The Algorithm $\mathcal{A}$

Our algorithm $\mathcal{A}$ is composed of two mutually inductive functions, called $\mathcal{A}_1$ and $\mathcal{A}_2$. It proceeds as follows: $\sigma \leqslant \tau$ is preprocessed into $\cup_i(\cap_j \sigma_{i,j}) \leqslant \cap_h(\cup_k \tau_{h,k})$, where all the $\sigma_{i,j}, \tau_{h,k}$ are in ANF; it is then processed by $\mathcal{A}_1$, which accepts or rejects it.

Definition 14 (Main function $\mathcal{A}_1$). *input:* $\cup_i(\cap_j \sigma_{i,j}) \leqslant \cap_h(\cup_k \tau_{h,k})$ *where all the $\sigma_{i,j}, \tau_{h,k}$ are ANF; output: boolean.*

- *if $\cap_h(\cup_k \tau_{h,k})$ is ω, then accept, else*
    if for all i and h, there exists some j and some k, such that $\mathcal{A}_2(\sigma_{i,j} \leqslant \tau_{h,k})$ is true, then accept, else reject.

Definition 15 (Subtyping function $\mathcal{A}_2$). *input:* $\sigma \leqslant \tau$, *where $\sigma \not\equiv \omega$ and $\tau \not\equiv \omega$ are ANFs; output: boolean.*

- *Case $\omega \leqslant \phi$: reject;*
- *Case $\omega \leqslant \sigma \to \tau$: reject;*
- *Case $\phi \leqslant \phi'$: if $\phi \equiv \phi'$ then accept, else reject;*
- *Case $\phi \leqslant \sigma \to \tau$: reject;*
- *Case $\sigma \to \tau \leqslant \phi$: reject;*
- *Case $\sigma \to \tau \leqslant \sigma' \to \tau'$: if $\mathcal{A}_1(\sigma' \leqslant \sigma)$ and $\mathcal{A}_1(\tau \leqslant \tau')$, then accept, else reject.*

The following two lemmas will be used to prove soundness and completeness of the algorithm $\mathcal{A}_1$.

Lemma 16

1. *$\sigma \cup \tau \leqslant \rho$ iff $\sigma \leqslant \rho$ and $\tau \leqslant \rho$;*
2. *$\sigma \leqslant \tau \cap \rho$ iff $\sigma \leqslant \tau$ and $\sigma \leqslant \rho$.*

Proof. The two parts can be proved by examining the subtyping rules of the (sub)type theory Ξ. $\square$

Lemma 17. *If all the σ_i and τ_j are ANFs, then:*

1. *If $\exists j, \cap_i \sigma_i \leqslant \tau_j$, then $\cap_i \sigma_i \leqslant \cup_j \tau_j$;*
2. *If $\exists i, \sigma_i \leqslant \cup \tau_j$, then $\cap_i \sigma_i \leqslant \cup_j \tau_j$.*

Proof. The two parts can be proved by induction on the subtyping rules of the (sub)type theory Ξ using the ANF definition. $\square$

The soundness proof is now straightforward.

Theorem 18 ($\mathcal{A}_1, \mathcal{A}_2$'s Soundness)

1. *Let σ (resp. τ) be in DANF (resp. CANF). If $\mathcal{A}_1(\sigma \leqslant \tau)$, then $\sigma \leqslant \tau$;*
2. *Let σ and τ be in ANF, such that $\tau \not\equiv \omega$. If $\mathcal{A}_2(\sigma \leqslant \tau)$, then $\sigma \leqslant \tau$.*

Proof. The proof follows the algorithm, therefore it proceeds by mutual induction.

1. *By case analysis on the algorithm $\mathcal{A}_1$ using Lemmas 16 and 17, and part 2;*
2. *By case analysis on the algorithm $\mathcal{A}_2$, and by looking at the subtyping rules.* $\square$

Theorem 19 ($\mathcal{A}_1, \mathcal{A}_2$'s Completeness)

1. *For any type σ', τ' such that $\sigma' \leqslant \tau'$, let $\cup_i(\cap_j \sigma_{i,j}) \equiv \mathcal{R}_3 \circ \mathcal{R}_4 \circ \mathcal{R}_1(\sigma')$ and $\cap_h(\cup_k \tau_{h,k}) \equiv \mathcal{R}_2 \circ \mathcal{R}_4 \circ \mathcal{R}_1(\tau')$. We have that $\mathcal{A}_1(\cup_i(\cap_j \sigma_{i,j}) \leqslant \cap_h(\cup_k \tau_{h,k}))$;*
2. *Let σ and τ be in ANF, such that $\tau \not\sim \omega$. If $\sigma \leqslant \tau$, then $\mathcal{A}_2(\mathcal{R}_1(\sigma) \leqslant \mathcal{R}_1(\tau))$.*

Proof. We know by Lemma 12 that rewriting preserves subtyping, therefore as $\sigma' \leqslant \tau'$, we know that $\cup_i(\cap_j \sigma_{i,j}) \leqslant \cup_j \cap_h (\cup_k \tau_{h,k})$. The proof proceeds by mutual induction.

1. *The proof of this point relies on Lemmas 16 and 17: it is not shown by lack of space (see [LS17]) ;*
2.   – *Case $\omega \leqslant \tau$: by hypothesis, $\omega \nleqslant \tau$, so this case is absurd;*
   - *Case $\phi \leqslant \phi'$: we can show that $\phi \equiv \phi'$;*
   - *Case $\sigma \to \tau \leqslant \phi$: it can be proved that this case is absurd;*
   - *Case $\phi \leqslant \sigma \to \tau$: we can show that $\phi \leqslant \sigma \to \tau$ iff $\sigma \to \tau \sim \omega$, and this contradicts the hypothesis $\sigma \to \tau \nsim \omega$: this is absurd;*
   - *Case $\sigma \to \tau \leqslant \sigma' \to \tau'$: we can show that $\tau \leqslant \tau'$, and $\sigma' \leqslant \sigma$. We conclude by induction hypothesis.* □

5   Conclusions

We mention some future research directions.

Completeness of $\mathcal{L}^{\cap\cup}$. We have not proven yet completeness for our logic towards NJ(β), but we conjecture that if G_Γ is a logical context and $G_\Gamma \vdash_{\mathsf{NJ}(\beta)} r_\sigma[M]$, then $\Gamma \vdash M : \sigma$.

Strong/Relevant Implication is another proof-functional connective: as well explained in [BM94], it can be viewed as a special case of implication *"whose related function space is the simplest one, namely the one containing only the identity function"*. Relevant implication is well-known in the literature, corresponding to Meyer and Routley's Minimal Relevant Logic B^+ [MR72]. Following our parallelism between type systems for lambda-calculi *à la* Curry, *à la* Church, and logics, we could conjecture that strong implication, denoted by $\supset_r$ in the logic, by $\to_r$ in the type theory, and by λ_r in the typed lambda-calculus, can lead to the following type (assignment) rules, proof-functional logical inference, and Mints' realizer in NJ(β), respectively:

$$\frac{\Gamma \vdash \mathsf{I} : \sigma \to \tau}{\Gamma \vdash \mathsf{I} : \sigma \to_r \tau} \; (\to_r I) \qquad\qquad \frac{\Gamma, x{:}\sigma \vdash x@\Delta : \tau}{\Gamma \vdash \lambda x.x@\lambda_r x{:}\sigma.\Delta : \sigma \to_r \tau} \; (\to_r I)$$

$$\frac{\Gamma, x{:}\sigma \vdash \Delta : \tau \quad \langle\Delta\rangle \equiv x}{\Gamma \vdash \lambda_r x{:}\sigma.\Delta : \sigma \to_r \tau} \; (\to_r I) \qquad\qquad \frac{G_\Gamma \vdash r_{\sigma\to\tau}[\mathsf{I}]}{G_\Gamma \vdash r_{\sigma\to_r\tau}[\mathsf{I}]} \; (\supset_r I)$$

As showed in Remark 8, even a stronger (sub)type theory of Ξ (*i.e.* the (sub)theory Π of [BDCd95]) cannot be overlapped with a sound and complete interpretation of (sub)types as (sub)sets. We conjecture that, by extending the proof-functional logic with relevant implication ($\mathcal{L}^{\cap\cup\to_r}_{\leqslant}$), we could achieve completeness, by combining explicit coercions and relevant abstractions, as the following derivation shows:

$$\frac{\dfrac{\Gamma \vdash x : \sigma \quad \sigma \leqslant \tau}{\dfrac{\Gamma \vdash (\tau)x : \tau \quad \langle(\tau)x\rangle \equiv x}{\Gamma \vdash \lambda_r x{:}\sigma.(\tau)x : \sigma \to_r \tau}} \quad \Gamma \vdash \Delta : \sigma}{\Gamma \vdash (\lambda_r x{:}\sigma.(\tau)x)\,\Delta : \tau}$$

Dependent Types/Logical Frameworks. Our aim is to build a small logical framework *à la* Edinburgh Logical Framework [HHP93], featuring dependent types and proof-functional logical connectives. We conjecture that, in addition to the usual machinery dealing with dependent types and a suitable upgrade of the essence function, the following typing rules can be good candidates for a proof-functional LF extension:

$$\frac{\Gamma, x{:}\sigma \vdash \Delta : \tau \quad \wr\Delta\wr \equiv x}{\Gamma \vdash \lambda^r x{:}\sigma.\Delta : \Pi^r x{:}\sigma.\tau} \ (\Pi^r I) \qquad \frac{\Gamma \vdash \Delta_1 : \sigma \quad \Gamma \vdash \Delta_2 : \tau \quad \wr\Delta_1\wr \equiv \wr\Delta_2\wr}{\Gamma \vdash \langle \Delta_1 , \Delta_2 \rangle : \sigma \cap \tau} \ (\cap I)$$

$$\frac{\begin{array}{c}\Gamma \vdash \Delta_1 : \Pi y{:}\sigma.\rho[\mathsf{in}_1^\tau \, y/x] \quad \wr\Delta_1\wr \equiv \wr\Delta_2\wr \\ \Gamma \vdash \Delta_2 : \Pi y{:}\tau.\rho[\mathsf{in}_2^\sigma \, y/x] \quad \Gamma \vdash \Delta_3 : \sigma \cup \tau\end{array}}{\Gamma \vdash [\Delta_1 , \Delta_2] \, \Delta_3 : \rho[\Delta_3/x]} \ (\cup E)$$

Studying the behavior of proof-functional connectives would be beneficial to existing interactive theorem provers such as Coq or Isabelle, and dependently typed programming languages such as Agda, Beluga, Epigram, or Idris.

Prototype Implementation. We are currently implementing a small kernel for a logical framework featuring union and intersection types, as the $\Lambda_{t\leqslant}^{\cap\cup}$ calculus and the proof-functional logic $\mathcal{L}_{\leqslant}^{\cap\cup}$ does. The actual type system also features an experimental implementation of dependent-types *à la* LF following the above type rules, and of a *Read-Eval-Print-Loop* (REPL). We will put our future efforts to integrate our algorithm $\mathcal{A}$ to the type checker engine. We conjecture that our subtyping algorithm could be rewritten nondeterministically for an alternating Turing machine in polynomial time: this would mean that this problem is in PSPACE. This could be coherent with the fact that inclusion problem for regular tree languages is PSPACE-complete [Sei90]. The aim of the prototype is to check the expressiveness of the proof-functional nature of the logical engine in the sense that when the user must prove *e.g.* a strong conjunction formula $\sigma_1 \cap \sigma_2$ obtaining (mostly interactively) a witness Δ_1 for σ_1, the prototype can "squeeze" the proof-functional essence M of Δ_1 to accelerate, and in some case automatize, the construction of a witness Δ_2 proof for the formula σ_2 having the same essence M of Δ_1. Existing proof assistants could get some benefit if extended with a proof-functional logic. We are also started an encoding of the proof-functional operators of intersection and union in Coq. The actual state of the prototype can be retrieved at https://github.com/cstolze/Bull.

Acknowledgment. We are grateful to Ugo de'Liguoro, Daniel Dougherty, and the anonymous referees for their useful comments and suggestions.

References

[Aik99] Aiken, A.: Introduction to set constraint-based program analysis. Sci. Comput. Program. **35**(2), 79–111 (1999)

[AW93] Aiken, A., Wimmers, E.L.: Type inclusion constraints and type inference. In: FPCA, pp. 31–41. ACM (1993)

[Bar84]   Barendregt, H.P.: The λ-Calculus. Studies in Logic and the Foundations of Mathematics. North-Holland, Amsterdam (1984)

[Bar13]   Barendregt, H.P.: The λ-Calculus with Types. Cambridge University Press, Association for Symbolic Logic (2013)

[BCDC83] Barendregt, H.P., Coppo, M., Dezani-Ciancaglini, M.: A filter lambda model and the completeness of type assignment. J. Symbol. Logic **48**(4), 931–940 (1983)

[BCL92]   Bruce, K.B., Di Cosmo, R., Longo, G.: Provable isomorphisms of types. Math. Struct. Comput. Sci. **2**(2), 231–247 (1992)

[BDCd95] Barbanera, F., Dezani-Ciancaglini, M., De'Liguoro, U.: Intersection and union types: syntax and semantics. Inf. Comput. **119**(2), 202–230 (1995)

[BM94]   Barbanera, F., Martini, S.: Proof-functional connectives and realizability. Arch. Math. Logic **33**, 189–211 (1994)

[Dam94]   Damm, F.M.: Subtyping with union types, intersection types and recursive types. In: Hagiya, M., Mitchell, J.C. (eds.) TACS 1994. LNCS, vol. 789, pp. 687–706. Springer, Heidelberg (1994). doi:10.1007/3-540-57887-0_121

[DCGV97] Dezani-Ciancaglini, M., Ghilezan, S., Venneri, B.: The "relevance" of intersection and union types. Notre Dame J. Formal Logic **38**(2), 246–269 (1997)

[DdLS16] Dougherty, D.J., De'Liguoro, U., Liquori, L., Stolze, C.: A realizability interpretation for intersection and union types. In: Igarashi, A. (ed.) APLAS 2016. LNCS, vol. 10017, pp. 187–205. Springer, Cham (2016). doi:10.1007/978-3-319-47958-3_11

[DL10]   Dougherty, D.J., Liquori, L.: Logic and computation in a lambda calculus with intersection and union types. In: Clarke, E.M., Voronkov, A. (eds.) LPAR 2010. LNCS, vol. 6355, pp. 173–191. Springer, Heidelberg (2010). doi:10.1007/978-3-642-17511-4_11

[DP04]   Dunfield, J., Pfenning, F.: Tridirectional typechecking. In: POPL, pp. 281–292 (2004)

[Dun14]   Dunfield, J.: Elaborating intersection and union types. J. Funct. Program. **24**(2–3), 133–165 (2014)

[FCB08]   Frisch, A., Castagna, G., Benzaken, V.: Semantic subtyping: dealing set-theoretically with function, union, intersection, and negation types. J. ACM **55**(4), 19:1–19:64 (2008)

[HHP93]   Harper, R., Honsell, F., Plotkin, G.: A framework for defining logics. J. ACM **40**(1), 143–184 (1993)

[Hin82]   Hindley, J.R.: The simple semantics for Coppo-Dezani-Sallé types. In: Dezani-Ciancaglini, M., Montanari, U. (eds.) Programming 1982. LNCS, vol. 137, pp. 212–226. Springer, Heidelberg (1982). doi:10.1007/3-540-11494-7_15

[How80]   Howard, W.A.: The formulae-as-types notion of construction. In: To H.B. Curry: Essays on Combinatory Logic, Lambda Calculus and Formalism, pp. 479–490. Academic Press, London (1980)

[LE85]   Lopez-Escobar, E.G.K.: Proof functional connectives. In: Di Prisco, C.A. (ed.) Methods in Mathematical Logic. LNM, vol. 1130, pp. 208–221. Springer, Heidelberg (1985). doi:10.1007/BFb0075313

[LR07]   Liquori, L., Rocca, S.R.D.: Intersection typed system à la church. Inf. Comput. **9**(205), 1371–1386 (2007)

[LS17]   Liquori, L., Stolze, C.: A decidable subtyping logic for intersection and union Types. Research report, Inria (2017). https://hal.inria.fr/hal-01488428

[Min89] Mints, G.: The completeness of provable realizability. Notre Dame J. Formal Logic **30**(3), 420–441 (1989)

[MPS86] MacQueen, D.B., Plotkin, G.D., Sethi, R.: An ideal model for recursive polymorphic types. Inf. Control **71**(1/2), 95–130 (1986)

[MR72] Meyer, R.K., Routley, R.: Algebraic analysis of entailment I. Logique et Analyse **15**, 407–428 (1972)

[Pfe93] Pfenning, F.: Refinement types for logical frameworks. In: TYPES, pp. 285–299 (1993)

[Pie91] Pierce, B.C.: Programming with intersection types, union types, and bounded polymorphism. Ph.D. thesis, Technical report CMU-CS-91-205, Carnegie Mellon University (1991)

[Pot80] Pottinger, G.: A type assignment for the strongly normalizable λ-terms. In: To H.B. Curry: Essays on Combinatory Logic, Lambda Calculus and Formalism, pp. 561–577. Academic Press (1980)

[Pra65] Prawitz, D.: Natural deduction: a proof-theoretical study. Ph.D. thesis, Almqvist & Wiksell (1965)

[Rey96] Reynolds, J.C.: Design of the programming language Forsythe. Technical report CMU-CS-96-146, Carnegie Mellon University (1996)

[Sei90] Seidl, H.: Deciding equivalence of finite tree automata. J. Symbolic Logic **19**(3), 424–437 (1990)

Container Combinatorics:
Monads and Lax Monoidal Functors

Tarmo Uustalu[(⊠)]

Department of Software Science, Tallinn University of Technology,
Akadeemia tee 21B, 12618 Tallinn, Estonia
tarmo@cs.ioc.ee

Abstract. Abbott et al.'s containers are a "syntax" for a wide class of set functors in terms of shapes and positions. Containers whose "denotation" carries a comonad structure can be characterized as directed containers, or containers where a shape and a position in it determine another shape, intuitively a subshape of this shape rooted by this position. In this paper, we develop similar explicit characterizations for container functors with a monad structure and container functors with a lax monoidal functor structure as well as some variations. We argue that this type of characterizations make a tool, e.g., for enumerating the monad structures or lax monoidal functors that some set functor admits. Such explorations are of interest, e.g., in the semantics of effectful functional programming languages.

1 Introduction

Abbott et al.'s containers [1], a notational variant of polynomials, are a "syntax" for a wide class of set functors. They specify set functors in terms of shapes and positions. The idea is that an element of $F X$ should be given by a choice of a shape and an element of X for each of the positions in this shape; e.g., an element of $\mathsf{List}\, X$ is given by a natural number (the length of the list) and a matching number of elements of X (the contents of the list). Many constructions of set functors can be carried out on the level of containers, for example the product, coproduct of functors, composition and Day convolution of functors etc. One strength of containers is their usefulness for enumerating functors with specific structure or properties or with particular properties. It should be pointed out from the outset that containers are equivalent to simple polynomials in the sense of Gambino, Hyland and Kock [8–10,13], except that in works on polynomials one is often mainly interested in Cartesian polynomial morphisms whereas in works on containers general container morphisms are focussed on. The normal functors of Girard [11] are more constrained: a shape can only have finitely many positions.

Ahman et al. [3,4] sought to find a characterization of those containers whose interpretation carries a comonad structure in terms of some additional structure on the container, using that comonads are comonoids in the monoidal category of

M.R. Mousavi and J. Sgall (Eds.): TTCS 2017, LNCS 10608, pp. 91–105, 2017.
DOI: 10.1007/978-3-319-68953-1_8

set functors. This additional structure, of what they called directed containers, turned out to be very intuitive: every position in a shape determines another shape, intuitively the subshape corresponding to this position; every shape has a distinguished root position; and positions in a subshape can be translated into positions in the shape. Directed containers are in fact the same as small categories, yet directed container morphisms are not functors, but cofunctors in the sense of Aguiar [2].

In this paper, we develop similar characterizations of container functors with a monad structure and those with a lax monoidal structure. We use that both monads and lax monoidal endofunctors are monoids in the category of set endofunctors wrt. its composition resp. Day convolution monoidal structures and that both monoidal structures are available also on the category of containers and preserved by interpretation into set functors. The relevant specializations of containers, which we here call mnd-containers and lmf-containers, are very similar, whereby every mnd-container turns out to also define an lmf-container.

Our motivation for this study is from programming language semantics and functional programming. Strong monads are a generally accepted means for organizing effects in functional programming since Moggi's seminal works. That strong lax monoidal endofunctors have a similar application was noticed first by McBride and Paterson [12] who called them applicative functors. That lax monoidal functors are the same as monoids in the Day convolution monoidal structure on the category of functors (under some assumptions guaranteeing that this monoidal structure is present) was noticed in this context by Capriotti and Kaposi [7]. It is sometimes of interest to find all monad or lax monoidal functor structures that a particular functor admits. Containers are a good tool for such explorations. We demonstrate this on a number of standard examples.

The paper is organized as follows. In Sect. 2, we review containers and directed containers as an explicit characterization of those containers whose interpretations carries a comonad structure. In Sect. 3, we analyze containers whose interpretation is a monad. In Sect. 4, we contrast this with an analysis of containers whose interpretation is a lax monoidal functor. In Sect. 5, we consider some specializations of monads and monoidal functors, to conclude in Sect. 6.

To describe our constructions on containers, we use type-theoretically inspired syntax, as we need dependent function and pair types throughout. For conciseness of presentation, we work in an informal extensional type theory, but everything we do can be formalized in intensional type theory. "Minor" ("implicit") arguments of functions are indicated as subscripts in Π-types, λ-abstractions and applications to enhance readability (cf. the standard notation for components of natural transformations). We use pattern-matching lambda-abstractions; _ is a "don't care" pattern.

The paper is a write-up of material that was presented by the author at the SSGEP 2015 summer school in Oxford[1], but was not published until now.

---

[1] See the slides at http://cs.ioc.ee/~tarmo/ssgep15/.

2 Containers, Directed Containers

2.1 Containers

We begin by a condensed review of containers [1].

A *container* is given by a set S (of shapes) and a S-indexed family P of sets (of positions in each shape).

A *container morphism* between two containers (S, P) and (S', P') is given by operations $t : S \to S'$ (the shape map) and $q : \Pi_{s:S}.\, P'\,(t\,s) \to P\,s$ (the position map). Note that while the shape map goes in the forward direction, the position map for a given shape goes in the backward direction.

The identity container morphism on (S, P) is $(\mathsf{id}_S, \lambda_s.\, \mathsf{id}_{P\,s})$. The composition of container morphisms $(t, q) : (S, P) \to (S', P')$ and $(t', q') : (S', P') \to (S'', P'')$ is $(t' \circ t, \lambda_s.\, q_s \circ q'_{t\,s})$. Containers and container morphisms form a category **Cont**.

A container (S, P) interprets into a set functor $[\![S, P]\!]^c = F$ where $F\,X = \Sigma s : S.\, P\,s \to X$, $F\,f = \lambda(s, v).\,(s, f \circ v)$.

A container morphism (t, q) between containers (S, P) and (S', P') interprets into a natural transformation $[\![t, q]\!]^c = \tau$ between $[\![S, P]\!]^c$ and $[\![S', P']\!]^c$ where $\tau\,(s, v) = (t\,s, v \circ q_s)$.

Interpretation $[\![-]\!]^c$ is a fully-faithful functor from **Cont** to $[\mathbf{Set}, \mathbf{Set}]$.

For example, the list functor can be represented by the container (S, P) where $S = \mathbb{N}$, because the shape of a list is a number—its length, and $P\,s = [0..s)$, as a position in a list of length s is a number between 0 and s, with the latter excluded. We have $[\![S, P]\!]^c\,X = \Sigma s : \mathbb{N}.\,[0..s) \to X \cong \mathsf{List}\,X$, reflecting that to give a list amounts to choosing a length together with the corresponding number of elements. The list reversal function is represented by the container endomorphism (t, q) on (S, P) where $t\,s = s$, because reversing a list yields an equally long list, and $q_s\,p = s - p$, as the element at position p in the reversed list is the element at position $s - p$ in the given list. But the list self-append function is represented by (t, q) where $t\,s = s + s$ and $q_s\,p = p \bmod s$.

There is an identity container defined by $\mathsf{Id}^c = (1, \lambda *.\, 1)$. Containers can be composed, composition is defined by $(S, P) \cdot^c (S', P') = (\Sigma s : S.\, P\,s \to S', \lambda(s, v).\, \Sigma p : P\,s.\, P'\,(v\,p))$. Identity and composition of containers provide a monoidal category structure on **Cont**.

Interpretation $[\![-]\!]^c$ is a monoidal functor from $(\mathbf{Cont}, \mathsf{Id}^c, \cdot^c)$ to the strict monoidal category $([\mathbf{Set}, \mathbf{Set}], \mathsf{Id}, \cdot)$. Indeed, $\mathsf{Id}\,X = X \cong \Sigma * : 1.\, 1 \to X = [\![\mathsf{Id}^c]\!]^c\,X$ and $([\![S, P]\!]^c \cdot [\![S', P']\!]^c)\,X = [\![S, P]\!]^c\,([\![S', P']\!]^c\,X) \cong \Sigma s : S.\, P\,s \to \Sigma s' : S'.\, P'\,s' \to X \cong \Sigma(s, v) : (\Sigma s : S.\, P\,s \to S').\,(\Sigma p : P\,s.\, P'\,(v\,p)) \to X = [\![(S, P) \cdot^c (S', P')]\!]^c\,X$.

Another monoidal category structure on **Cont** is symmetric. Define Hancock's tensor by $(S, P) \circledast^c (S', P') = (S \times S', \lambda(s, s').\, P\,s \times P'\,s)$. Now $(\mathbf{Cont}, \mathsf{Id}^c, \circledast^c)$ form a symmetric monoidal category.

Interpretation $[\![-]\!]^c$ is a symmetric monoidal functor from $(\mathbf{Cont}, \mathsf{Id}^c, \circledast^c)$ to the symmetric monoidal category $([\mathbf{Set}, \mathbf{Set}], \mathsf{Id}, \circledast)$ where $\circledast$ is the Day convolution defined by $(F \circledast G)\,Z = \int^{X, Y} (X \times Y \to Z) \times (F\,X \times G\,Y)$. Indeed,

$$\llbracket S, P \rrbracket^c \circledast \llbracket S', P' \rrbracket^c Z$$
$$= \int^{X,Y} (X \times Y \to Z) \times ((\Sigma s : S. \, P \, s \to X) \times (\Sigma s' : S'. \, P' \, s' \to Y))$$
$$\cong \Sigma (s, s') : S \times S'. \int^{X,Y} (X \times Y \to Z) \times ((P \, s \to X) \times (P' \, s' \to Y))$$
$$\cong \Sigma (s, s') : S \times S'. \, P \, s \times P' \, s' \to Z$$
$$= \llbracket (S, P) \circledast^c (S, P) \rrbracket^c Z$$

2.2   Directed Containers

Next we review directed containers as a characterization those containers whose interpretation carries a comonad structure; we rely on [3,4].

A *directed container* is defined as a container (S, P) with operations

- $\downarrow \, : \Pi s : S. \, P \, s \to S$ (the subshape corresponding to a position in a shape),
- $\mathsf{o} : \Pi_{s:S}. \, P \, s$ (the root position), and
- $\oplus : \Pi_{s:S}. \, \Pi p : P \, s. \, P \, (s \downarrow p) \to P \, s$ (translation of a position in a position's subshape)

satisfying

- $s \downarrow \mathsf{o}_s = s$
- $s \downarrow (p \oplus_s p') = (s \downarrow p) \downarrow p'$
- $p \oplus_s \mathsf{o}_{s \downarrow p} = p$
- $\mathsf{o}_s \oplus_s p = p$
- $(p \oplus_s p') \oplus_s p'' = p \oplus_s (p' \oplus_{s \downarrow p} p'')$

The data $(\mathsf{o}, \oplus)$ resemble a monoid structure on P. However, P is not a set, but a family of sets, and $\oplus$ operates across the family. Similarly, $\downarrow$ resembles a right action of $(P, \mathsf{o}, \oplus)$ on S. When none of $P \, s$, o_s, $p \oplus_s p'$ depends on s, these data form a proper monoid structure and a right action.

A *directed container morphism* between two directed containers $(S, P, \downarrow, \mathsf{o}, \oplus)$ and $(S', P', \downarrow', \mathsf{o}', \oplus')$ is a morphism (t, q) between the underlying containers satisfying

- $t \, (s \downarrow q_s \, p) = t \, s \downarrow' p$
- $\mathsf{o}_s = q_s \, \mathsf{o}'_{t \, s}$
- $q_s \, p \oplus_s q_{s \downarrow q_s \, p} \, p' = q_s \, (p \oplus'_{t \, s} p')$

Directed containers form a category **DCont** whose identities and composition are inherited from **Cont**.

A directed container $(S, P, \downarrow, \mathsf{o}, \oplus)$ interprets into a comonad $\llbracket S, P, \downarrow, \mathsf{o}, \oplus \rrbracket^{dc} = (D, \varepsilon, \delta)$ where

- $D = \llbracket S, P \rrbracket^c$
- $\varepsilon \, (s, v) = v \, \mathsf{o}_s$
- $\delta \, (s, v) = (s, \lambda p. \, (s \downarrow p, \lambda p'. \, v \, (p \oplus_s p')))$

A directed container morphism (t, q) between $(S, P, \downarrow, \mathsf{o}, \oplus)$ and $(S', P', \downarrow', \mathsf{o}', \oplus')$ interprets into a comonad morphism $[\![t, q]\!]^{\mathrm{dc}} = [\![t, q]\!]^{\mathrm{c}}$ between $[\![S, P, \downarrow, \mathsf{o}, \oplus]\!]^{\mathrm{dc}}$ and $[\![S', P', \downarrow', \mathsf{o}', \oplus']\!]^{\mathrm{dc}}$.

$[\![-]\!]^{\mathrm{dc}}$ is a fully-faithful functor between **DCont** and **Comonad(Set)**. Moreover, the functor $[\![-]\!]^{\mathrm{dc}}$ is the pullback of the fully-faithful functor $[\![-]\!]^{\mathrm{c}} : \mathbf{Cont} \to [\mathbf{Set}, \mathbf{Set}]$ along $U : \mathbf{Comonad(Set)} \to [\mathbf{Set}, \mathbf{Set}]$ and the category **DCont** is isomorphic to the category of comonoids in $(\mathbf{Cont}, \mathsf{Id}^{\mathrm{c}}, \cdot^{\mathrm{c}})$.

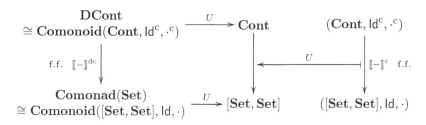

Here are some standard examples of directed containers and corresponding comonads.

Nonempty list functor (free semigroup functor). Let $D\,X = \mathsf{NEList}\,X = \mu Z.\,X \times (1 + Z) \cong \Sigma s : \mathbb{N}.\,[0..s] \to X$. We have $D\,X \cong [\![S, P]\!]^{\mathrm{c}}\,X$ for $S = \mathbb{N}$, $P\,s = [0..s]$.

The container (S, P) carries a directed container structure given by $s \downarrow p = s - p$, $\mathsf{o}_s = 0$, $p \oplus_s p' = p + p'$. Note that all three operations are well-defined: $p \le s$ implies that $s - p$ is well-defined; $0 \le s$; and $p \le s$ and $p' \le s - p$ imply $p + p' \le s$.

The corresponding comonad has $\varepsilon\,(x : xs) = x$ (the head of xs), $\delta\,[x] = [[x]]$, $\delta\,(x : xs) = (x : xs) : \delta\,xs$ (the nonempty list of all nonempty suffixes of xs).

There are other directed container structures on (S, P). One is given by $s \downarrow p = s$, $\mathsf{o}_s = 0$, $p \oplus_s p' = (p + p') \mod s$. This directed container interprets into the comonad defined by $\varepsilon\,xs = \mathsf{hd}\,xs$, $\delta\,xs = \mathsf{shifts}\,xs$ (the nonempty list of all cyclic shifts of xs).

Exponent functor. Let $D\,X = U \to X \cong 1 \times (U \to X)$ for some set U. We have $D\,X \cong [\![S, P]\!]^{\mathrm{c}}\,X$ for $S = 1$, $P\,* = U$.

Directed container structures on $[\![S, P]\!]^{\mathrm{c}}$ are in a bijection with monoid structures on U. Given a monoid structure $(\mathsf{i}, \otimes)$, the corresponding directed container structure is given by $* \downarrow p = *$, $\mathsf{o}_* = \mathsf{i}$, $p \oplus_* p' = p \otimes p'$.

The corresponding comonad has $\varepsilon\,f = f\,\mathsf{i}$, $\delta\,f = \lambda p.\,\lambda p'.\,f\,(p \otimes p')$.

Via the isomorphism $\mathsf{Str}\,X = \nu Z.\,X \times Z \cong \mathbb{N} \to X$, the special case of $(U, \mathsf{i}, \otimes) = (\mathbb{N}, 0, +)$ corresponds to the familiar stream comonad defined by $D\,X = \mathsf{Str}\,X$, $\varepsilon\,xs = \mathsf{hd}\,xs$ (the head of xs), $\delta\,xs = xs : \delta\,(\mathsf{tl}\,xs)$ (the stream of all suffixes of xs). A different special case $(U, \mathsf{i}, \otimes) = (\mathbb{N}, 1, *)$ corresponds to a different stream comonad given by $\varepsilon\,xs = \mathsf{hd}\,(\mathsf{tl}\,xs)$, $\delta\,xs = \mathsf{samplings}\,xs$ (the stream of all samplings of xs, where by the sampling of a stream $[x_0, x_1, x_2, \ldots]$ at rate p we mean the stream $[x_0, x_p, x_{p*2}, \ldots]$).

Product functor. Let $D\,X = V \times X = V \times (1 \to X)$ for some set V. We have that $T\,X \cong [\![S, P]\!]^c\, X$ for $S = V$, $P_- = 1$.

Evidently there is exactly one directed container structure on (S, P); it is given by $s \downarrow * = s$, $\mathsf{o}_s = *$, $* \oplus_s * = *$.

The corresponding comonad has $\varepsilon\,(v, x) = x$, $\delta\,(v, x) = (v, (v, x))$.

We defined directed containers as containers with specific additional structure. But they are in a bijection (up to isomorphism) with something much more familiar—small categories. Indeed, a directed container $(S, P, \downarrow, \mathsf{o}, \oplus)$ defines a small category as follows: the set of objects is S, the set of maps between s and s' is $\Sigma p : P\,s.(s \downarrow p = s')$; the identities and composition are given by o and $\oplus$. Any small category arises from a directed container uniquely in this fashion. The free category on a set V of objects (the discrete category with V as the set of objects), for example, arises from the directed container for the product comonad for V. However, directed container morphisms do not correspond to functors, since the shape map and position map of a container morphism go in opposite directions. A directed container morphism is reminiscent of a split opcleavage, except that, instead of a functor, it relies on an object mapping without an accompanying functorial action and accordingly the lift maps cannot be required to be opCartesian. A directed container morphism is a cofunctor (in the opposite direction) in the sense of Aguiar [2]. The category of directed containers is equivalent to the opposite of the category of small categories and cofunctors.

3 Containers ∩ Monads

There is no reason why the analysis of container functors with comonad structure could not be repeated for other types of functors with structure, the most obvious next candidate target being monads. The additional structure on containers corresponding to monads was sketched already in the original directed containers work [3]. Here we discuss the same characterization in detail.

We define an *mnd-container* to be a container (S, P) with operations

- $\mathsf{e} : S$
- $\bullet : \Pi s : S.\,(P\,s \to S) \to S$
- $q_0 : \Pi s : S.\,\Pi v : P\,s \to S.\,P\,(s \bullet v) \to P\,s$
- $q_1 : \Pi s : S.\,\Pi v : P\,s \to S.\,\Pi p : P\,(s \bullet v).\,P\,(v\,(v \nwarrow_s p))$

where we write $q_0\,s\,v\,p$ as $v \nwarrow_s p$ and $q_1\,s\,v\,p$ as $p \nearrow_v s$, satisfying

- $s = s \bullet (\lambda_-.\,\mathsf{e})$
- $\mathsf{e} \bullet (\lambda_-.\,s) = s$
- $(s \bullet v) \bullet (\lambda p''.\,w\,(v \nwarrow_s p'')\,(p'' \nearrow_v s)) = s \bullet (\lambda p'.\,v\,p' \bullet w\,p')$
- $p = (\lambda_-.\,\mathsf{e}) \nwarrow_s p$
- $p \nearrow_{\lambda_-.\,s} \mathsf{e} = p$
- $v \nwarrow_s ((\lambda p''.\,w\,(v \nwarrow_s p'')\,(p'' \nearrow_v s)) \nwarrow_{s \bullet v} p) = (\lambda p'.\,v\,p' \bullet w\,p') \nwarrow_s p$

$-\ ((\lambda p''.\,w\,(v\,\diagdown_s\,p'')\,(p''\,\diagup_v\,s))\,\diagdown_{s\bullet v}\,p)\,\diagup_v\,s =$
$$\mathsf{let}\ u\,p' \leftarrow v\,p' \bullet w\,p'\ \mathsf{in}\ w\,(u\,\diagdown_s\,p)\,\diagdown_{v\,(u\,\diagdown_s\,p)}\,(p\,\diagup_u\,s)$$
$-\ p\,\diagup_{\lambda p''.\,w\,(v\,\diagdown_s\,p'')\,(p''\,\diagup_v\,s)}\,(s\bullet v) =$
$$\mathsf{let}\ u\,p' \leftarrow v\,p' \bullet w\,p'\ \mathsf{in}\ (p\,\diagup_u\,s)\,\diagup_{w\,(u\,\diagdown_s\,p)}\,v\,(u\,\diagdown_s\,p)$$

We can see that the data $(\mathsf{e}, \bullet)$ are like a monoid structure on S modulo the 2nd argument of the multiplication being not an element of S, but a function from $P\,s$ to S where s is the 1st argument. Similarly, introducing the visual $\diagdown$, $\diagup$ notation for the data q_0, q_1 helps us see that they are reminiscent of a biaction (a pair of agreeing right and left actions) of this monoid-like structure on P. But a further difference is also that P is not a set, but a S-indexed family of sets.

We also define an *mnd-container morphism* between $(S, P, \mathsf{e}, \bullet, \diagdown, \diagup)$ and $(S', P', \mathsf{e}', \bullet', \diagdown', \diagup')$ to be a container morphism (t, q) between (S, P) and (S', P') such that

$-\ t\,\mathsf{e} = \mathsf{e}'$
$-\ t\,(s \bullet v) = t\,s \bullet' (t \circ v \circ q_s)$
$-\ v \diagdown_s q_{s\bullet v}\,p = q_s\,((t \circ v \circ q_s)\,\diagdown'_{t\,s}\,p)$
$-\ q_{s\bullet v}\,p \diagup_v s = q_{v\,(v\,\diagdown_s q_{s\bullet v}\,p)}\,(p\,\diagup'_{t\circ v\circ q_s}\,(t\,s))$

Mnd-containers form a category **MCont** whose identity and composition are inherited from **Cont**.

Every mnd-container $(S, P, \mathsf{e}, \bullet, \diagdown, \diagup)$ interprets into a monad $[\![S, P, \mathsf{e}, \bullet, \diagdown, \diagup]\!]^{mc} = (T, \eta, \mu)$ where

$-\ T = [\![S, P]\!]^c$
$-\ \eta\,x = (\mathsf{e}, \lambda p.\,x)$
$-\ \mu\,(s, v) = \mathsf{let}\ (v_0\,p, v_1\,p) \leftarrow v\,p\ \mathsf{in}\ (s \bullet v_0, \lambda p.\,v_1\,(v_0\,\diagdown_s\,p)\,(p\,\diagup_{v_0}\,s))$

Every mnd-container morphism (t, q) between $(S, P, \mathsf{e}, \bullet, \diagdown, \diagup)$ and $(S', P', \mathsf{e}', \bullet', \diagdown', \diagup')$ interprets into a monad morphism $[\![t, q]\!]^{mc} = [\![t, q]\!]^c$ between $[\![S, P, \mathsf{e}, \bullet, \diagdown, \diagup]\!]^{mc}$ and $[\![S', P', \mathsf{e}', \bullet', \diagdown', \diagup']\!]^{mc}$.

$[\![-]\!]^{mc}$ is a fully-faithful functor between **MCont** and **Monad(Set)**. Moreover, the functor $[\![-]\!]^{mc}$ is the pullback of the fully-faithful functor $[\![-]\!]^c :$ **Cont** $\rightarrow$ **[Set, Set]** along $U :$ **Monad(Set)** $\rightarrow$ **[Set, Set]** and the category **MCont** is isomorphic to the category of monoids in $(\textbf{Cont}, \mathsf{Id}^c, \cdot^c)$.

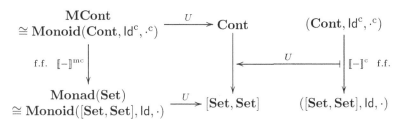

We consider as examples some containers interpreting into functors with a monad structure used in programming language semantics or functional programming.

Coproduct functor. Let $TX = X + E$ for some set E. We have that $TX \cong [\![S, P]\!]^c X$ for $S = 1 + E$, $P(\text{inl} *) = 1$, $P(\text{inr} \_) = 0$.

In a hypothetical mnd-container structure on (S, P), we cannot have $e = \text{inr}\, e_0$ for some $e_0 : E$, since then $P\, e = 0$, but all elements of $0 \to S \cong 1$ are equal, in particular, $\lambda\_. \text{inl} * = \lambda\_. \text{inr}\, e_0 : 0 \to S$, so the 2nd mnd-container equation $e \bullet (\lambda\_. s) = s$ cannot hold for both $s = \text{inl} *$ and $s = \text{inr}\, e_0$.

Therefore it must be that $e = \text{inl} *$. By the 2nd mnd-container equation then $\text{inl} * \bullet v = e \bullet (\lambda*. v *) = v *$ (since $P(\text{inl} *) = 1$) whereas $\text{inr}\, e \bullet v = \text{inr}\, e \bullet (\lambda\_. e) = \text{inr}\, e$ by the 1st mnd-container equation (since $P(\text{inr}\, e) = 0$).

To have $p : P(s \bullet v)$ is only possible, if $s = \text{inl} *$, $v = \lambda*. \text{inl} *$. In this case, $P(s \bullet v) = 1$ and $p = *$, and we can define $v \diagdown_s p = *$ and $p \diagup_v s = *$.

This choice of $(e, \bullet, \diagdown, \diagup)$ satisfies all 8 equations of a mnd-container.

We see that the container (S, P) carries exactly one mnd-container structure. The corresponding monad structure on T is that of the exception monad, with $\eta\, x = \text{inl}\, x$, $\mu(\text{inl}\, c) = c$, $\mu(\text{inr}\, e) = \text{inr}\, e$.

List functor (free monoid functor). Let T be the list functor: $TX = \text{List}\, X = \mu Z. 1 + X \times Z \cong \Sigma s : \mathbb{N}. [0..s) \to X$. We have that $TX \cong [\![S, P]\!]^c X$ for $S = \mathbb{N}$, $P\, s = [0..s)$.

The container (S, P) carries the following mnd-container structure:

- $e = 1$
- $s \bullet v = \sum_{p:[0..s)} v\, p$
- $v \diagdown_s p = $ greatest $p_0 : [0..s)$ such that $\sum_{p':[0..p_0)} v\, p' \leq p$
- $p \diagup_v s = p - \sum_{p':[0..v \diagdown_s p)} v\, p'$

The corresponding monad structure on T is the standard list monad with $\eta\, x = [x]$, $\mu\, xss = \text{concat}\, xss$.

This is not the only mnd-container structure available on (S, P). Another is $e = 1$, $s \bullet \lambda\_. 1 = s$, $1 \bullet \lambda 0. s = s$, $s \bullet v = 0$ otherwise, $\lambda\_. 1 \diagdown_s p = p$, $\lambda 0. s \diagdown_1 p = 0$, $p \diagup_{\lambda\_. 1} s = 0$, $p \diagup_{\lambda 0. s} 1 = p$.

The corresponding monad structure on T has $\eta\, x = [x]$, $\mu[[x_0], \ldots, [x_{v\,0-1}]] = [x_0, \ldots, x_{v\,0-1}]$, $\mu[xs] = xs$, $\mu\, xss = []$ otherwise.

Exponent functor. Let $TX = U \to X$ for some set U and $S = 1$, $P* = U$.

There is exactly one mnd-container structure on (S, P) given by

- $e = *$
- $* \bullet (\lambda\_. *) = *$
- $(\lambda\_. *) \diagdown_* p = p$
- $p \diagup_{\lambda\_. *} * = p$

Indeed, first note that the 1st to 3rd equations of an mnd-container are trivialized by $S = 1$. Further, $S = 1$ and the 4th and 5th equations force the definitions of $\diagdown$ and $\diagup$ and the remaining equations hold.

The corresponding monad structure on T is given by $\eta\, x = \lambda u. x$, $\mu\, f = \lambda u. f\, u\, u$. This is the well-known reader monad.

Product functor. Let $TX = V \times X$ for some set V and $S = V$, $P\_ = 1$.
Any mnd-container structure on (S, P) must be of the form

- $e = i$
- $s \bullet (\lambda*.\, s') = s \otimes s'$
- $(\lambda*.\, s') \,\backslash_s * = *$
- $* \,\nearrow_{\lambda*.\, s'}\, s = *$

for some $i : V$ and $\otimes : V \to V \to V$. The 1st to 3rd equations of an mnd-
container reduce to the equations of a monoid while the remaining equations are
trivialized by $P\_ = 1$. So mnd-container structures on (S, P) are in a bijective
correspondence with monoid structures on V.

The corresponding monad structures on T have $\eta\, x = (i, x)$, $\mu\,(p, (p', x)) = (p \otimes p', x)$. They are the writer monads for the different monoid structures on V.

Underlying functor of the state monad. Let $TX = U \to U \times X \cong (U \to U) \times (U \to X)$ for some set U. We have $TX \cong [\![S, P]\!]^c X$ for $S = U \to U$ and $P\_ = U$.
The container (S, P) admits the mnd-container structure defined by

- $e = \lambda p.\, p$
- $s \bullet v = \lambda p.\, v\, p\, (s\, p)$
- $v \,\backslash_s p = p$
- $p \,\nearrow_v s = s\, p$

The corresponding monad structure on T is that of the state monad for U,
given by $\eta\, x = \lambda u.\, (u, x)$ and $\mu\, f = \lambda u.\, \text{let } (u', g) \leftarrow f\, u' \text{ in } g\, u'$.
This mnd-container structure is not unique; as a simplest variation, one can
alternatively choose $s \bullet v = \lambda p.\, v\, p\, (s^n\, p)$, $p \,\nearrow_v s = s^n\, p$ for some fixed $n : \mathbb{N}$, with
s^n denoting n-fold iteration of s.

Underlying functor of update monads. Let $TX = U \to V \times X \cong (U \to V) \times (U \to X)$ for some sets U and V. We have $TX \cong [\![S, P]\!]^c X$ for $S = U \to V$ and
$P\_ = U$.

If $(i, \otimes)$ is a monoid structure on V and $\downarrow$ its right action on U, then the
container (S, P) admits the mnd-container structure defined by

- $e = \lambda\_.\, i$
- $s \bullet v = \lambda p.\, s\, p \otimes v\, p\, (s\, p)$
- $v \,\backslash_s p = p$
- $p \,\nearrow_v s = p \downarrow s\, p$

The corresponding monad structure on T is that of the update monad [5] for
U, $(V, i, \otimes)$ and $\downarrow$ given by $\eta\, x = \lambda u.(i, x)$ and $\mu\, f = \lambda u.\, \text{let } (p, g) \leftarrow f\, u; (p', x) \leftarrow g\, (u \downarrow p) \text{ in } (p \otimes p', x)$.
It should be clear that not every monad structure on T arises from some
$(i, \otimes)$ and $\downarrow$ in this manner.

The list functor example can be generalized in the following way. Let
$(O, \#, \text{id}, \circ)$ be some non-symmetric operad, i.e., let O be a set of operations,

$\#:O \to \mathbb{N}$ a function fixing the arity of each operation and $\mathsf{id}:O$ and $\circ:\Pi o:O.\,(\# o \to O) \to O$ an identity operation and a parallel composition operator, with $\#\,\mathsf{id}=1$ and $\#\,(o \circ v) = \sum_{i:[0,\# o)} \#\,(v\,i)$, satisfying the equations of a non-symmetric operad. We can take $S=O$, $P\,o=[0..\# o)$, $\mathsf{e}=\mathsf{id}$, $\bullet = \circ$ and $\diagdown,\diagup$ as in the definition of the (standard) list mnd-container. This choice of $(S,P,\mathsf{e},\bullet,\diagdown,\diagup)$ gives an mnd-container. The list mnd-container corresponds to a special case where there is exactly one operation for every arity, in which situation we can w.l.o.g. take $O=\mathbb{N}$, $\# o=o$. Keeping this generalization of the list monad example in mind, we can think of mnd-containers as a version of non-symmetric operads where operations may also have infinite arities and, importantly, arguments may be discarded and duplicated in composition.

Altenkirch and Pinyo [6] have proposed to think of an mnd-container $(S,P,\mathsf{e},\bullet,\diagdown,\diagup)$ as a "lax" $(1,\Sigma)$-type universe à la Tarski, namely, to view S as a set of types ("codes for types"), P as an assignment of a set to each type, e as a type 1, $\bullet$ as a Σ-type former, $\diagdown$ and $\diagup$ as first and second projections from the denotation of a Σ-type. The laxity is that there are no constructors for the denotations of 1 and Σ-types, and of course the equations governing the interaction of the constructors and the eliminators are then not enforced either. Thus 1 need not really denote the singleton set and Σ-types need not denote dependent products.

4   Containers ∩ Lax Monoidal Functors

We proceed to analyzing containers whose interpretation carries a lax monoidal functor structure wrt. the $(1,\times)$ monoidal category structure on **Set**. We will see that the corresponding additional structure on containers is very similar to that for monads, but simpler.

Recall that a *lax monoidal functor* between monoidal categories $(\mathcal{C},I,\otimes)$ and $(\mathcal{C}',I',\otimes')$ is defined as a functor F between $\mathcal{C}$ and $\mathcal{C}'$ with a map $\mathsf{m}^0:I' \to FI$ and natural transformation with components $\mathsf{m}_{X,Y}:FX \otimes' FY \to F(X \otimes Y)$ cohering with the unitors and associators of the two categories. A *lax monoidal transformation* between two lax monoidal functors $(F,\mathsf{m}^0,\mathsf{m})$ and $(F',\mathsf{m}^{0'},\mathsf{m}')$ is a natural transformation $\tau:F \to F'$ such that $\tau_I \circ \mathsf{m}^0 = \mathsf{m}^{0'}$ and $\tau_{X\otimes Y} \circ \mathsf{m}_{X,Y} = \mathsf{m}'_{X,Y} \circ \tau_X \otimes' \tau_Y$.

We define an *lmf-container* as a container (S,P) with operations

$-$ $\mathsf{e}:S$
$-$ $\bullet:S \to S \to S$
$-$ $q_0:\Pi s:S.\,\Pi s':S.\,P\,(s \bullet s') \to P\,s$
$-$ $q_1:\Pi s:S.\,\Pi s':S.\,P\,(s \bullet s') \to P\,s'$

where we write $q_0\,s\,s'\,p$ as $s' \diagdown_s p$ and $q_1\,s\,s'\,p$ as $p \diagup_{s'} s$, satisfying

$-$ $\mathsf{e} \bullet s = s$
$-$ $s = s \bullet \mathsf{e}$
$-$ $(s \bullet s') \bullet s'' = s \bullet (s' \bullet s'')$

- $e \nwarrow_s p = p$
- $p \nearrow_s e = p$
- $s' \nwarrow_s (s'' \nwarrow_{s \bullet s'} p) = (s' \bullet s'') \nwarrow_s p$
- $(s'' \nwarrow_{s \bullet s'} p) \nearrow_{s'} s = s'' \nwarrow_{s'} (p \nearrow_{s' \bullet s''} s)$
- $p \nearrow_{s''} (s \bullet s') = (p \nearrow_{s' \bullet s''} s) \nearrow_{s''} s'$

Differently from the mnd-container case, the data $(S, e, \bullet)$ of a lmf-container form a proper monoid. The data $(\nwarrow, \nearrow)$ resemble a biaction of $(S, e, \bullet)$.

We also define an *lmf-container morphism* between $(S, P, e, \bullet, \nwarrow, \nearrow)$ and $(S', P', e', \bullet', \nwarrow', \nearrow')$ to be a container morphism (t, q) between (S, P) and (S', P') such that

- $t\, e = e'$
- $t\,(s \bullet s') = t\, s \bullet' t\, s'$
- $s' \nwarrow_s q_{s \bullet s'}\, p = q_s\, (t\, s' \nwarrow'_{t\, s}\, p)$
- $q_{s \bullet s'}\, p \nearrow_{s'} s = q_{s'}\, (p \nearrow'_{t\, s'}\, t\, s)$

Lmf-containers form a category **LCont** whose identity and composition are inherited from **Cont**.

Every lmf-container $(S, P, e, \bullet, \nwarrow, \nearrow)$ interprets into a lax monoidal endofunctor $[\![S, P, e, \bullet, \nwarrow, \nearrow]\!]^{\mathrm{lc}} = (F, \mathsf{m}^0, \mathsf{m})$ on $(\mathbf{Set}, 1, \times)$ where

- $F = [\![S, P]\!]^{\mathrm{c}}$
- $\mathsf{m}^0 * = (e, \lambda_\_. *)$
- $\mathsf{m}\,((s, v), (s', v')) = (s \bullet s', \lambda p.\,(v\,(s' \nwarrow_s p), v'\,(p \nearrow_{s'} s)))$

Every lmf-container morphism (t, q) between $(S, P, e, \bullet, \nwarrow, \nearrow)$ and $(S', P', e', \bullet', \nwarrow', \nearrow')$ interprets into a lax monoidal transformation $[\![t, q]\!]^{\mathrm{lc}} = [\![t, q]\!]^{\mathrm{c}}$ between $[\![S, P, e, \bullet, \nwarrow, \nearrow]\!]^{\mathrm{mc}}$ and $[\![S', P', e', \bullet', \nwarrow', \nearrow']\!]^{\mathrm{lc}}$.

$[\![-]\!]^{\mathrm{lc}}$ is a fully-faithful functor between **LCont** and the category **LMF(Set)** of lax endofunctors on $(\mathbf{Set}, 1, \times)$. The functor $[\![-]\!]^{\mathrm{lc}}$ is the pullback of the fully-faithful functor $[\![-]\!]^{\mathrm{c}} : \mathbf{Cont} \to [\mathbf{Set}, \mathbf{Set}]$ along $U : \mathbf{LMF(Set)} \to [\mathbf{Set}, \mathbf{Set}]$. The category **LCont** is isomorphic to the category of monoids in $(\mathbf{Cont}, \mathsf{Id}^{\mathrm{c}}, \circledast^{\mathrm{c}})$.

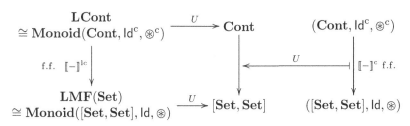

The similarity between the additional structures on containers for monads and lax monoidal functors may at first appear unexpected, but the reasons become clearer, if one compares the types of the "accumulating" Kleisli extension $\lambda(c, f).\ \mu\,(T\,(\lambda x.\, T\,(\lambda y.\,(x, y))\,(f\, x))\, c) : T\, X \times (X \to T\, Y) \to T\,(X \times Y)$ and the monoidality constraint $\mathsf{m} : F\, X \times F\, Y \to F\,(X \times Y)$.

It is immediate from the definitions that any mnd-container $(S, P, e, \bullet, \nwarrow, \nearrow)$ carries an lmf-container structure $(e', \bullet', \nwarrow', \nearrow')$ given by

- $e' = e$
- $s \bullet' s' = s \bullet (\lambda\_.\, s')$
- $s' \searrow'_s p = (\lambda\_.\, s') \searrow'_s p$
- $p \nearrow'_{s'} s = p \nearrow'_{\lambda\_.\, s'} s$

This is in agreement with the theorem that any strong monad defines a strong lax monoidal functor. Since any set functor is uniquely strong and all natural transformations between set functors are strong, the strength assumption and conclusion trivialize in our setting.

Another immediate observation is that, for any lmf-container structure $(e, \bullet, \searrow, \nearrow)$ on (S, P), there is also a reverse lmf-container structure $(e', \bullet', \searrow', \nearrow')$ given by

- $e' = e$
- $s \bullet' s' = s' \bullet s$
- $s' \searrow'_s p = p \nearrow_s s'$
- $p \nearrow'_{s'} s = s \searrow_{s'} p$

The corresponding statement about lax monoidal functors holds for any symmetric monoidal category.

Let us now revisit our example containers and see which lmf-container structures they admit.

Coproduct functor. Let $T X = X + E$ for some set E and $S = 1 + E$, $P\,(\text{inl}\,*) = 1$, $P\,(\text{inr}\,\_) = 0$.

Any lmf-container structure on (S, P) must have $e = \text{inl}\,*$. Indeed, if it were the case $e = \text{inr}\,e_0$ for some $e_0 : E$, then we would have $\text{inr}\,e_0 \bullet \text{inl}\,* = \text{inl}\,*$ by the 1st lmf-container equation. But then $q_0\,(\text{inr}\,e_0)\,(\text{inl}\,*) : 1 \to 0$, which cannot be.

Similarly, for all $e_0 : E$, $s : S$, it must be that $\text{inr}\,e_0 \bullet s \neq \text{inl}\,*$ and $s \bullet \text{inr}\,e_0 \neq \text{inl}\,*$. Hence, by the 1st and 2nd lmf-container equations, it must be the case that $\text{inl}\,* \bullet s = s$, $\text{inr}\,e \bullet \text{inl}\,* = \text{inr}\,e$, $\text{inr}\,e \bullet \text{inr}\,e' = \text{inr}\,(e \otimes e')$. The 3rd lmf-container equation forces that $\otimes$ is a semigroup structure on E. The other lmf-container equations hold trivially. Therefore, lmf-container structures on (S, P) are in a bijection with semigroup structures on E.

The corresponding lax monoidal functors have $m^0\,* = \text{inl}\,*$, $m\,(\text{inl}\,x, \text{inl}\,x') = \text{inl}\,(x, x')$, $m\,(\text{inl}\,x, \text{inr}\,e) = \text{inr}\,e$, $m\,(\text{inr}\,e, \text{inl}\,x) = \text{inr}\,e$, $m\,(\text{inr}\,e, \text{inr}\,e') = \text{inr}\,(e \otimes e')$.

The unique mnd-container structure on (S, P) corresponds to the particular case of the left zero semigroup, i.e., the semigroup where $e \otimes e' = e$.

List functor. Let $T X = \text{List}\,X$ and $S = \mathbb{N}$, $P\,s = [0..s)$.

The standard mnd-container structure on (S, P) gives this lmf-container structure:

- $e = 1$
- $s \bullet s' = s * s'$
- $s' \searrow_s p = p \ \text{div}\ s'$
- $p \nearrow_{s'} s = p \ \text{mod}\ s'$

The corresponding lax monoidal functor structure on T is given by $\mathsf{m}^0 * = [*]$, $\mathsf{m}\,(xs, ys) = [(x, y) \mid x \leftarrow xs, y \leftarrow ys]$.

The other mnd-container structure we considered gives $\mathsf{e} = 1$, $s \bullet 1 = s$, $1 \bullet s = s$, $s \bullet s' = 0$ otherwise, $1 \searrow_s p = p$, $s \searrow_1 p = 0$, $p \nearrow_1 s = 0$, $p \nearrow_s 1 = p$.

The corresponding lax monoidal functor structure on T is $\mathsf{m}^0 * = [*]$, $\mathsf{m}\,(xs, [y]) = [(x, y) \mid x \leftarrow xs]$, $\mathsf{m}\,([x], ys) = [(x, y) \mid y \leftarrow ys]$, $\mathsf{m}\,(xs, ys) = []$ otherwise.

But there are further lmf-container structures on (S, P) that do not arise from an mnd-container structure, for example this:

- $\mathsf{e} = 1$
- $s \bullet s' = s \min s'$
- $s' \searrow_s p = p$
- $p \nearrow_{s'} s = p$

The corresponding lax monoidal functor structure is $\mathsf{m}^0 * = [*]$, $\mathsf{m}\,(xs, ys) = \mathsf{zip}\,(xs, ys)$.

Exponent functor. Let $T\,X = U \to X$ for some set U and $S = 1$, $P * = U$.
There is exactly one lmf-container structure on (S, P) given by

- $\mathsf{e} = *$
- $* \bullet * = *$
- $* \searrow_* p = p$
- $p \nearrow_* * = p$

and that is the lmf-container given by the unique mnd-container structure.

The corresponding lax monoidal functor structure on T is given by $\mathsf{m}^0 * = \lambda u.\,*$, $\mathsf{m}\,(f, f') = \lambda u.\,(f\,u, f'\,u)$.

Product functor. Let $T\,X = V \times X$ for some set V and $S = V$, $P_- = 1$.
Any lmf-container structure on (S, P) must be of the form

- $\mathsf{e} = \mathsf{i}$
- $s \bullet s' = s \otimes s'$
- $s' \searrow_s * = *$
- $* \nearrow_{s'} s = *$

for $(\mathsf{i}, \otimes)$ a monoid structure on V, so the only lmf-container structures are those given by mnd-structures.

The corresponding lax monoidal functor structures on T are given by $\mathsf{m}^0 * = (\mathsf{i}, *)$, $\mathsf{m}\,((p, x), (p', x')) = (p \otimes p', (x, x'))$.

Similarly to the monad case, we can generalize the list functor example. Now we are interested in relaxation of non-symmetric operads where parallel composition is only defined when the given n operations composed with the given n-ary operation are all the same, i.e., we have O a set of operations, $\# : O \to \mathbb{N}$ a function fixing the arity of each operation and $\mathsf{id} : O$ and $\circ : O \to O \to O$

an identity operation and a parallel composition operator, with $\# \, \mathsf{id} = 1$ and $\# \, (o \circ o') = \# \, o * \# \, o'$, satisfying the equations of an ordinary non-symmetric operad. If we now choose $S = O$, $P \, o = [0..\# \, o)$, $\mathsf{e} = \mathsf{id}$, $\bullet = \circ$ and take $\diagdown$, $\diagup$ as in the definition of the standard list lmf-container, we get a non-symmetric operad in this relaxed sense.

Under the lax type universe view, an lmf-container is a lax $(1, \times)$-universe, i.e., it is only closed under non-dependent lax Σ-types.

5   Further Specializations

There are numerous special types of monads and lax monoidal functors that can be analyzed similarly. Here are some examples.

The lax monoidal functor interpreting an lmf-container is symmetric (i.e., satisfies $F \, \sigma_{X,Y} \circ \mathsf{m}_{X,Y} = \mathsf{m}_{Y,X} \circ \sigma_{FX,FY}$) if and only if the lmf-container is identical to its reverse, i.e., it satisfies

- $s \bullet s' = s' \bullet s$,
- $s' \diagdown_s p = p \diagup_s s'$

In this case, the monoid $(S, \mathsf{e}, \bullet)$ is commutative and each of the two action-like operations $\diagdown$, $\diagup$ determines the other.

The monad interpreting an mnd-container is commutative (which reduces to the corresponding lax monoidal functor being symmetric) if and only if

- $s \bullet (\lambda \_. \, s') = s' \bullet (\lambda \_. \, s)$
- $(\lambda \_. \, s') \diagdown_s p = p \diagup_{\lambda \_. \, s} s'$

Note that, in this case, $\diagdown$ and $\diagup$ are constrained, but not to the degree of fully determining each other.

The monad interpreting an mnd-container is Cartesian (which means that all naturality squares of η and μ are pullbacks) if and only if

- the function $\lambda \_. * : P \, \mathsf{e} \to 1$ is an isomorphism
- for any $s : S$ and $v : P \, s \to S$, the function $\lambda p. \, (v \diagdown_s p, p \diagup_v s) : P \, (s \bullet v) \to \Sigma p : P \, s. \, P \, (v \, p)$ is an isomorphism.

Such mnd-containers with additional conditions are proper $(1, \Sigma)$-type universes: 1 and Σ-types denote the singleton set and dependent products.

6   Conclusion

We showed that the containers whose interpretation into a set functor carries a monad or a lax monoidal functor structure admit explicit characterizations similar to the directed container (or small category) characterization of those containers whose interpretation is a comonad. It was not surprising that such characterizations are possible, as we could build on the very same observations that were used in the analysis of the comonad case. But the elaboration of the characterizations is, we believe, novel. We also believe that it provides useful insights into the nature of monad or lax monoidal functor structures on container functors. In particular, it provides some clues on why monads and lax monoidal functors on **Set** and, more generally, in the situation of canonical strengths enjoy analogous properties. In future work, we would like to reach a better understanding of the connections of containers to operads.

Acknowledgments. I am very grateful to Thorsten Altenkirch, Pierre-Louis Curien, Conor McBride, Niccolò Veltri for discussions. Paul-André Melliès pointed me to Aguiar's work. The anonymous reviewers of TTCS 2017 provided very useful feedback. This work was supported by the Estonian Ministry of Education and Research institutional research grant IUT33-13.

References

1. Abbott, M., Altenkirch, A., Ghani, N.: Containers: constructing strictly positive types. Theor. Comput. Sci. **342**(1), 3–27 (2005). doi:10.1016/j.tcs.2005.06.002
2. Aguiar, M.: Internal Categories and Quantum Groups. Ph.D. thesis. Cornell University, Ithaca, NY (1997). http://www.math.cornell.edu/~maguiar/thesis2.pdf
3. Ahman, D., Chapman, J., Uustalu, T.: When is a container a comonad? Log. Methods Comput. Sci. **10**(3), article 14 (2014). doi:10.2168/lmcs-10(3:14)2014
4. Ahman, D., Uustalu, T.: Directed containers as categories. In: Atkey, R., Krishnaswami, N. (eds.) Proceedings of 6th Workshop on Mathematically Structured Functional Programming, MSFP 2016. Electron. Proc. in Theor. Comput. Sci., vol. 207, pp. 89–98. Open Publishing Assoc., Sydney (2016). doi:10.4204/eptcs.207.5
5. Ahman, D., Uustalu, T.: Update monads: cointerpreting directed containers. In: Matthes, R., Schubert, A. (eds.) Proceedings of 19th Conference on Types for Proofs and Programs, Leibniz Int. Proc. in Inf., vol. 26, pp. 1–23. Dagstuhl Publishing, Saarbrücken/Wadern (2014). doi:10.4230/lipics.types.2013.1
6. Altenkirch, T., Pinyo, G.: Monadic containers and universes (abstract). In: Kaposi, A. (ed.) Abstracts of 23rd International Conference on Types for Proofs and Programs, TYPES 2017, pp. 20–21. Eötvös Lórand University, Budapest (2017)
7. Capriotti, P., Kaposi, A.: Free applicative functors. In: Levy, P., Krishnaswami, N. (eds.) Proceedings of 5th Workshop on Mathematically Structured Functional Programming, MSFP 2014, Electron. Proc. in Theor. Comput. Sci., vol. 153, pp. 2–30. Open Publishing Assoc., Sydney (2014). doi:10.4204/eptcs.153.2
8. Curien, P.-L.: Syntactic presentation of polynomial functors. Note, May 2017
9. Gambino, N., Hyland, M.: Wellfounded trees and dependent polynomial functors. In: Berardi, S., Coppo, M., Damiani, F. (eds.) TYPES 2003. LNCS, vol. 3085, pp. 210–225. Springer, Heidelberg (2004). doi:10.1007/978-3-540-24849-1_14
10. Gambino, N., Kock, J.: Polynomial functors and polynomial monads. Math. Proc. Cambridge Philos. Soc. **154**(1), 153–192 (2013). doi:10.1017/s0305004112000394
11. Girard, J.-Y.: Normal functors, power series and lambda-calculus. Ann. Pure Appl. Log. **37**(2), 129–177 (1988). doi:10.1016/0168-0072(88)90025-5
12. McBride, C., Paterson, R.: Applicative programming with effects. J. Funct. Program. **18**(1), 1–13 (2008). doi:10.1017/s0956796807006326
13. Weber, M.: Polynomials in categories with pullbacks. Theor. Appl. Categ. **30**, 533–598 (2015). http://www.tac.mta.ca/tac/volumes/30/16/30-16abs.html

Unification of Hypergraph λ-Terms

Alimujiang Yasen and Kazunori Ueda[✉]

Department of Computer Science and Engineering,
Waseda University, Tokyo, Japan
{ueda,alim}@ueda.info.waseda.ac.jp

Abstract. We developed a technique for modeling formal systems involving name binding in a modeling language based on hypergraph rewriting. A hypergraph consists of graph nodes, edges with two endpoints and edges with multiple endpoints. The idea is that hypergraphs allow us to represent terms containing bindings and that our notion of a graph type keeps bound variables distinct throughout rewriting steps. We previously encoded the untyped λ-calculus and the evaluation and type checking of System $F_{<:}$, but the encoding of System $F_{<:}$ type inference requires a unification algorithm. We studied and successfully implemented a unification algorithm modulo α-equivalence for hypergraphs representing untyped λ-terms. The unification algorithm turned out to be similar to nominal unification despite the fact that our approach and nominal approach to name binding are very different. However, some basic properties of our framework are easier to establish compared to the ones in nominal unification. We believe this indicates that hypergraphs provide a nice framework for encoding formal systems involving binders and unification modulo α-equivalence.

1 Introduction

Unification solves equations over terms. For a unification problem $M = N$, a unification algorithm finds a substitution $\delta = [X := P, Y := Q, \ldots]$ for unknown variables X and Y occurring in terms M and N so that applying δ to the original problem make $\delta(M)$ and $\delta(N)$ equal. Depending on the terms occurring in the unification problem, a unification algorithm is classified as (standard) *first-order* unification and *higher-order* unification, where higher-order unification solves equations over higher-order terms such as λ-terms. First-order unification is simple in theory and efficient in implementation [7,11], whereas higher-order unification is more complex both in theory and implementation [5].

The reason why higher-order unification is complex is that they solve equations of terms modulo α-, β- and possibly η-equivalence, denoted as $=_{\alpha\beta\eta}$. Alpha-equivalence equates two λ-terms M and N up to the renaming of their bound variables, denoted as $M =_{\alpha} N$; β-equivalence equates two terms under $(\lambda a.M)N =_{\beta} M[a := N]$; and η-equivalence states that $(\lambda a.Ma) =_{\eta} M$ where a does not occur free in M. Although higher-order unification is required in logic programming languages and proof assistants based on higher-order approach [9],

M.R. Mousavi and J. Sgall (Eds.): TTCS 2017, LNCS 10608, pp. 106–124, 2017.
DOI: 10.1007/978-3-319-68953-1_9

full higher-order unification is undecidable and may not generate most general unifiers. Higher-order pattern unification is a simple version of higher-order unification which solves terms modulo $\alpha\beta_0\eta$-equivalence [8], where β_0-equivalence is a form of β-equivalence $(\lambda x.M)N =_{\beta_0} M[x := N]$ where N must be a variable not occurring free in $\lambda x.M$. Most importantly, it is an efficient process with linear-time decidability [8,18]. Higher-order pattern unification is popular in practice because of that. For instance, the latest implementation of $\lambda Prolog$ is actually an implementation of a sublanguage of $\lambda Prolog$ called L_λ, which only uses higher-order pattern unification [10]. However, the infrastructure for implementing a variant of the λ-calculus is not lightweight, and a restriction to β_0-equivalence asks users for good programming practice to avoid cases which do not respect the restriction. A first-order style unification algorithm for terms involving name binding is preferred in these respects.

One such unification algorithm is nominal unification [14], which solves equations of nominal terms. In nominal terms, *names* are equipped with the *swapping* operation and the *freshness* condition [4]. The work in [2,6] shows the connection between nominal unification and higher-order pattern unification; if two nominal terms are unifiable, then their translated higher-order pattern counterparts are also unifiable. Alpha-equivalence is assumed for higher-order terms in theory. Yet, in the higher-order approach, implementing a meta-language (a variant of the typed λ-calculus) means that one must also consider $=_{\beta_0\eta}$. In nominal unification, only $=_\alpha$ is needed, and variable capture is allowed during the unification in the sense that a unifier may bring a name a into the scope of a as in $(\lambda a.X)[X := a]$. Nominal unification solves problems in two phases; solving equations of terms and solving freshness constraints.

Using graphs to represent λ-terms has a long history [19,20]. In our earlier work, we studied a hypergraph-based technique for representing terms involving name binding [16], using HyperLMNtal [13] as a representation and implementation language. The idea was that hypergraphs could naturally express terms containing bindings; atoms (nodes of graphs) represent constructors such as abstraction and application; hyperlinks (edges with multiple endpoints) represent variables; and regular links (edges with two endpoints) connect constructors with each other. In this technique, two isomorphic (but not identical) hypergraphs representing α-equivalent terms containing bindings have two syntactically different textual representations in HyperLMNtal. For example, two instances of the λ-term $\lambda a.aa$ are represented by α-equivalent but syntactically different hypergraphs such as `abs(A,(app(A,A)),L)` and `abs(B,(app(B,B)),R)` as shown in Fig. 1.

In Fig. 1, circles are atoms, straight lines are regular links and eight-point stars with curved lines are hyperlinks. The arrowheads on circles indicate the first arguments of atoms and the ordering of their arguments. These two hypergraphs, rooted at L and R, are isomorphic, i.e., have the same shape, but are syntactically not identical. (Later, we explain why regular links between `abs` and `app` atoms are implicit in the above two terms.)

(a)   (b)

Fig. 1. Two α-equivalent terms represented as hypergraphs

Our idea was first proposed in [16], where we developed the theory with the encoding of the untyped λ-calculus. Our formalism separates bound and free variables by Barendregt's variable convention [1] and also requires bound variables to be distinct from each other. A graph type called *hlground* (meaning ground graphs made up of hyperlinks) keeps bound variables distinct during the substitution. For example, $\lambda a.M$ and $\lambda a.N$ do not exist at the same time, and if $\lambda a.M$ exists, a may occur in M only. Such conventions may look too strict, but our experiences show that it brings great convenience in practice. For example, in our recent work [17], we encoded System $F_{<:}$ easily in HyperLMNtal; implementing the type checking of System $F_{<:}$ required the equality checking of types containing type variable binders, which was handled by directly applying α-equality rules in theory. As the next step, we want to implement the type inference of System $F_{<:}$, which means that we should study the unification of terms containing name binding within our formalism.

Hypergraphs representing λ-terms are called *hypergraph λ-terms*. This paper considers unification problems for equations over hypergraph λ-terms modulo $=_\alpha$. Hypergraph λ-terms have nice properties; for two abstractions L=abs(A,M) and R=abs(B,N), A does not occur in N and B does not occur in M, and A and B are always different hyperlinks. These properties greatly simplified the reasoning in our previous work, and we expect such simplicity in this work as well.

The outline of the paper is as follows. In Sect. 2, we briefly describe *hypergraph λ-terms* and the definition of substitutions. In Sect. 3, we present the unification algorithm and related proofs. In Sect. 4, we give some examples. In Sect. 5, we briefly describe the implementation of the unification algorithm. In Sect. 6, we review related work and conclude the paper.

2   Hypergraph λ-Terms

HyperLMNtal is a modeling language based on hypergraph rewriting [13] that is intended to be a substrate language of diverse computational models, especially those addressing concurrency, mobility and multiset rewriting. Moreover, we have successfully encoded the λ-calculus with strong reduction in HyperLMNtal in two different ways, one in the fine-grained approach [12] and the other in the coarse-grained approach [16]. This paper takes the latter approach that uses hyperlinks to represent binders, where the representation of λ-terms is called *hypergraph λ-terms*. We briefly describe HyperLMNtal and hypergraph λ-terms.

2.1 HyperLMNtal

In HyperLMNtal, *hypergraphs* consist of graph nodes called *atoms*, undirected edges with two endpoints called *regular links* and edges with multiple endpoints called *hyperlinks*. The simplified syntax of hypergraphs in HyperLMNtal is as follows,

$$(\textit{Hypergraphs}) \ P :: = 0 \mid p(A_1, \ldots, A_m) \mid P, P$$

where *link names* (denoted by A_i) and *atom names* (denoted by p) are presupposed. *Hypergraphs* are the principal syntactic category: 0 is an empty hypergraph; $p(A_1, \ldots, A_m)$ is an atom with arity m; and P, P is parallel composition. A hypergraph P is transformed by a rewrite rule of the form $H \text{ :- } G \mid B$ when a subgraph of P matches (i.e., is isomorphic to) H and auxiliary conditions specified in G are satisfied, in which case the subgraph of P is rewritten into another hypergraph B. The auxiliary conditions include type constraints and equality constraints. In HyperLMNtal programs, names starting with lowercase letters denote atoms and names starting with uppercase letters denote links. An abbreviation called *term notation* is frequently used in HyperLMNtal programs. It allows an atom b without its final argument to occur as an argument of a when these two arguments are interconnected by regular links. For instance, `f(a,b)` represents the graph `f(A,B),a(A),b(B)`, and `C=app(A,B)` represents the graph `app(A,B,C)`. The latter example shows that an n-ary constructor can be represented by an $(n + 1)$-ary HyperLMNtal atom whose final argument stands for the root link of the constructor.

In a rewrite rule, placing a constraint `new(A,a)` in the guard means that `A` is created as a hyperlink with an *attribute* a given as a natural number. A type constraint specified in the guard describes a class of graphs with specific shapes. For example, a graph type `hlink(A)` ensures that A is a hyperlink occurrence. A graph type `hlground(A, a_1, \ldots, a_n)` identifies a subgraph rooted at the link A, where $a_1, \ldots, a_n$ are the attributes of hyperlinks which are allowed to occur in the subgraph. The identified subgraph may be copied or removed according to rewrite rules. Details appear in Sect. 2.2.

2.2 Hypergraph λ-Terms

We write *hypergraph λ-terms* by the following syntax.

$$
\begin{array}{llll}
(\textit{Terms}) & M ::= & A & \textit{variables} \\
& & \mathsf{abs}(A, M) & \textit{abstractions} \\
& & \mathsf{app}(M, M) & \textit{applications}
\end{array}
$$

Here, the A are hyperlinks whose attributes are determined as follows: hyperlinks representing variables bound inside M or in a larger term containing M are given attribute 1 (denoted A^1), while those not bound anywhere are given attribute 2 (denoted A^2). Hypergraph λ-terms are straightforwardly obtained from λ-terms. For example, the Church numeral 2

$$\lambda x.\lambda y.x(xy)$$

is written as

```
R=abs(A,abs(B,app(A,app(A,B)))).
```

Note that both `abs` and `app` are ternary atoms, where their third arguments, made implicit by the term notation, are links connected to their parent atoms or represented by the leftmost `R`.

The following rewrite rules shows how to work with hypergraph λ-terms in HyperLMNtal.

```
N=n(2) :- new(A,1), new(B,1) | N=abs(A,abs(B,app(A,app(A,B)))).
init :- r=app(n(2),n(2)).
init.
```

The first rule creates a hypergraph representing the Church numeral 2. The second rule creates an application of two Church numerals.

The idea behind the hypergraph-based approach is that it applies the principle of *Barendregt's variable convention* (bound variables should be separated from free variables to allow easy reasoning) also to bound variables; all bound variables should be distinct from each other upon creation and should be kept distinct from each other during substitution. Besides keeping bound variables distinct, one should avoid variable capture during substitution.

In a substitution $(\lambda y.M)[x := N]$, replacing x with N in M will not lead to variable capture if y is kept distinct from the variables of N. The idea is to ensure that variables appear distinctly in M_1 and M_2 in an application $M_1 M_2$. Concretely, in a substitution $(M_1 M_2)[x := N]$, we generate two α-equivalent but syntactically different copies of N, say N_1 and N_2, to have $(M_1[x := N_1])(M_2[x := N_2])$. For a hypergraph λ-term with distinct variables, applying such strategy in the substitution ensures that $y \notin fv(N)$ for $(\lambda y.M)[x := N]$. To summarize, we use distinct hyperlinks with appropriate attributes to represent distinct variables of λ-terms and don't allow multiple binders of the same variable.

We use `sub` atoms to represent substitutions; $R=\texttt{sub}(X, N, M)$ represents $M[x := N]$. The definition of substitutions for hypergraph λ-terms is given in Fig. 2, where each rule is prefixed by a rule name. The rule `beta` implements β-reduction, and the other four rules implement substitutions. When the rule `var2` is applied, a subgraph matched with `hlground(N,1)` is removed. When the rule `app` is applied, two α-equivalent but syntactically different copies of a subgraph matched by `hlground(N,1)` are created. The `hlink(X)` checks if `X` is a hyperlink.

```
beta@@ R=app(abs(X,M),N)      :- R=sub(X,N,M).
var1@@ R=sub(X,N,X)           :- hlink(X) | R=N.
var2@@ R=sub(X,N,Y)           :- X\=Y, hlground(N,1) | R=Y.
abs@@  R=sub(X,N,abs(Y,M))    :- R=abs(Y,sub(X,N,M)).
app@@  R=sub(X,N,app(M1,M2)):- hlink(X), hlground(N,1) |
                               R=app(sub(X,N,M1), sub(X,N,M2)).
```

Fig. 2. Definition of substitutions on hypergraph λ-terms

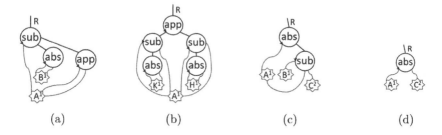

(a)   (b)   (c)   (d)

Fig. 3. Applying a substitution on an application

The graph type `hlground(N,1)` identifies a subgraph rooted at N, then rewriting may copy or remove the subgraph. When copying a subgraph identified by `hlground(N,1)` in a rule, it creates fresh copies of hyperlinks which have the attribute 1 and have no occurrences outside of the subgraph, while it shares hyperlinks which have the attribute 1 but have occurrences outside of the subgraph between the copies of the subgraph. It always shares hyperlinks which have an attribute different from 1 between the copies of the subgraph. When removing a subgraph identified by `hlground(N,1)` in a rule, it removes the subgraph along with all hyperlink endpoints in the subgraph.

For example, the rule `app` rewrites `R=sub(A,abs(B,B),app(A,A))` in Fig. 3a to `R=app(sub(A,abs(K,K),A),sub(A,abs(H,H),A))` in Fig. 3b, where the constraint `hlground(N,1)` identifies a subgraph `N=abs(B,B)` which is copied into `abs(K,K)` and `abs(H,H)`. The rule `var2` rewrites `R=abs(A,sub(B,A,C))` in Fig. 3c to `R=abs(A,C)` in Fig. 3d, where `hlground(N,1)` identifies a subgraph `N=A` and then the subgraph containing one endpoint of A is removed. For more details of `hlground`, readers are referred to our previous work [16].

3   Unification

We extend hypergraph λ-terms with *unknown variables* of unification problems, denoted by $X, Y, \ldots$, in a standard manner. Let A, B, C, D be hyperlinks, M, N, P be some hypergraph λ-terms, and L, R be regular links occurring as the last arguments of the atoms representing λ-term constructors.

The assumed equality between hypergraph λ-terms in our unification is α-equivalence with freshness constraints. When no confusion may arise, we write $=$ instead of $=_\alpha$ for the sake of simplicity. For a unification problem $M = N$ of two hypergraphs M and N containing unknown variables $X, Y, \ldots$, the goal is to find hypergraph λ-terms which replace $X, Y, \ldots$ and ensure the α-equivalence of M and N. To reason about the equality of non-ground hypergraph λ-terms (hypergraphs containing unknown variables), we use the concepts of *swapping* $\leftrightarrow$ and *freshness* $\#$ from the nominal approach [4].

Lemma 1. *In hypergraph λ-terms, for an abstraction L=abs(A,M), the hyperlink A occurs in M only.*

Proof. Follows from the construction of hypergraph λ-terms.   □

Henceforth, note that the last arguments of atoms representing λ-term constructors are implicit in terms related by $=$ and $\#$.

Lemma 2. *For two α-equivalent hypergraph λ-terms*

$$abs(A, M) = abs(B, N) ,$$

the following holds,

- *$A \# N$ and $B \# M$,*
- *$M = [A \leftrightarrow B]N$ and $[A \leftrightarrow B]M = N$,*

where $A \# N$ denotes that A is fresh for N (or A is not in N) and $[A \leftrightarrow B]N$ denotes the swapping of A and B in N.

Proof. Follows from Lemma 1 and the fact that hyperlinks representing bound variables are distinct in hypergraph λ-terms.   □

In Lemma 2, we could use renaming $M = [A/B]N$ and $[B/A]M = N$ instead of swapping, where $[A/B]N$ means replacing B by A in N. Moving $[A/B]$ to the left-hand side of $=$ requires the switching of A and B. Using swapping saves us from such switching operation in the implementation. Another point is that it is clear from their definitions that swapping subsumes renaming. In $[A \leftrightarrow B]N$, swapping $[A \leftrightarrow B]$ applies to every hyperlink in N until it reaches an unknown variable X occurring in N. We *suspend* swapping when it encounters an unknown variable X until X is instantiated to a non-variable term in the future.

Definition 1. *Let π be a list of swappings $[A_1 \leftrightarrow B_1, \ldots, A_n \leftrightarrow B_n]$, $var(\pi) = \{A_1, B_1, \ldots, A_n, B_n\}$, and $\pi^{-1} = [A_n \leftrightarrow B_n, \ldots, A_1 \leftrightarrow B_1]$. Applying π to a term M is written as $\pi \cdot M$. When M is an unknown variable X, we call $\pi \cdot M$ a suspension. The inductive definition of applying swappings to hypergraph λ-terms is defined as follows, where $\pi @ \pi'$ is a concatenation of π and π'.*

$$\pi @[A \leftrightarrow C] \cdot B \overset{def}{=} \pi \cdot B \qquad (A \neq B, B \neq C)$$

$$\pi @[A \leftrightarrow C] \cdot A \overset{def}{=} \pi \cdot C$$

$$\pi @[C \leftrightarrow A] \cdot A \overset{def}{=} \pi \cdot C$$

$$\pi \cdot \mathbf{abs}(A, M) \overset{def}{=} \mathbf{abs}(A, \pi \cdot M)$$

$$\pi \cdot \mathbf{app}(M, N) \overset{def}{=} \mathbf{app}(\pi \cdot M, \pi \cdot N)$$

$$\pi \cdot (\pi' \cdot M) \overset{def}{=} \pi @ \pi' \cdot M$$

$$[\,] \cdot M \overset{def}{=} M$$

We don't apply swapping to hyperlinks representing the bound variables of an $\mathtt{abs}$ (the fourth rule in Definition 1) because all bound variables are distinct in hypergraph λ-terms, and a swapping is only created from two abstractions using the rule =abs in Fig. 4. We use a *freshness constraint* $\#$ in the equality judgment of non-ground hypergraph λ-terms, and write $\theta \vdash M = N$ to denote that M and N are α-equal terms under a set θ of freshness constraints called a *freshness environment*. For example,

$$\{\mathtt{A}\#X, \mathtt{B}\#X\} \vdash \mathtt{abs}(\mathtt{A}, \ X) = \mathtt{abs}(\mathtt{B}, \ X)$$

is a valid judgment. Likewise, we write $\theta \vdash A\#M$ to say that $A\#M$ holds under θ. For example, $\mathtt{A}\#X \vdash \mathtt{A}\#\mathtt{app}(X, \mathtt{B})$ is a valid judgment. With swapping and freshness constraints, judging the equality of two non-ground hypergraph λ-terms is simple, as shown in Fig. 4.

The soundness of most of the rules in Fig. 4 should be self-evident. Below we give some lemmas to justify =susp and #susp. It is important to note that the rules in Fig. 4 are assumed to be used in a goal-directed manner starting from hypergraph λ-terms M and N. In the following lemmas, *"obtained by applying rules in Fig. 4 and Definition 1"* means that we use the rules in Fig. 4 in goal-directed, backward manner and the rules in Definition 1 in the left-to-right direction. By doing so, we come up with a set of unification rules which works on two unifiable terms and fails for two non-unifiable terms.

When judging the equality of two non-ground hypergraph λ-terms using the rules in Fig. 4, swappings are only generated by the rule =abs, and these swappings are applied to terms by the rules in Definition 1. During such process, we may have terms such as $\theta \vdash \pi \cdot M = \pi' \cdot N$ and $\theta \vdash A\#\pi \cdot M$. As mentioned before, a swapping is always created from two abstractions which have distinct bound hyperlinks. Therefore, in a judgment, swappings enjoy the following properties: Each swapping always has two distinct hyperlinks, and two swappings generated by the rule =abs have no hyperlinks in common. For example, in a judgment, there are no swappings such as $[A \leftrightarrow A]$ and $[A \leftrightarrow B, B \leftrightarrow C]$.

Lemma 3. *If the judgment*

$$\theta \vdash \pi \cdot M = \pi' \cdot N$$

$$\overline{\theta \vdash A = A} \quad \text{=hlink}$$

$$\frac{\theta \vdash M = [A \leftrightarrow B] \cdot N \quad \theta \vdash A\#N \quad \theta \vdash B\#M}{\theta \vdash \mathtt{abs}(A, M) = \mathtt{abs}(B, N)} \quad \text{=abs}$$

$$\frac{\theta \vdash M_1 = M_2 \quad \theta \vdash N_1 = N_2}{\theta \vdash \mathtt{app}(M_1, N_1) = \mathtt{app}(M_2, N_2)} \quad \text{=app}$$

$$\frac{(A\#X) \in \theta \text{ for all } A \in var(\pi@\pi')}{\theta \vdash \pi \cdot X = \pi' \cdot X} \quad \text{=susp}$$

$$\frac{A \neq B}{\theta \vdash A\#B} \quad \text{\#hlink}$$

$$\frac{\theta \vdash A\#N}{\theta \vdash A\#\mathtt{abs}(B, N)} \quad \text{\#abs}$$

$$\frac{\theta \vdash A\#M \quad \theta \vdash A\#N}{\theta \vdash A\#\mathtt{app}(M, N)} \quad \text{\#app}$$

$$\frac{(\pi^{-1} \cdot A\#X) \in \theta}{\theta \vdash A\#\pi \cdot X} \quad \text{\#susp}$$

Fig. 4. The equality and freshness judgments for non-ground hypergraph λ-terms

is obtained by applying rules in Fig. 4 and Definition 1, then $var(\pi) \cap var(\pi') = \emptyset$ holds.

Proof. Follows from the fact that hyperlinks of a swapping are distinct.   □

Note that the rules in Fig. 4 and Definition 1 generate non-empty swappings only to the right-hand side of equations, so the π above is actually empty. Nevertheless, we have non-empty swappings in the left-hand side in this and the following lemmas because the claims generalize to equations generated by the unification algorithm described later in Fig. 5.

Lemma 4. *If the judgment*

$$\theta \vdash \pi \cdot \mathit{abs}(A, M) = \pi' \cdot \mathit{abs}(B, N),$$

is obtained by applying rules in Fig. 4 and Definition 1, then $A \notin var(\pi@\pi')$ and $B \notin var(\pi@\pi')$ hold.

Proof. The same as the proof of Lemma 3.   □

The next lemma states how swappings move between two sides of $=$ in a judgment.

Lemma 5. $\theta \vdash M = \pi \cdot N$ *obtained by applying rules in Fig. 4 and Definition 1 holds if and only if $\theta \vdash \pi^{-1} \cdot M = N$ holds.*

Proof. ($\Rightarrow$) Let $\pi = [A_1 \leftrightarrow B_1, \ldots, A_n \leftrightarrow B_n]$. Because freshness constraints are generated only from the rule =abs, we can assume that $A_1, \ldots, A_n$ occur only in

N, that $B_1, \ldots, B_n$ occur only in M, and that θ contains $\{A_1 \# M, \ldots, A_n \# M,$ $B_1 \# N, \ldots, B_n \# N\}$. If $N = A_i$ for some i, then $M = B_i$ by assumption and the rule =hlink, in which case $\pi^{-1} \cdot M = A_i$ and the lemma holds. If N is a hyperlink not in $var(\pi)$, then M and N are the same hyperlink not in $var(\pi)$ and the lemma holds obviously. If N is an unknown variable, the lemma is again obvious from the rule =susp. The other cases are straightforward by structural induction.

($\Leftarrow$) The proof of the other direction is similar. $\square$

The next lemma justifies the rule #susp in Fig. 4.

Lemma 6. $\theta \vdash A \# \pi \cdot M$ *obtained by applying rules in Fig. 4 and Definition 1 holds if and only if* $\theta \vdash \pi^{-1} \cdot A \# M$ *holds.*

Proof. ($\Rightarrow$) By Lemma 4 and the fact that freshness constraints are created by the rule =abs, we know that $A \notin var(\pi)$. Therefore, if $\theta \vdash A \# \pi \cdot M$, $\theta \vdash \pi^{-1} \cdot A \# M$ holds.
($\Leftarrow$) For the same reason, $A \notin var(\pi^{-1})$. Therefore, if $\theta \vdash \pi^{-1} \cdot A \# M$ holds, $\theta \vdash A \# \pi \cdot M$ holds. $\square$

The next lemma justifies the rule =susp in Fig. 4.

Lemma 7. $\theta \vdash \pi \cdot M = \pi' \cdot M$ *obtained by applying rules in Fig. 4 and Definition 1 holds for* π *and* π' *if and only if* $A \# M \in \theta$ *for all* $A \in var(\pi @ \pi')$.

Proof. ($\Rightarrow$) By lemma 3, we know that $var(\pi) \cap var(\pi') = \emptyset$. Therefore, in order for $\theta \vdash \pi \cdot M = \pi' \cdot M$ to hold, π and π' should have no effects on M, which means $var(\pi @ \pi') \cap var(M) = \emptyset$, which is the same as $A \# M \in \theta$ for all $A \in var(\pi @ \pi')$.
($\Leftarrow$) If $A \# M \in \theta$ for all $A \in var(\pi @ \pi')$, obviously, $\theta \vdash \pi \cdot M = \pi' \cdot M$ holds. $\square$

Theorem 1. *The relation* $=$ *defined in Fig. 4 is an equivalence relation, i.e.,*

(a) $\theta \vdash M = M$,
(b) $\theta \vdash M = N$ *implies* $\theta \vdash N = M$,
(c) $\theta \vdash M = N$ *and* $\theta \vdash N = P$ *implies* $\theta \vdash M = P$.

Proof.

(a) When M is a hyperlink A, then $A = A$ follows from the rule =hlink. When M is an abstraction, note that M stands for an α-equivalence class. For example, M stands for either $M = $ abs(A,A) or $M = $ abs(B,B). Assume $P = P$ (as induction hypothesis), $A \# P$, and that B occurs in P, then $P = [A \leftrightarrow B] @ [B \leftrightarrow A] \cdot P$ holds. Let $N = [B \leftrightarrow A] \cdot P$, then it is clear that $B \# N$. Clearly, abs(B,P) $= $ abs(A,N) holds, therefore $M = M$ holds for abstractions. When M is an application, the proof is again by structural induction. The equivalence of terms containing suspension follows from the rule =susp and Lemma 7.

=hln	$\{A = A\} \cup P, \delta \Longrightarrow P, \delta$
=abs	$\{\text{abs}(A, M) = \text{abs}(B, N)\} \cup P, \delta \Longrightarrow \{M = [B \leftrightarrow A]N, A\#N, B\#M\} \cup P, \delta$
=app	$\{\text{app}(M_1, N_1) = \text{app}(M_2, N_2)\} \cup P, \delta \Longrightarrow \{M_1 = M_2, N_1 = N_2\} \cup P, \delta$
=rm	$\{\pi \cdot X = \pi' \cdot X\} \cup P, \delta \Longrightarrow P, \delta$
=var	$\left.\begin{array}{l}\{M = \pi \cdot X\}\\\{\pi \cdot X = M\}\end{array}\right\} \cup P, \delta \Longrightarrow \quad \delta'(P), \delta' \circ \delta, \text{ where } \delta' = [X := \pi^{-1} \cdot M]$ provided X does not occur in M
#hln	$\{A\#B\} \cup P, \delta, \Longrightarrow P, \delta$
#abs	$\{A\#\text{abs}(B, N)\} \cup P, \delta \Longrightarrow \{A\#N\} \cup P, \delta$
#app	$\{A\#\text{app}(M, N)\} \cup P, \delta \Longrightarrow \{A\#M, A\#N\} \cup P, \delta$
#sus	$\{A\#\pi \cdot X\} \cup P, \delta \Longrightarrow \{\pi^{-1} \cdot A\#X\} \cup P, \delta$

Fig. 5. Unification of hypergraph λ-terms

(b) When M and N are hyperlinks, $\vdash M = N$ by the rule =hlink simply implies $\vdash N = M$. When M and N are $M = \text{abs}(A, N_1)$ and $N = \text{abs}(B, N_2)$ respectively, $\vdash M = N$ leads to $\vdash N_1 = [A \leftrightarrow B] \cdot N_2$, $\vdash A\#N_2$ and $\vdash B\#N_1$ by the rule =abs. By Lemma 5 and the induction hypothesis, we have $\vdash N_2 = [A \leftrightarrow B] \cdot N_1$, $\vdash A\#N_2$ and $\vdash B\#N_1$ which leads to $\text{abs}(B, N_2) = \text{abs}(A, N_1)$. When M and N are applications, the proof is by the rule =app and using the induction hypothesis twice. The equivalence of terms containing suspension follows from the rule =susp and Lemma 7.

(c) When M, N and P are hyperlinks, it holds. When M, N and P are $M = \text{abs}(A, M_1)$, $N = \text{abs}(B, M_2)$ and $P = \text{abs}(C, M_3)$, we have $\vdash M_1 = [A \leftrightarrow B] \cdot M_2$, $\vdash A\#M_2$, $\vdash B\#M_1$ and $\vdash M_2 = [B \leftrightarrow C] \cdot M_3$, $\vdash B\#M_3$, $\vdash C\#M_2$ by =abs. By Lemma 1, we know that $A\#M_3$ and $C\#M_1$. By Lemma 5 and the induction hypothesis, we have $\{A\#M_3, C\#M_1\} \vdash M_1 = [A \leftrightarrow B]@[B \leftrightarrow C] \cdot M_3$, which is the same as $\{A\#M_3, C\#M_1\} \vdash M_1 = [A \leftrightarrow C] \cdot M_3$, which leads to $\vdash \text{abs}(A, M_1) = \text{abs}(C, M_3)$ by =abs. The proof of applications is trivial. The equivalence of terms containing suspension follows from the rule =susp and Lemma 7. $\qquad \square$

A substitution δ is a finite set of mappings from unknown variables to terms, written as $[X := M_1, Y := M_2, \dots]$ where its domain, $dom(\delta)$, is a set of distinct unknown variables $\{X, Y, \dots\}$. Applying δ to a term M is written as $\delta(M)$ and is defined in a standard manner. A composition of substitutions is written as $\delta \circ \delta'$ and defined as $(\delta \circ \delta')(M) = \delta(\delta'(M))$. The ε denotes an identity substitution. Substitution commutes with *swapping*; i.e., $\delta(\pi \cdot M) = \pi \cdot (\delta(M))$. For example, applying $[X := A]$ to $[A \leftrightarrow B] \cdot \text{app}(N, X)$ will result in $\text{app}(N, B)$. For two sets of freshness constraints θ and θ', and substitutions δ and δ', writing $\theta' \vdash \delta(\theta)$ means that $\theta' \vdash A\#\delta(X)$ holds for all $(A\#X) \in \theta$, and $\theta \vdash \delta = \delta'$ means that $\theta \vdash \delta(X) = \delta'(X)$ for all $X \in dom(\delta) \cup dom(\delta')$.

The definitions of unification, most general unifiers and idempotent unifiers are similar to the ones in nominal unification [14]. A unification problem P is a finite set of equations over hypergraph λ-terms and freshness constraints. Each equation $M = N$ may contain unknown variables $X, Y, \ldots$. A solution of P is a unifier denoted as (θ, δ), consisting of a set θ of freshness constraints and a substitution δ. A unifier (θ, δ) of a problem P equates every equation in P, i.e., establishes $\theta \vdash \delta(M) = \delta(N)$. $\mathcal{U}(P)$ denotes the set of unifiers of a problem P. For P, a unifier $(\theta, \delta) \in \mathcal{U}(P)$ is a *most general unifier* if for any unifier $(\theta', \delta') \in \mathcal{U}(P)$, there is a substitution δ'' such that $\theta' \vdash \delta''(\theta)$ and $\theta' \vdash \delta'' \circ \delta = \delta'$. A unifier $(\theta, \delta) \in \mathcal{U}(P)$ is idempotent if $\theta \vdash \delta \circ \delta = \delta$.

The unification algorithm is described in Fig. 5, where P is a given unification problem and δ is a substitution which is usually initialized to ε. Each rule arbitrarily selects an equation or a freshness constraint from P and transforms it accordingly. The rule `=abs` transforms an equation and creates two freshness constraints, where all freshness constraints we need are obtained. That is why the rule `=rm` simply deletes an equation without creating any freshness constraints. The rule `=var` creates a substitution δ' from an equation (if $X \notin M$), applies δ' to P and adds δ' to δ. The rules in Fig. 5 essentially correspond to the rules in Fig. 4 except for the rule `=var`. The next lemma justifies the rule `=var`.

Lemma 8. *Substitution generated by the rule =var in Fig. 5 preserves = and #
obtained by applying rules in Fig. 4. That is,*

(a) If $\theta' \vdash \delta(\theta)$ and $\theta \vdash M = N$ hold, then $\theta' \vdash \delta(M) = \delta(N)$ holds.
(b) If $\theta' \vdash \delta(\theta)$ and $\theta \vdash A \# M$ hold, then $\theta' \vdash A \# \delta(M)$ holds.

Proof. The proof of both is by structural induction. *(a)* We only show the case of abstraction. Assume $M = \texttt{abs(A,X)}$, $N = \texttt{abs(B,Y)}$, $\delta = [\texttt{X} := P_1, \texttt{Y} := P_2]$. Then we have $\theta = \{\texttt{A\#Y}, \texttt{B\#X}\}$, $\theta \subseteq \theta'$, $\texttt{A\#}P_2$, and $\texttt{B\#}P_1$. From $\theta \vdash M = N$, we have $\texttt{X} = [\texttt{B} \leftrightarrow \texttt{A}]Y$. Using $\texttt{A\#}P_2$ and $\texttt{B\#}P_1$, and by the induction hypothesis, $P_1 = [\texttt{B} \leftrightarrow \texttt{A}]P_2$ holds. Therefore, $\theta' \vdash \delta(\texttt{abs(A,X)}) = \delta(\texttt{abs(B,Y)})$ holds. *(b)* The proof is by structural induction. □

Terms in the hypergraph approach and the nominal approach are first-order terms without built-in β-reduction. To represent bound variables, the nominal approach uses concrete names and the hypergraph approach uses hyperlinks which are identified by names when writing hypergraph terms as text. Our unification and nominal unification both assume α-equality for terms. Therefore, it is not surprising that our unification algorithm happens to be similar to the nominal unification algorithm. Nevertheless, there are differences. Our algorithm does not have a rule for handling two abstractions with the same bound variable. Also, the rule `=rm` is different from the $\approx?$-`suspension` rule in nominal unification [14]. This is because Lemma 7 is different from its counterpart in nominal unification: the former states the freshness of every variable of $\pi @ \pi'$ and the latter states the freshness of the variables in the *disagreement set* of π and π'.

Theorem 2. *For a given unification problem P, the unification algorithm in Fig. 5 either fails if P has no unifier or successfully produces an idempotent most general unifier.*

Proof. Given in Appendix with related lemmas. The structure of the proof in [14] applies to our case basically, though our formalization allows the interleaving of the = and # rules of the algorithm.   □

4   Examples of the Unification

We apply the unification algorithm in Fig. 5 to three unification problems.

Example 1. A unification problem

$$\text{abs}(\text{A},\text{abs}(\text{B},X)) = \text{abs}(\text{C},\text{abs}(\text{D},X))$$

has a solution.

$\{\text{abs}(\text{A},\text{abs}(\text{B},X)) = \text{abs}(\text{C},\text{abs}(\text{D},X))\}$, ε
$\{\text{abs}(\text{B},X) = [\text{C} \leftrightarrow \text{A}] \cdot \text{abs}(\text{D},X), \text{A}\#\text{abs}(\text{D},X), \text{C}\#\text{abs}(\text{B},X)\}$, ε (=abs)
$\{X = [\text{D} \leftrightarrow \text{B}, \text{C} \leftrightarrow \text{A}] \cdot X, \text{A}\#X, \text{C}\#X, \text{B}\#[\text{C} \leftrightarrow \text{A}] \cdot X, \text{D}\#X\}$, ε (=abs,#abs,#hln)
$\{\text{A}\#X, \text{C}\#X, \text{B}\#X, \text{D}\#X\}$, ε (=rm,#sus)
Success

The problem has the most general unifier $(\{\text{A}\#X, \text{C}\#X, \text{B}\#X, \text{D}\#X\}, \varepsilon)$, which says that X can be any term not containing A, B, C or D.

Example 2. A unification problem

$$\text{abs}(\text{A},\text{abs}(\text{B},\text{app}(X,\text{B}))) = \text{abs}(\text{C},\text{abs}(\text{D},\text{app}(\text{D},X)))$$

has no solution.

$\{\text{abs}(\text{A},\text{abs}(\text{B},\text{app}(X,\text{B}))) = \text{abs}(\text{C},\text{abs}(\text{D},\text{app}(\text{D},X)))\}$, ε
$\{\text{abs}(\text{B},\text{app}(X,\text{B})) = [\text{C} \leftrightarrow \text{A}] \cdot \text{abs}(\text{D},\text{app}(\text{D},X)),$ (=abs)
$\quad \text{A}\#\text{abs}(\text{D},\text{app}(\text{D},X)), \text{C}\#\text{abs}(\text{B},\text{app}(X,\text{B}))\}$, ε
$\{\text{app}(X,\text{B}) = [\text{D} \leftrightarrow \text{B}] \cdot \text{app}(\text{D},[\text{C} \leftrightarrow \text{A}] \cdot X),$ (=abs,#abs,#app,#hln)
$\quad \text{A}\#X, \text{C}\#X, \text{B}\# \text{app}(\text{D},[\text{C} \leftrightarrow \text{A}] \cdot X), \text{D}\#\text{app}(X,\text{B})\}$, ε
$\{X = \text{B}, \text{B} = [\text{D} \leftrightarrow \text{B}, \text{C} \leftrightarrow \text{A}] \cdot X, \text{A}\#X, \text{C}\#X, \text{D}\#X, \text{B}\#X\}$, ε (=app,#app,#hln,#sus)
$\{\text{B} = \text{D}, \text{B}\#\text{B}\}$, $[X := \text{B}]$ (=var,#hln)
Failure

The problem is unsolvable; it fails due to both B = D and B#B.

Example 3. A unification problem

$$\text{abs}(\text{A},\text{app}(X,Y)) = \text{abs}(\text{B},\text{app}(\text{app}(\text{B},Y),X))$$

has no solution.

$\{\texttt{abs(A,app}(X,Y)) = \texttt{abs(B,app(app(B},Y)\texttt{,}X))\}, \varepsilon$
$\{\texttt{app}(X,Y) = [\texttt{B} \leftrightarrow \texttt{A}] \cdot \texttt{app(app(B},Y)\texttt{,}X),$ (=abs)
$\texttt{A\#app(app(B},Y)\texttt{,}X), \texttt{B\#app}(X,Y)\}, \varepsilon$
$\{X = \texttt{app(A,}[\texttt{B} \leftrightarrow \texttt{A}] \cdot Y), Y = [\texttt{B} \leftrightarrow \texttt{A}] \cdot X,$ (=app,#app,#hln)
$\texttt{A\#}X, \texttt{A\#}Y, \texttt{B\#}X, \texttt{B\#}Y\}, \varepsilon$
$\{Y = [\texttt{B} \leftrightarrow \texttt{A}] \cdot \texttt{app(A,}[\texttt{B} \leftrightarrow \texttt{A}] \cdot Y), \texttt{A\#app(A,}[\texttt{B} \leftrightarrow \texttt{A}] \cdot Y),$ (=var)
$\texttt{A\#}Y, \texttt{B\#app(A,}[\texttt{B} \leftrightarrow \texttt{A}] \cdot Y), \texttt{B\#}Y\}, [X := \texttt{app(A,}[\texttt{B} \leftrightarrow \texttt{A}] \cdot Y)]$
$\{Y = \texttt{app(B,}[\texttt{B} \leftrightarrow \texttt{A,B} \leftrightarrow \texttt{A}] \cdot Y), \texttt{A\#}Y, \texttt{B\#}Y, \texttt{A\#}Y, \texttt{A\#A}, \texttt{B\#}Y\},$ (#app,#hln,#sus)
$[X := \texttt{app(A,}[\texttt{B} \leftrightarrow \texttt{A}] \cdot Y)]$
Failure

The problem is unsolvable; it fails due to $\texttt{A\#A}$.

5   Implementation

We implemented the unification of hypergraph λ-terms in HyperLMNtal in a straightforward manner[1]. There are a total of 52 rewrite rules in the implementation; 12 rewrite rules corresponding to the 9 rules in Fig. 5 (4 rules for the =var rule), 14 rules for the occur-check, 7 rules for implementing applying swapping to terms, 7 rewrite rules for substitution, and several auxiliary rules for list management. Interestingly, the implementation of substitution $M[X := N]$ turned out to be essentially the same as that for the λ-calculus, i.e., $\mathsf{sub}(X, N, M)$ in Fig. 2. The implementation solved a number of unification problems, including the examples in this paper. HyperLMNtal brought simplicity in the sense that the rewrite rules of the implementation are extremely close to the unification rules discussed in this paper.

6   Related Work and Conclusion

Complexity of formalizing unification over terms containing name binding is largely determined by the approach taken for representing such terms. There are two prominent unification algorithms: higher-order pattern unification [8] and nominal unification [14].

A higher-order approach implements a variant of the λ-calculus as a meta-language, which is used to encode formal systems involving name binding [9]. The meta-language implicitly handles substitution and implicitly restricts bound variables to be distinct. Users reason about formal systems indirectly through the meta-language, in which terms are higher-order terms. Higher-order pattern unification unifies equations of terms modulo $=_{\alpha\beta_0\eta}$. It finds functions to substitute unknown variables, which means that variable capture never happens. The characteristics of higher-order pattern unification are the result of letting the meta-language handle everything implicitly. In the nominal approach, bound-able *names* are equipped with *swapping* and *freshness* to ensure correct substitutions [4]. Users reason on formal systems through nominal terms which are

---

[1] Implementation is available at https://gitlab.com/alimjanyasin.

first-order terms. As the result, nominal unification solves equations of terms modulo $=_\alpha$, because $=_{\beta\eta}$ is not needed for first-order terms, and allows for variable capture in the unification while preserving α-equivalence. We believe that having no restrictions on bound variables is the cause of somewhat complex proofs in the nominal unification. One observation is that using a higher-order meta-language implicitly ensures the distinctness of bound variables in the higher-order approach. In the nominal approach, such restriction on bound variables does not exist.

Our approach uses hyperlinks to represent variables, hypergraphs to represent terms and `hlground` followed by hypergraph copying to avoid variable capture. Unlike the nominal approach, we use fresh hyperlinks whenever needed and `hlground` manages hyperlinks. In our approach, it is natural to restrict a hyperlink to be bound only once and every abstraction is syntactically unique. Just like nominal unification, our unification only considers α-equivalence and allows variable capture in the unification. The key idea of our technique is that implementing α-renaming (as the copying of hypergraphs identified by `hlground`) leads to the simplification of overall reasoning. Urban pointed out that the proofs of nominal unification in [14] are clunky and presented simpler proofs in [15]. Proofs in this paper are even somewhat simpler than the proofs in [15]. In our unification algorithm, the basic properties are easy to establish; Lemmas 4, 5, 6 and 7 are intuitive and simple. In particular, we proved equivalence relation (Theorem 1) without much efforts.

To conclude, we worked on the unification of hypergraph λ-terms and the result shows that our approach has taken the promising strategy as indicated by simple proofs of fundamental properties needed for the unification algorithm. We successfully implemented the unification algorithm in HyperLMNtal. This work suggests that our hypergraph rewriting framework provides a convenient platform to work with formal systems involving name bindings and unification of their terms. In the future, we plan to use this unification algorithm to encode type inferences of formal systems involving name binding. Besides, it should be interesting to reformalize logic programming languages such as αProlog [3] using our hypergraph-based approach and implement them in HyperLMNtal to see how much simplicity our approach can provide in practice.

Acknowledgement. The authors are indebted to anonymous referees for their useful comments and pointers to the literature. This work is partially supported by Grant-In-Aid for Scientific Research ((B)26280024), JSPS, Japan, and Waseda University Grant for Special Research Projects.

A   Appendix

A.1   Adequacy of Equivalence

The relation $=$ defined in Fig. 4 and the standard α-equivalence $=_\alpha$ (based on graph isomorphism) for ground hypergraph λ-terms are the same.

Proposition 1 (adequacy). *For ground hypergraph λ-terms M and N, the relation $M =_\alpha N$ holds if and only if $\emptyset \vdash M = N$ holds in Fig. 4, and $\emptyset \vdash A\#M$ holds if and only if A in not in the set $fv(M)$, defined by*

$$fv(A) \stackrel{def}{=} \{A\} \quad (A \text{ is a hyperlink}),$$

$$fv(\mathtt{abs}(A, M)) \stackrel{def}{=} fv(M)\backslash\{A\},$$

$$fv(\mathtt{app}(M, N)) \stackrel{def}{=} fv(M) \cup fv(N).$$

Proof Let M and N be hyperlinks. If $M =_\alpha N$ holds, then $\emptyset \vdash M = N$ holds by the rule =hlink. The other direction is similar. Let M and N be $\mathtt{abs}(A, M_1)$ and $\mathtt{abs}(B, N_1)$, respectively. If $M =_\alpha N$, this means $M_1 =_\alpha N_1[B := A]$, A is not in N_1 and B is not in M_1. Therefore, $\emptyset \vdash M = N$ holds by the rule =abs. If $\emptyset \vdash M = N$, $M =_\alpha N$ is clear from the premise of =abs. Let M and N be $M_1 M_2$ and $N_1 N_2$. If $M =_\alpha N$, then we have $M_1 =_\alpha N_1$ and $M_2 =_\alpha N_2$. Clearly, $\emptyset \vdash M = N$ from the rule =app. The other direction is similar.

It is easy to see that $\emptyset \vdash A\#M$ in Fig. 4 and A not being in $fv(M)$ are the same for ground hypergraph λ-terms. If one of them holds, so does the other. □

A.2   Correctness of Unification

Here, we give the details of the correctness proof of the unification algorithm in Fig. 5.

Lemma 9. *The unification algorithm always terminates.*

Proof. To show that the algorithm terminates, we need to define the size of terms $|M|$ as follows.

$$|A| \stackrel{def}{=} 1$$

$$|\mathtt{abs}(A, M)| \stackrel{def}{=} 1 + |M|$$

$$|\mathtt{app}(M, N)| \stackrel{def}{=} 1 + |M| + |N|$$

$$|\pi \cdot X| \stackrel{def}{=} 1$$

For a unification problem P, a measure of the size of P is a lexicographically ordered pair of natural numbers (n, m), where n is the number of different unknown variables in P and m is the size of all equations in P, defined as

$$m \stackrel{def}{=} \sum_{(M=N)\in P} |M| + |N|.$$

The = rules in Fig. 5 decrease (n, m). The rule =var eliminates one unknown variable, so n decreases. The rule =rm decreases m and may decrease n. Other = rules decrease m and do not change n.

The **#** rules decrease the size of freshness constraints, which is $\sum_{(A\#M)\in P} |M|$. Eventually, all remaining freshness constraints in a solvable problem P will have the form $A\#X$, for which there are no applicable rules.

For an unsolvable problem P, the algorithm terminates with P containing terms of equations which cannot be made α-equivalent and invalid freshness constraints: (i) $A = B$ where A and B are different hyperlinks; (ii) $M = N$ where M and N start with different constructors such as abs and app; (iii) one of M and N is a hyperlink and another is a constructor; (iv) $\pi \cdot X = M$ where M is either abs(A, M_1) or app(M_2, N) with X occurring in M_1, M_2 and N; (v) having a freshness constraint such as $A\#A$.

By these facts, we can conclude that the algorithm terminates in both success and failure cases. □

Lemma 10. *if* $\theta \vdash \delta(\pi \cdot X) = \delta(M)$ *then* $\theta \vdash \delta \circ [X := \pi^{-1} \cdot M] = \delta$.

Proof. By commuting δ and π and by Theorem 1 (b), we have $\theta \vdash \delta(M) = \pi \cdot \delta(X)$. By Lemma 5 and commuting again, we have $\theta \vdash \delta(\pi^{-1} \cdot M) = \delta(X)$, which implies $\theta \vdash \delta \circ [X := \pi^{-1} \cdot M] = \delta$. □

Lemma 11. *For a problem* P, $(\theta, \delta) \in \mathcal{U}(\delta_1(P))$ *iff* $(\theta, \delta \circ \delta_1) \in \mathcal{U}(P)$.

Proof. Follows from the definition of substitution composition. □

In Fig. 5, the only rule that creates substitution is the rule =var. It is easy to see that =var creates a substitution $[X := \pi^{-1} \cdot M]$ with $X \notin dom(\delta)$.

When applying the unification rules, the =hln, =app, =rm and all **#** rules just simplifies some of equations and freshness constraints or removes some of them, without creating anything really new. Interesting ones are the rule =abs which creates new freshness constraints and the rule =var which creates a new mapping. Therefore, in the following Lèmmas, we focus on these two rules.

Lemma 12.

(a) *If* $(\theta, \delta) \in \mathcal{U}(P)$ *and* $P, \delta \Longrightarrow P', \delta'' \circ \delta$ *using the rule* =var *creating* $\delta'' = [X := \pi^{-1} \cdot M]$, *then* $(\theta, \delta) \in \mathcal{U}(P')$ *and* $\theta \vdash \delta \circ \delta'' = \delta$.
(b) *If* $(\theta, \delta) \in \mathcal{U}(P)$ *and* $P, \delta \Longrightarrow P', \delta$ *using the rule* =abs *creating* $\theta'' = \{A\#N, B\#M\}$, *then* $(\theta, \delta) \in \mathcal{U}(P')$ *and* $\theta \vdash \delta(\theta'')$.

Proof.

(a) We can write $P, \delta \Longrightarrow P', \delta'' \circ \delta$ as $P, \delta \Longrightarrow \delta''(P), \delta'' \circ \delta$. By $(\theta, \delta) \in \mathcal{U}(P)$ and $(\pi \cdot X = M)$ or $(M = \pi \cdot X)$ is in P, $\theta \vdash \delta(\pi \cdot X) = \delta(M)$ holds, which leads to $\theta \vdash \delta \circ \delta'' = \delta$ by Lemma 10. By Lemma 11, we have $(\theta, \delta) \in \mathcal{U}(P')$ which is the same as $(\theta, \delta \circ \delta'') \in \mathcal{U}(P)$.
(b) By the assumption, we have $\theta \vdash \delta(\text{abs}(A, M)) = \delta(\text{abs}(B, N))$ and $\theta'' = \{A\#N, B\#M\}$. In order to derive the above, Fig. 4 tells that we must have $\theta \vdash A\#\delta(N)$, $\theta \vdash B\#\delta(M)$ and $\theta \vdash \delta(M) = [A \leftrightarrow B] \cdot \delta(N)$, from which the conclusions follow. □

Lemma 13.

(a) If $(\theta, \delta) \in \mathcal{U}(P')$ and $P, \delta \Longrightarrow P', \delta'' \circ \delta$ using the rule *=var* creating $\delta'' = [X := \pi^{-1} \cdot M]$, then $(\theta, \delta \circ \delta'') \in \mathcal{U}(P)$.
(b) If $(\theta, \delta) \in \mathcal{U}(P')$ and $P, \delta \Longrightarrow P', \delta$ using the rule *=abs* creating $\theta'' = \{A\#N, B\#M\}$, then $(\theta, \delta) \in \mathcal{U}(P)$.

Proof.

(a) $P, \delta \Longrightarrow P', \delta'' \circ \delta$ can be written as $P, \delta \Longrightarrow \delta''(P), \delta'' \circ \delta$. Clearly, $(\theta, \delta \circ \delta'') \in \mathcal{U}(P)$ follows from Lemma 11 and the assumption $(\theta, \delta) \in \mathcal{U}(\delta''(P))$.
(b) The proof is similar to the proof of second part of Lemma 12, but in the opposite direction. $\square$

Theorem 2. *For a given unification problem P, the unification algorithm in Fig. 5 either fails if P has no unifier or successfully produces an idempotent most general unifier.*

Proof. For a unification problem which has no unifiers, the algorithm fails as explained in Lemma 9. For a solvable unification problem P_0, the proof proceeds in three steps: (i) a unifier is generated, (ii) it is most general, and (iii) it is idempotent.

First, the algorithm transforms P_0 as

$$P_0, \delta_0 \Longrightarrow P_1, \delta_1 \Longrightarrow \ldots \Longrightarrow P_n, \delta_n \not\Longrightarrow$$

by substitutions $\delta'_1, \ldots, \delta'_n$ and freshness constraints $\theta'_1, \ldots, \theta'_m$ where $\delta_0 = \varepsilon$, $\delta_1 = \delta'_1 \circ \delta_0, \ldots, \delta_n = \delta'_n \circ \delta_{n-1}$, and the θ'_i stands for freshness constraints created by the ith application of the rule *=abs*. By the # rules in Fig. 5, we know that P_n consists only of freshness constraints of the form $A\#X$. Let us denote P_n as θ. By Lemma 13 and $(\theta, \varepsilon) \in \mathcal{U}(P_n)$, we have $(\theta, \delta) \in \mathcal{U}(P_0)$ where $\delta = \delta'_n \circ \ldots \circ \delta'_1$.

Second, for any other unifier $(\theta', \delta') \in \mathcal{U}(P_0)$, by Lemma 12 we have $\theta' \vdash \delta' \circ \delta'_1 = \delta', \ldots, \theta' \vdash \delta' \circ \delta'_n = \delta'$ and $\theta' \vdash \delta'(\theta'_1), \ldots, \theta' \vdash \delta'(\theta'_m)$. From the former, we have $\theta' \vdash \delta' \circ \delta'_n \circ \ldots \circ \delta'_1 = \delta'$, which is the same as $\theta' \vdash \delta' \circ \delta = \delta'$. From the latter, we have $\theta' \vdash \delta'(\theta'')$ where $\theta'' = \theta'_1 \cup \ldots \cup \theta'_m$. From $\theta' \vdash \delta' \circ \delta = \delta'$ and $\theta' \vdash \delta'(\theta'')$, we have $\theta' \vdash (\delta' \circ \delta)(\theta'')$. Since we know that $\delta(\theta'')$ is transformed into θ, we have $\theta' \vdash \delta'(\theta)$. Therefore (θ, δ) is the most general unifier.

Third, since δ' is any unifier, we have $\theta \vdash \delta \circ \delta = \delta$. Therefore (θ, δ) is the idempotent most general unifier. $\square$

References

1. Barendregt, H.: The Lambda Calculus: its Syntax and Semantics. Studies in Logic and the Foundations of Mathematics, vol. 103. North-Holland, Amsterdam (1984)
2. Cheney, J.: Relating higher-order pattern unification and nominal unification. In: Proceedings of the 19th International Workshop on Unification, UNIF 2005, pp. 104–119 (2005)
3. Cheney, J., Urban, C.: αProlog: a logic programming language with names, binding and *alpha*-equivalence. In: Demoen, B., Lifschitz, V. (eds.) ICLP 2004. LNCS, vol. 3132, pp. 269–283. Springer, Heidelberg (2004). doi:10.1007/978-3-540-27775-0_19
4. Gabbay, M.J., Pitts, A.M.: A new approach to abstract syntax with variable binding. Formal Aspects Comput. **13**, 341–363 (2002)
5. Huet, G.J.: A unification algorithm for typed λ-Calculus. Theoret. Comput. Sci. **1**(1), 27–57 (1975)
6. Levy, J., Villaret, M.: Nominal unification from a higher-order perspective. In: Voronkov, A. (ed.) RTA 2008. LNCS, vol. 5117, pp. 246–260. Springer, Heidelberg (2008). doi:10.1007/978-3-540-70590-1_17
7. Martelli, A., Montanari, U.: An efficient unification algorithm. ACM Trans. Program. Lang. Syst. **4**(2), 258–282 (1982)
8. Miller, D.: A logic programming language with lambda-abstraction, function variables, and simple unification. J. Logic Comput. **1**, 497–536 (1991)
9. Pfenning, F., Elliott, C.: Higher-order abstract syntax. In: Proceedings of the ACM SIGPLAN Conference on Programming Language Design and Implementation, pp. 199–208 (1988)
10. Qi, X.: An Implementation of the Language Lambda Prolog Organized around Higher-Order Pattern Unification. Ph.D. thesis, University of Minnesota (2009)
11. Robinson, J.A.: A machine-oriented logic based on the resolution principle. J. ACM **12**(1), 23–41 (1965)
12. Ueda, K.: Encoding the pure lambda calculus into hierarchical graph rewriting. In: Voronkov, A. (ed.) RTA 2008. LNCS, vol. 5117, pp. 392–408. Springer, Heidelberg (2008). doi:10.1007/978-3-540-70590-1_27
13. Ueda, K., Ogawa, S.: HyperLMNtal: an extension of a hierarchical graph rewriting model. Küstliche Intelligenz **26**(1), 27–36 (2012)
14. Urban, C., Pitts, A.M., Gabbay, M.J.: Nominal unification. J. Theor. Comput. Sci. **323**(1–3), 473–497 (2004)
15. Urban, C.: Nominal unification revisited. In: Proceedings of the 24th International Workshop on Unification, UNIF 2010, pp. 1–11 (2010)
16. Yasen, A., Ueda, K.: Hypergraph representation of lambda-terms. In: Proceedings of 10th International Symposium on Theoretical Aspects of Software Engineering, pp. 113–116 (2016)
17. Yasen, A., Ueda, K.: Name Binding is Easy with Hypergraphs. submitted
18. Qian, Z.: Linear unification of higher-order patterns. In: Gaudel, M.-C., Jouannaud, J.-P. (eds.) CAAP 1993. LNCS, vol. 668, pp. 391–405. Springer, Heidelberg (1993). doi:10.1007/3-540-56610-4_78
19. Bourbaki, N.: Théorie des ensembless, Hermann (1970)
20. Mackie, I.: Efficient λ-evaluation with interaction nets. In: van Oostrom, V. (ed.) RTA 2004. LNCS, vol. 3091, pp. 155–169. Springer, Heidelberg (2004). doi:10.1007/978-3-540-25979-4_11

Erratum to: Topics in Theoretical Computer Science

Mohammad Reza Mousavi[1][⊠] and Jiří Sgall[2]

[1] University of Leicester, Leicester, UK
m.r.mousavi@hh.se
[2] Charles University, Prague, Czech Republic

Erratum to:
M.R. Mousavi and J. Sgall (Eds.):
Topics in Theoretical Computer Science, LNCS 10608,
https://doi.org/10.1007/978-3-319-68953-1

The paper starting on p. 41 was incorrectly listed under the topical section heading "Logic, Semantics, and Programming Theory" in the original version of the table of contents. This has been corrected and the paper is now listed under the "Algorithms and Complexity" section.

The updated online version of this book can be found at
https://doi.org/10.1007/978-3-319-68953-1

Author Index

Printed in the United States
By Bookmasters